Ride the Wave

Jaap Tuinman

CONSULTANTS
Sharon Anderson
Elaine Baker
John Drysdale
Julie Kniskern
Joanne McCabe
Claudia Mitchell
Maureen Neuman
Sharon Rich
Kathleen Rosborough

PROGRAM EDITOR
Kathleen Doyle

GINN

Ginn Publishing Canada Inc.

JOURNEYS

Ride the Wave

Anthology 6

© Copyright 1988 by Ginn Publishing
Canada Inc.
ALL RIGHTS RESERVED.

EDITORS
Sharon Stewart
Anne MacInnes

EDITORIAL CONSULTANT
Nicki Scrimger

ART/DESIGN
Sandi Meland Cherun/
Word & Image Design Studio

C97611
ISBN 0-7702-1226-3

Printed and bound in Canada.

CDEFGHIJK 976543210

Acknowledgments

For kind permission to reprint the following copyrighted material, acknowledgment is hereby made:

Excerpt (pp. 7–33) from *Dear Mr. Henshaw.* Copyright © 1983 by Beverly Cleary, with illustrations by Paul O. Zelinsky. Reprinted by permission of William Morrow & Company, Inc.

Chapter One from *Mama's Going to Buy You a Mockingbird.* Copyright © Jean Little, 1984. Reprinted by permission of Penguin Books Canada Limited.

"The Young Maple Tree" by Edith Jane Harrison, originally published in *Crackers* magazine, Number 5, 1982.

Excerpt from *Henry Reed's Baby-Sitting Service.* Copyright © 1966 by Keith Robertson. Reprinted by permission of Viking Penguin Inc.

Excerpt from *Anastasia on Her Own.* Copyright © 1985 by Lois Lowry. Reprinted by permission of Houghton Mifflin Company.

Excerpt from *A Boy Called Nam.* Copyright © 1984 by Leo Heaps. Reprinted with the permission of the author.

Text for "The Ghost Pond" and "The Rescued Pond" is reprinted from *OWL* Magazine, April 1979, with permission of the publisher, The Young Naturalist Foundation.

"And They Lived Happily Ever After for a While" from *Fast and Slow.* Copyright © 1975 by John Ciardi. Reprinted by permission of Houghton Mifflin Company.

Text and illustration for "Elmo E. Man, Environmental Detective" by Jan Gray, reprinted from *OWL* Magazine, May 1986, with permission of the publisher, The Young Naturalist Foundation.

Excerpt from *Burnish Me Bright.* Copyright © 1970 by Julia Cunningham. Reprinted by permission of Pantheon Books, a Division of Random House, Inc.

Chapter Two from *Crazy Ideas.* Copyright © 1984 by Ken Roberts. A Groundwood Book. Reprinted with the permission of Douglas & McIntyre Ltd.

Chapter Four from *The Phantom Tollbooth.* Copyright © 1961 by Norton Juster. Reprinted by permission of Random House, Inc.

"Take Sky" from *One at a Time.* Copyright © 1961, 1962 by David McCord. Reprinted by permission of Little, Brown and Company.

Selections from *Charlie and the Chocolate Factory.* Copyright © 1964 by Roald Dahl. Reprinted by permission of Alfred A. Knopf, Inc.

Chapter Two from *As Ever, Booky.* Copyright © 1985 by Bernice Thurman Hunter. Reprinted with the permission of Scholastic-TAB Publications Ltd.

"The Cremation of Sam McGee," copyright 1907 by the Estate of Robert W. Service; with illustrations, copyright © 1986 by Ted Harrison. Reprinted with the permission of M.W. Krasilovsky for the Estate of Robert Service, and the publisher, Kids Can Press Ltd., Toronto, for Ted Harrison.

"Silverspot" from *Wild Animals I Have Known* by Ernest Thompson Seton was originally published by Charles Scribner's Sons of New York.

"The Ways of Living Things" by Jack Prelutsky is from *The Random House Book of Poetry for Children.* Copyright © 1983 by Random House, Inc. Reprinted by permission of the publisher.

"What the Wind Said" from *The Pedaling Man and Other Poems.* Copyright © 1968 by Russell Hoban. Reprinted by permission of Harold Ober Associates Incorporated for the author.

"The Elusive Secret of Oak Island." Copyright © 1979 by Jean Booker, originally published in *The Canadian Children's Annual 1980.* Reprinted here by permission of the author.

Excerpt (pp. 61–69) from *Captain Grey* by Avi. Copyright © 1977 by Avi Wortis. Reprinted by permission of Pantheon Books, a Division of Random House, Inc.

"Ghost Ship" from *Strange Mysteries from Around the World.* Copyright © 1980 by Seymour Simon. Reprinted by permission of the author.

Selections and photographs from *Dove.* Copyright © 1972 by Robin Lee Graham and Derek L.T. Gill. Reprinted by permission of Harper & Row, Publishers, Inc.

Chapter Ten of *Island of the Blue Dolphins.* Copyright © 1960 by Scott O'Dell. Reprinted by permission of Houghton Mifflin Company.

"My Friend the Grouper" adapted from pp. 156–163 in *The Living Sea* by Jacques Yves Cousteau with James Dugan. Copyright © 1963 by Harper & Row, Publishers, Inc. Reprinted with the permission of the publisher.

"The Vigil" by Jan Andrews was originally published, in this version, in *Ahoy* magazine, Spring 1981, and is reprinted here by permission of the author.

"The Singing Float." Copyright © 1986 by Monica Hughes. Reprinted by permission of the author.

"Susan: Super Sleuth and the Diamond Dilemma" by William Ettridge, from *The Canadian Children's Annual 1976.* Copyright © 1975 Potlatch Publications Limited. Reprinted with the permission of the publisher.

"The Case of the Kidnapped Nephew" (second part) from *Whatever Happened to Uncle Albert? And Other Puzzling Plays.* Copyright © 1980 by Sue Alexander. Reprinted by permission of Clarion Books/Ticknor & Fields, a Houghton Mifflin Company.

Excerpt from "The Village over the Mountain" in *Fog Magic.* Copyright 1943/renewed © 1970 by Julia L. Sauer. All rights reserved. Reprinted by permission of Viking Penguin Inc.

Selections from *Tom's Midnight Garden* by A. Philippa Pearce. Copyright © Oxford University Press, 1958. Reprinted by permission of the publisher.

Acknowledgments continued on p. 430.

Contents

Detail of *Six Figures in a Landscape* by Charles Pachter

Working It Out

Dear Mr. Henshaw

by Beverly Cleary

Boyd Henshaw is Leigh Botts's favorite author. Ever since Leigh was in grade two he has written a letter to Mr. Henshaw every year. Now Leigh's teacher has assigned an author report, so it's time for another letter. . . .

September 20

Dear Mr. Henshaw,

This year I am in the sixth grade in a new school in a different town. Our teacher is making us do author reports to improve our writing skills, so of course I thought of you. Please answer the following questions.

1. How many books have you written?
2. Is Boyd Henshaw your real name or is it fake?
3. Why do you write books for children?
4. Where do you get your ideas?
5. Do you have any kids?
6. What is your favorite book that you wrote?
7. Do you like to write books?
8. What is the title of your next book?
9. What is your favorite animal?
10. Please give me some tips on how to write a book. This is important to me. I really want to know so I can get to be a famous author and write books exactly like yours.

from Dear Mr. Henshaw

Please send me a list of your books that you wrote, an autographed picture, and a bookmark. I need your answer by next Friday. This is urgent!

Sincerely,

Leigh Botts

De Liver
De Letter
De Sooner
De Better
De Later
De Letter
De Madder
I Getter

Dear Mr. Henshaw,   November 15

At first I was pretty upset when I didn't get an answer to my letter in time for my report, but I worked it out OK. I read what it said about you on the back of *Ways to Amuse a Dog* and wrote real big on every other line so I filled up the paper. On the book it said you lived in Seattle, so I didn't know you had moved to Alaska although I should have guessed from *Moose on Toast*.

When your letter finally came I didn't want to read it to the class, because I didn't think Miss Martinez would like silly answers, like your real name is Messing A. Round, and you don't have kids because you don't raise goats. She said I had to read it. The class laughed and Miss Martinez smiled, but she didn't smile when I came to the part about your favorite animal was a purple monster who ate children who sent authors long lists of questions for reports instead of learning to use the library.

Your writing tips were OK. I could tell you meant what you said. Don't worry. When I write something, I won't send it to you. I understand how busy you are with your own books.

I hid the second page of your letter from Miss Martinez. That list of questions you sent for me to answer really made me mad. Nobody else's author put in a list of questions to be answered, and I don't think it's fair to make me do more work when I already wrote a report.

Anyway, thank you for answering my questions. Some kids didn't get any answers at all, which made them mad, and one girl almost cried, she was so afraid she would get a bad grade. One boy got a letter from an author who sounded real excited about getting a letter and wrote such a long answer the boy had to write a long report. He guessed nobody ever wrote to that author before, and he sure wouldn't again. About ten kids wrote to the same author, who wrote one answer to all of them. There was a big argument about who got to keep it until Miss Martinez took the letter to the office and duplicated it.

About those questions you sent me. I'm not going to answer them, and you can't make me. You're not my teacher.

Yours truly,

Leigh Botts

P.S. When I asked you what the title of your next book was going to be, you said, Who knows? Did you mean that was the title or you don't know what the title will be? And do you really write books because you have read every book in the library and because writing beats mowing the lawn or shovelling snow?

November 16

Dear Mr. Henshaw,

Mom found your letter and your list of questions which I was dumb enough to leave lying around. We had a big argument. She says I have to answer your questions because authors are working people like anyone else, and if you took time to answer my questions, I should answer yours. She says I can't go through life expecting everyone to do everything for me. She used to say the same thing to Dad when he left his socks on the floor.

Well, I got to go now. It's bedtime. Maybe I'll get around to answering your ten questions, and maybe I won't. There isn't any law that says I have to. Maybe I won't even read any more of your books.

Disgusted reader,

Leigh Botts

P.S. If my Dad was here, he would tell you to go climb a tree.

12/1305

Dear Mr. Henshaw,   November 20

Mom is nagging me about your dumb old questions. She says if I really want to be an author, I should follow the tips in your letter. I should read, look, listen, think, and <u>write</u>. She says the best way she knows for me to get started is to apply the seat of my pants to a chair and answer your questions and answer them fully. So here goes.

1. Who are you?

Like I've been telling you, I am Leigh Botts. Leigh Marcus Botts. I don't like Leigh for a name because some people don't know how to say it or think it's a girl's name. Mom says with a last name like Botts I need something fancy but not too fancy. My Dad's name is Bill and Mom's name is Bonnie. She says Bill and Bonnie Botts sounds like something out of a comic strip.

I am just a plain boy. This school doesn't say I am Gifted and Talented, and I don't like soccer very much the way everybody at this school is supposed to. I am not stupid either.

2. What do you look like?

I already sent you my picture, but maybe you lost it. I am sort of medium. I don't have red hair or anything like that. I'm not real big like my Dad. Mom says I take after her family, thank goodness. That's the way she always says it. In first and second grades kids used to call me Leigh the Flea, but I have grown. Now when the class lines up according to height, I am in the middle. I guess you could call me the mediumest boy in the class.

This is hard work. To be continued, maybe.

Leigh Botts

November 22

Dear Mr. Henshaw,

I wasn't going to answer any more of your questions, but Mom won't get the TV repaired because she says it was rotting my brain. This is Thanksgiving vacation and I am so bored I decided to answer a couple of your rotten questions with my rotten brain. (Joke.)

3. What is your family like?

Since Dad and Bandit went away, my family is just Mom and me. We all used to live in a mobile home outside of Bakersfield which is in California's Great Central Valley we studied about in school. When Mom and Dad got divorced, they sold the mobile home, and Dad moved into a trailer.

Dad drives a big truck, a cab-over job. That means the cab is over the engine. Some people don't know that. The truck is why my parents got divorced. Dad used to drive for someone else, hauling stuff like cotton, sugar beets, and other produce around Central California and Nevada, but he couldn't get owning his own rig for cross-country hauling out of his head. He worked practically night and day and saved a down payment. Mom said we'd never get out of that mobile home when he had to make such big payments on that rig, and she'd never know where he was when he hauled cross-country. His big rig sure is a beauty, with a bunk in the cab and everything. His rig, which truckers call a tractor but everyone else calls a truck, has ten wheels, two in front and eight in back so he can hitch up to anything—flatbeds, refrigerated vans, a couple of gondolas.

In school they teach you that a gondola is some kind of boat in Italy, but in the U.S. it is a container for hauling loose stuff like carrots.

My hand is all worn out from all this writing, but I try to treat Mom and Dad the same so I'll get to Mom next time.

Your pooped reader,
Leigh Botts

November 23

Mr. Henshaw:

Why should I call you "dear," when you are the reason I'm stuck with all this work? It wouldn't be fair to leave Mom out so here is Question 3 continued.

Mom works part time for Catering by Katy which is run by a real nice lady Mom knew when she was growing up in Taft, California. Katy says all women who grew up in Taft had to be good cooks because they went to so many potluck suppers. Mom and Katy and some other ladies make fancy food for weddings and parties. They also bake cheesecake and apple strudel for restaurants. Mom is a good cook. I just wish she would do it more at home, like the mother in *Moose on Toast*. Almost every day Katy gives Mom something good to put in my school lunch.

Mom also takes a couple of courses at the community college. She wants to be an LVN which means Licensed Vocational Nurse. They help real nurses except they don't stick needles in people. She is almost always home when I get home from school.

Your ex-friend,
Leigh Botts

November 24

Mr. Henshaw:
Here we go again.

4. Where do you live?

After the divorce Mom and I moved from Bakersfield to Pacific Grove which is on California's Central Coast about thirty kilometres from the sugar refinery at Spreckels where Dad used to haul sugar beets before he went cross-country. Mom said all the time she was growing up in California's Great Central Valley she longed for a few ocean breezes, and now we've got them. We've got a lot of fog, especially in the morning. There aren't any crops around here, just golf courses for rich people.

We live in a little house, a *really* little house, that used to be somebody's summer cottage a long time ago before somebody built a two-storey duplex in front of it. Now it is what they call a garden cottage. It is sort of falling apart, but it is all we can afford. Mom says at least it keeps the rain off, and it can't be hauled away on a flatbed truck. I have a room of my own, but Mom sleeps on a couch in the living room. She fixed the place up real nice with things from the thrift shop down the street.

Next door is a gas station that goes ping-ping, ping-ping every time a car drives in. They turn off the pinger at 10:00 P.M., but most of the time I am asleep by then. Mom doesn't want me to hang around the gas station. On our street, besides the thrift shop, there is a pet shop, a sewing machine shop, an electric shop, a couple of junk stores they call antique shops, plus a Taco King and a Softee Freeze. I am not supposed to hang around those places either. Mom is against hanging around anyplace.

15

Sometimes when the gas station isn't pinging, I can hear the ocean and the sea lions barking. They sound like dogs, and I think of Bandit. To be continued unless we get the TV fixed.

Still disgusted,
Leigh Botts

November 26

Mr. Henshaw:

If our TV was fixed I would be looking at "Highway Patrol," but it isn't so here are some more answers from my rotten brain. (Ha-ha.)

5. Do you have any pets?

I do not have any pets. (My teacher says always answer questions in complete sentences.) When Mom and Dad got divorced and Mom got me, Dad took Bandit because Mom said she couldn't work and look after a dog, and Dad said he likes to take Bandit in his truck because it is easier to stay awake on long hauls if he has him to talk to. I really miss Bandit, but I guess he's happier riding around with Dad. Like the father said in *Ways to Amuse a Dog,* dogs get pretty bored just lying around the house all day. That is what Bandit would have to do with Mom and me gone so much.

Bandit likes to ride. That's how we got him. He just jumped into Dad's cab at a truck stop in Nevada and sat there. He had a red bandanna around his neck instead of a collar, so we called him Bandit.

Sometimes I lie awake at night listening to the gas station ping-pinging and thinking about Dad and Bandit hauling tomatoes or cotton bales on Interstate 5, and I am glad Bandit is there to keep Dad awake. Have you ever seen Interstate 5? It is straight and boring with nothing much but cotton fields and a big feedlot that you can smell a long way before you come to it. It is so boring that the cattle on the feedlot don't even bother to moo. They just stand there. They don't tell you that part in school when they talk about California's Great Central Valley.

I'm getting writer's cramp from all this writing. I'll get to No. 6 next time. Mom says not to worry about the postage, so I can't use that as an excuse for not answering.

Pooped writer,
Leigh Botts

Mr. Henshaw:

Here we go again. I'll never write another list of questions for an author to answer, no matter what the teacher says.

6. Do you like school?

School is OK, I guess. That's where the kids are. The best thing about sixth grade in my new school is that if I hang in, I'll get out.

7. Who are your friends?

I don't have a whole lot of friends in my new school. Mom says maybe I'm a loner, but I don't know. A new boy in school has to be pretty cautious until he gets to know who's who. Maybe I'm just a boy nobody pays much attention to. The only time anybody paid much attention to me was in my last school when I gave the book report on *Ways to Amuse a Dog*. After my report some people went to the library to get the book. The kids here pay more attention to my lunch than they do to me. They really watch to see what I have in my lunch because Katy gives me such good things.

I wish somebody would ask me over sometime. After school I stay around kicking a soccer ball with some of the other kids so they won't think I am stuck-up or anything, but nobody asks me over.

8. Who is your favorite teacher?

I don't have a favorite teacher, but I really like Mr. Fridley. He's the custodian. He's always fair about who gets to pass out milk at lunchtime, and once when he had to clean up after someone who threw up in the hall, he didn't even look cross. He just said, "Looks like somebody's been whooping it up," and started sprinkling sawdust around. Mom used to get mad at Dad for whooping it up, but she didn't mean throwing up. She meant he stayed too long at that truck stop outside of town.

Two more questions to go. Maybe I won't answer them. So there. Ha-ha.

Leigh Botts

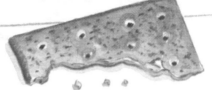

Mr. Henshaw:

OK, you win, because Mom is still nagging me, and I don't have anything else to do. I'll answer your last two questions if it takes all night.

9. What bothers you?

What bothers me about what? I don't know what you mean. I guess I'm bothered by a lot of things. I am bothered when someone steals something out of my lunchbag. I don't know enough about the people in the school to know who to suspect. I am bothered about little kids with runny noses. I don't mean I am fussy or anything like that. I don't know why. I am just bothered.

I am bothered about walking to school *slow*. The rule is nobody is supposed to be on the school grounds until ten minutes before the first bell rings. Mom has an early class. The house is so lonely in the morning when she is gone that I can't stand it and leave when she does. I don't mind being alone after school, but I do in the morning before the fog lifts and our cottage seems dark and damp.

Mom tells me to go to school but to walk slow which is hard work. Once I tried walking around every square in the sidewalk, but that got boring. So I did walking heel-toe, heel-toe. Sometimes I walk backwards except when I cross the street, but I still get there so early I have to sort of hide behind the shrubbery so Mr. Fridley won't see me.

I am bothered when my Dad telephones me and finishes by saying, "Well, keep your nose clean, kid." Why can't he say he misses me, and why can't he call me Leigh? I am bothered when he doesn't phone at all which is most of the time. I have a book of road maps and try to follow his trips when I hear from him. When the TV worked I watched the weather on the news so I would know if he was driving through blizzards, tornadoes, hail like golf balls, or any of that fancy weather they have other places in the U.S.

10. What do you wish?

I wish somebody would stop stealing the good stuff out of my lunchbag. I guess I wish a lot of other things, too. I wish someday Dad and Bandit would pull up in front in the rig. Maybe Dad would be hauling a twelve-metre reefer (that means refrigerated trailer) which would make his outfit add up to eighteen wheels altogether. Dad would yell out of the cab, "Come on, Leigh. Hop in and I'll give you a lift to school." Then I'd climb in and Bandit would wag his tail and lick my face. We'd take off with all the men in the gas station staring after us. Instead of going straight to school, we'd go barrelling along the freeway looking down on the tops of ordinary cars, then down the offramp and back to school just before the bell rang. I guess I wouldn't seem so medium then, sitting up there in the cab in front of a twelve-metre reefer. I'd jump out, and Dad would say, "So long, Leigh. Be seeing you," and Bandit would give a little bark like goodbye. I'd say, "Drive carefully, Dad," like I always do. Dad would take a minute to write in the truck's logbook, "Drove my son to school." Then the truck would pull away from the curb with all the kids staring and wishing their Dads drove big trucks, too.

There, Mr. Henshaw. That's the end of your crummy questions. I hope you are satisfied for making me do all this extra work.

Fooey on you,
Leigh Botts

December 4

Dear Mr. Henshaw,

I am sorry I was rude in my last letter when I finished answering your questions. Maybe I was mad about other things, like Dad forgetting to send this month's support payment. Mom tried to phone him at the trailer park where, as Mom says, he hangs his hat. He has his own phone in his trailer so the broker who lines up jobs for him can reach him. I wish he still hauled sugar beets over to the refinery in Spreckels so he might come to see me. The judge in the divorce said he has a right to see me.

When you answered my questions, you said the way to get to be an author was to <u>write</u>. You underlined it twice. Well, I sure did a lot of writing, and you know what? Now that I think about it, it wasn't so bad when it wasn't for a book report or a report on some country in South America or anything where I had to look things up in the library. I even sort of miss writing now that I've finished your questions. I get lonesome. Mom is working overtime at Catering by Katy because people give a lot of parties this time of year.

When I write a book maybe I'll call it *The Great Lunchbag Mystery*, because I have a lot of trouble with my lunchbag. Mom isn't so great on cooking roasts and steaks now that Dad is gone, but she makes me good lunches with sandwiches on whole wheat bread from the health food store with good filling spread all the way to the corners. Katy sends me little cheesecakes baked just for me or stuffed mushrooms and little things she calls canapés (kȧ-nȧ-pāýs). Sometimes I get a slice of quiche (kēēsh).

Today I was supposed to have a devilled egg. Katy buys the smallest eggs for parties so half an egg can be eaten in one bite and won't spill on people's carpets. She puts a little curry powder in with the mashed-up yolk which she squirts out of a tube so it looks like a rose. At lunchtime when I opened my lunchbag, my egg was gone. We leave our lunchbags and boxes (mostly bags because no sixth grader wants to carry a lunchbox) lined up along the wall under our coathooks at the back of the classroom behind a sort of partition.

Are you writing another book? Please answer my letter so we can be pen pals.

Still your No. 1 fan,
Leigh Botts

Sarah and Jeremy

by Jean Little

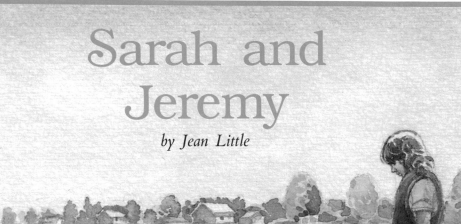

"Can I come, too?" Sarah asked.

Jeremy jumped. The dreamy look left his eyes. Lost in his thoughts, he had not known that she was there until she spoke. Now he looked up at her standing on the dock above him.

from Mama's Going to Buy You a Mockingbird

"No," he said.

"I have my life jacket on."

"No," he repeated, his voice hard.

He gave her no reason for his decision. He knew better. Give Sarah any excuse for an argument and you were asking for trouble. She was like a bulldog; she never gave up. Now, instead of going away, she stayed right where she was and drooped with disappointment. She looked so sad and small that he wanted to hit her.

"You heard me," he told her, stung into speech by her waiting silence. "I said 'No' and I meant it. Do me a favor and scram."

Sarah's lips parted, but if she had thought of answering him back, she stopped herself. He had no business ordering her off the dock, and she knew she could get him into trouble with Aunt Margery by telling on him. She also knew that if she tattled, she would never get to go out in the rowboat with him. Well, not today, anyway. She held her tongue and went on waiting.

Jeremy turned away. Let her stand there forever. He couldn't care less.

Go ahead and bawl, he thought. See how far it gets you. He pushed back his brown hair which badly needed cutting and studied the cloud formations above the cottage. Then he began to whistle as if he had entirely forgotten her presence.

But Sarah Talbot, though she was nearly four years younger than her brother, still knew a few important things about him. One of these was when not to cry. Another was that, tough as he tried to sound, he had a soft heart. She remained visibly hopeful.

Having ignored her for a full minute, Jeremy could not resist darting a glance at her to see how she was taking it. Her head was lowered so that her hair fell forward on either side of her face. She made no sound, not even a whisper of a sigh. Jeremy remembered Dad telling him about a man called Gandhi who had changed the history of India by simply sitting still and waiting for his enemies to give in. At that moment, Jeremy saw why it had worked. Sarah had not begged him or bribed him or threatened him or even tried to explain to him how she was feeling. Yet in some mysterious way, she had put him in the wrong.

Of course, he already knew how she was feeling. She was lonely, maybe even lonelier than he was. After all, he was older. Dad and Mom told him more and it was easier for him to piece together bits of over-heard conversation and make sense out of them.

It was Dad's illness that had changed everything. Mom said that he had been sick for quite awhile before he went for a check-up after school closed at the end of June. Then the doctor had made him go right into the hospital for tests, even though they had already started packing to go to the cottage. The next thing Jeremy knew, Mom was telling Sarah and him that Dad had to have an operation. Aunt Margery was going to take them to the lake so that Mom would be free to visit their father and do all she could to help him to get better fast.

"It's wonderful of Margery to do this," she said. "Otherwise you two would be stuck here in the city with nothing to do but perish from heat prostration."

All their friends were away and it had already been hot in Riverside, so he and Sarah had been glad to go. Dad had had the operation the day after they left. But Jeremy didn't know for sure what had happened. Dad must be better, yet Aunt Margery got upset every time he tried to ask about it. Mom had phoned but never when he and Sarah were in the cottage, and Aunt Margery said it would be no use calling her back because she used a pay phone at the hospital. Finally, last night, he had had a chance to speak with her, but as she handed him the receiver Aunt Margery had hissed, "Don't plague her with questions, Jeremy. She has enough to bear without that." Then Mom herself had sounded so tired and worried that he hadn't been able to ask her about all that he wanted to know.

Well, they'd be here in a couple of weeks. That much he had found out. Till then the trick was to think of other things. It would have been easier if Aunt Margery were different. Not that she wasn't nice to them. It was just that she wasn't . . . well, she wasn't Mom. Mom laughed more and had fewer rules.

Jeremy went back to watching Sarah. Even if she were putting on that mournful look, he could see that underneath it lay real misery. It showed in the hunch of her skinny shoulders and her ducked-down head, in her bitten fingernails, even in the way her toes kept bunching up and then flattening out. He felt sorry for her but he still did not want to be both-ered with her. If he could fix things for her it would be different, but he couldn't even fix things for himself.

Irritated at his momentary weakness, he did his best to appear menacing, shifting his weight as though he were about to come after her. Her head jerked up. Her eyes widened a little. But she stood her ground. He liked her toughness. He could beat her up with one hand tied behind him and she knew it, yet she wouldn't run.

"Anyway, I'm not going anywhere," he told her.

Before he had the words out of his mouth, he knew they were a mistake. Dad always said, "Give Sarah a foot and she'll take a leg and an arm as well."

"You've got the paddles hooked into their things," she pointed out, her voice mild, her eyes gleaming. "And you've untied the rope at the back."

"For crying out loud, Sarah," he snapped, "they're not paddles, they're *oars*. And those are oarlocks, you dummy. You don't call it the back of the boat, either. You say the stern."

Straightening her out on so many things at once made him feel better. Sarah looked properly impressed.

"Oh, yeah," she said. "I guess I forgot."

"You're plenty old enough to remember."

He heard himself sounding like Dad and nearly smiled. In the short silence that followed, Jeremy could see her making up her mind what to try next.

"Why do you have the oars in the oarlocks," she asked, "if you aren't going anywhere? And why . . ."

" . . . did I untie the stern?" he finished for her. "Well, sister dear, if it is any of your business, which it isn't, I thought I might want to go somewhere later so I got ready just in case. Satisfied?"

He should have known better.

"If you do go later, can I come?" she said.

He hardened his heart.

"No. I want to go by myself."

"Did Aunt Margery say you could take the boat out?" she asked softly.

Outraged at this veiled threat, he stopped feeling even faintly sorry for her.

"I don't have to ask Aunt Margery and you know it. Last summer

Dad said I was old enough to take it out whenever I liked. Buzz off, you little brat. Go play with Paul and quit bothering me."

Instead of departing, Sarah squatted down on the dock so that she was even closer to him.

"I hate Paul!" she said, her voice trembling. "I'm never going to speak to him again. Never ever!"

Jeremy had heard that before. Paul Denver, the only child Sarah's age at their end of the lake, was a whiner, and Jeremy didn't like him any more than she did. He was worse than useless when they played games needing imagination, and yet he could twist the truth so cleverly when he tattled that it was hard to deny what he said even though you knew he was lying.

But now Jeremy realized that something worse than usual must have happened. Sarah wasn't just mad. This particular upset was somehow different.

"What did Paul do?" he asked, keeping his tone matter-of-fact.

Sarah lifted her head, looked at him, and then went back to examining her toes.

"He said that his mother said that Daddy is a very sick man. And she told him that I was a poor little girl and he was supposed to be kind to me no matter how bad I am. He said his mother feels sorry for us."

She spoke in such a low voice that Jeremy could barely understand her, but as her words registered, he felt inside himself her bewilderment and outrage.

"So what did you do?" he asked, knowing that she would not have let that pass.

"I punched him in the stomach and he went bawling to Mrs. Denver and Aunt Margery. He yelled that I hit him and he hadn't done anything to me first. And Aunt Margery . . ."

She choked and Jeremy put his hand up and patted the foot nearest to him.

"Slow down and don't be a bawl-baby like Paul Denver. Now tell me about Aunt Margery."

Sarah had control of herself again.

"She said Paul's younger and smaller than me and she made me say I was sorry."

"I wish I had been there," her brother said, his hands tightening into fists. "I'd have fixed him. Catch me saying 'sorry'!"

Sarah glanced up at him again.

"You would have," she said flatly.

She was right and he knew it. What chance did a kid have when grown-ups took sides with a wart like Paul Denver? But what was Sarah going on about now? He must have missed something.

"Hey, stop talking to your big toe," he said. "I can't hear you when you mumble. Tell me that last part again."

She took a deep breath, raised her chin slightly, and repeated herself. "When Paul left, I had a swing and then I went inside to get Fiona. I didn't want Aunt Margery to know I was there. She was busy talking to Paul's mother. So I tiptoed . . ."

She was still squatting there on the dock and, as she spoke, she somehow coiled herself as tightly as a spring with her shadowed face tucked down against her knees. All Jeremy could see of her were her legs and arms and the top of her head, but he noticed she was trembling. If only Mom were here! But she wasn't. He would have to do his best. He stayed where he was and waited.

"I heard them talking. Aunt Margery was telling her that Mom said that the doctor said . . ."

She hesitated. Jeremy felt he would fly apart.

"Yeah, yeah, go *on*," he urged.

" . . . the doctor said Daddy had left something too late and now there's only a fifty-fifty chance. Aunt Margery said she had warned them but they wouldn't listen . . . I can't remember exactly. When she saw me, she got really mad. She said I sneaked up. But the door was open. Mom says to knock if the door is shut. Jeremy, what's a fifty-fifty chance?"

For a long moment, Jeremy sat absolutely still. Then he reached out to untie the knot that tethered the bow of the boat and said in an ordinary, everyday voice, "Get in. I've changed my mind. I'll take you for a row."

The Young Maple Tree

by Edith Jane Harrison

We had lived next door to old Mr. and Mrs. Benson for as long as I could remember. Mr. Benson had been retired for years, but he couldn't bear just to sit around the house. That's why his yard always looked so much better than anyone else's in the block. He mowed his lawn before it needed it, didn't give the hedge a chance to grow, and was always planting something.

This year he'd got a young maple tree. Mrs. Benson had sighed to Ma when he brought it home, "There are so many trees here now that the house is shaded from all sides. But Ben just can't sit. Where he'll find a place for it is beyond me."

I'd come out of the house early that Saturday morning, hoping I could sneak off and go fishing before Ma thought of a reason why I shouldn't, and I could see Mr. Benson looking for a place to plant his tree. First he wheeled it in his old barrow out near the front sidewalk. He stood back and looked at it from all sides, then shook his head and wheeled it to another position.

When he caught sight of me, he waved and called, "Come on over, Bill, and see my tree."

28

I was kind of anxious to get fishing before Ma saw me, but I thought the world and all of Mr. Benson, who never turned down a ticket or a Boy Scout apple or anything I'd ever sold, so I went over to talk to him.

"Looks like a good tree," I said, and squatted on the ground, pulling a blade of grass and chewing on it. Mr. Benson took out his pipe and packed it with tobacco.

"It *is* a good tree," he said. "There's nothing like a maple to make you feel that it's worthwhile doing something and that what you do maybe does matter." He pointed with his pipe stem to the full-grown tree near the corner of the house. "See that maple? My dad helped me plant it when I was just a boy. We grew together, that tree and I. And times when I thought I'd have to give up, like when Biff got killed overseas, I'd go out and look at that tree." He paused, and seemed to be thinking of how to explain what he felt to me. I could see him struggling for the words, trying to get them right.

I knew what he wanted to say, and I didn't want him to worry about getting the words just right, so I nodded to show him I knew what he meant.

"It's always helped me, Bill. I'd think, there's my tree. It's been through storm and hail and wind, and it's still standing straight and strong and beautiful. Then I'd feel better."

I listened to him talk, and all the time I could feel the words that he didn't know how to say. I'd always been able to talk with Mr. Benson. Better than with my own dad. All Dad ever talked about was school work and mowing lawns and not leaving my bike in the driveway. Mr. Benson was interested in anything I did, even if I was only out back digging fish worms.

I didn't say anything, because I wanted Mr. Benson to go on talking. He had something on his mind, I could tell.

"Suppose you're wondering why I'm planting another young maple, when I'm an old man, eh?" His eyes seemed unnaturally bright in the lined face under the white hair.

I had been wondering that, because he couldn't possibly see it grow till it was a big tree, and they had no family to leave the property to, now that Biff was gone. But I figured if he wanted to plant a tree, why shouldn't he?

"You're not so old," I said, not knowing what else to say.

"Thanks, Bill, but you and I both know it's not true. I am old. And maybe foolish. If I tell you why I want to plant this tree, you'll probably think I'm a foolish old man."

By then I was real curious and I kept my eyes on his face, afraid that if I glanced away, he might decide not to tell me.

"Do you know how old I am, Bill?" He drew on his pipe and looked at me.

"Seventy?" I guessed. He was probably more.

"Seventy-six." He glanced around the yard, and I knew he was seeing the perfect spring day it was with the shining blue of the sky, the uncurling leaves of the trees, and his own neat garden that he was so proud of.

"Did you ever plant anything, Bill?"

To tell the truth, I'm not much of a gardener. The only gardening I've ever done is hoeing or weeding or helping Ma plant some seeds. "No," I said. "Well, maybe a few seeds. But nothing like a tree."

He puffed on his pipe, with a faraway look in his eyes. "I have a feeling that every time I plant something, a part of me is planted with it. That as it grows and strengthens, I'm growing and strengthening too. Do you understand?"

I nodded, knowing that he was very anxious for me to understand.

"You remind me of Biff when he was your age," he said, and then he stood there not saying anything for a while. "I wanted to plant one more tree . . ." He stared at the ground, and I looked down at my feet.

Neither of us could put what we felt into words. I got up and stood in front of Mr. Benson, wondering what I could say to let him know I understood.

"Maybe I'll plant a maple tree, too," I said, then I went to get my bike. Mr. Benson stood and waved, then took up his wheelbarrow again.

I didn't have much luck fishing that morning. Mostly this doesn't bother me, I just sit there anyway. Besides, I never go fishing just to catch fish. It's kind of nice to hold a fishing pole and think about next

Saturday's baseball game, or how I'm going to get Dad to let me buy that new baseball mitt, or what Ma'll have for lunch when I get home.

But that morning something was itching me; for some reason I felt that I should get home. I shrugged off the feeling, but it kept coming back strong. I'd been there a couple of hours, so I jumped on my bike and started home. I was just turning into our driveway when an ambulance pulled out of Mr. Benson's driveway.

I sort of half-fell off my bike and stood there staring at the ambulance as it went up the street. Somehow I got my feet moving and went into the house.

"Ma," I said, "I saw an ambulance over at Mr. Benson's. It's him, isn't it?"

"Yes, Bill." She was mixing something at the kitchen table, and she kept right on stirring, not looking at me. "It happened right after you left."

"He's . . . dead?" My stomach felt hollow.

Ma nodded. "Bill? Are you all right?"

"Ma," I said, and the hollow in my stomach felt bigger every minute, "what happened to the tree?"

"Land sakes, Bill," Ma said, "worrying about a tree! Bill, where are you going?"

I went out to the porch. I walked down the steps and down the driveway. There was something I had to do.

The tree was still in the wheelbarrow, in a corner of Mr. Benson's backyard.

I got a little spade from our garage and went over to Mr. Benson's yard and started digging. When I had it about right, I took the maple tree out of the wheelbarrow and I planted it.

I filled the hole up, and smoothed it over, then I got the hose and I watered that tree until the water oozed up out of the ground and ran over my shoes.

The Crystal Ball Sees All

by Keith Robertson

Five-year-old Belinda Osborn liked to hide, and that meant big trouble for the Henry Reed Baby-Sitting Service. Henry and Midge, his partner, spent half their time worrying that something terrible had happened to her. Then a visit to Mr. Adams's electronic workshop gave Henry a bright idea.

Mr. Adams was puttering around with a lot of electronic equipment that looked very interesting, so I stayed quite a while. As I was leaving he showed me a little walkie-talkie set that was no bigger than two little battery radios.

"They're good for about a half a kilometre," Mr. Adams said. "More a toy than anything, although Craig and I have found them useful when we've gone fishing together. You know, when we're fishing a small stream where there's no danger from deep water, I can let him be off by himself and still keep in touch."

"Would you rent those to me for a few hours?" I asked Mr. Adams. "They might be the solution to a tough baby-sitting problem."

"You're welcome to use them at no cost. Just bring them back in good shape."

I hurried on home with Agony yelping dismally as he lost

from Henry Reed's Baby-Sitting Service

33

ground. I telephoned Midge as soon as I got in the house and explained what I had in mind.

"I want to add an extra touch," Midge said. "Go over to our garage and you'll find one of those polished metal balls that people put on pedestals on the lawn. Somebody gave it to Mom one time and she's never used it. Bring it with you. If you get here fast you can get all set while Belinda is still asleep."

I left Agony with Aunt Mabel and went to Midge's for the metal globe. Then I pedalled to the Osborns' as fast as I could. Belinda was still asleep so I made a quick survey of the backyard. A big maple tree seemed the most likely spot. I gave one of the walkie-talkies to Midge and with the other in my pocket I climbed the tree. Midge had to give me a boost to reach the first limb, but after that it was simple. The leaves were so thick that it wasn't easy to find a location where I could see reasonably well in all directions, but finally I found a spot.

"I'm all set," I said into the walkie-talkie. "Testing—one, two, three—can you read me?"

"Loud and clear," Midge said. "Maybe too loud and clear. She might be able to hear you without a receiver."

We did a little experimenting and found that we could talk in scarcely more than a whisper and still hear each other perfectly.

"Why don't you go and make some noise so she'll wake up?" I suggested. "Perching up in this tree is going to be uncomfortable after a while."

"Gladly," Midge said. "I'm looking forward to this." She disappeared and a few minutes later came back with Belinda trailing behind her. Midge had carefully placed the metal globe in the centre of the lawn. Belinda spotted it immediately.

"What's that?" she asked.

"My crystal ball," Midge said.

"What's it for?"

"I can look into that and see things. I can tell what's happening in faraway places. I brought it so that I can look in it and tell where you are when you run away and hide."

Belinda didn't say a word. She had her back toward me but I knew she was staring at Midge with that peculiar stare of hers, plotting something.

"So if you want to do your runaway act, go right ahead," Midge said. "I'm going to sit down in this chair and relax."

She sat down and closed her eyes. Belinda stood watching her for several minutes. Then she marched over and stared at the crystal ball. She must not have seen anything to scare her because she promptly began a slow circle of Midge's chair. When she was directly behind Midge she backed slowly toward the corner of the house. By the time she got to the corner she was out of Midge's sight but I could still see her from my perch in the tree. There was an enormous spreading yew near the drive and she ducked under one of the branches and disappeared into the centre of it.

"Midge from sky lookout," I whispered into the walkie-talkie. "Come in, please."

"I'm in," Midge said. "Where is she?"

"Around the corner of the house, hiding in the middle of that big spreading yew by the driveway."

"Good," Midge said. "I'll discombobulate her."

She picked up the big metal ball and began walking around the backyard. She moved over to where she could be seen by Belinda but turned her back toward the yew.

"Crystal ball, tell me where Belinda is hiding!" she said in a loud voice, holding one hand to her forehead. She didn't look much like a gypsy fortuneteller since she was wearing shorts instead of long flowing robes, but otherwise her act was pretty good.

"I see something. I see something!" she announced. "The picture is becoming clearer. I see a little girl hiding in a yew near the driveway. I also see a bee buzzing over the tree. It is going to sting her if she doesn't quit hiding and get back where she belongs."

The yew began to shake and a minute later Belinda appeared. She looked as though she would like to murder Midge, but she didn't say a word. Midge put the ball back on the lawn and sat down in her chair again.

"Would you like to play a game or go swimming?" she suggested.

"No!"

"All right," Midge said. "Do anything you like."

Belinda stood looking at the ball for about five minutes. Whatever else Belinda is, she isn't dumb. There was an empty plastic bucket sitting just outside the garden tool house. Belinda marched over, picked it up, and returned to the centre of the lawn. She looked at Midge to be certain that she wasn't being watched and then put the bucket upside down over the ball. After hesitating a minute she slowly sidled toward the garage.

"She just put a bucket over your crystal ball," I said.

"The crystal ball will see everything, bucket or no bucket," Midge said softly. "Where's she going?"

"She just disappeared into the garage," I said. "I don't know whether you know it or not, but there's a little loft at the back end of the garage. I can't see it but she may climb up there."

"Okay!" Midge answered. "Madam Glass will now go into one of her famous trances."

"Belinda, it's no use," she called. "If you don't come back immediately I'll have to consult my crystal ball again. And putting that bucket over it doesn't do a thing."

Belinda wasn't convinced. She didn't stir. Midge picked up the ball and walked around the yard with it in her hand.

When she got over in front of the garage she said, "I begin to see a picture. It's cloudy, but it's becoming clearer. I can make out a little girl hiding in a garage."

She had been speaking in a deep, sort of ghostly voice. She dropped the ghostly tone and said in a very sharp voice, "Belinda, come right out of the garage immediately before I come in after you." She put some real authority in her voice and sounded just like Mrs. Houghton, our history teacher, does when she is annoyed.

Belinda came out of the garage a minute later, her chin down almost to her chest. She looked unhappy.

"Want to go swimming?" Midge asked.

"No."

"All right, try running away and hiding, if you'd rather," Midge said, flopping in her chair.

Belinda went back to staring at the metal ball. She was thinking hard and she had a real inspiration this time. She picked up the crystal ball and made off with it. I was laughing so hard that for a minute I forgot to watch and almost lost her. Finally, I saw her as she disappeared around the edge of the little garden tool house. A second later I saw the end of a board swing out and drop back again. I didn't actually see Belinda disappear, but I had a good idea of what had happened.

I did an imitation of Dracula and said into my walkie-talkie, "The crystal ball sees everything but who can see the crystal ball?"

"What are you talking about?" Midge asked.

"She hooked your crystal ball and headed for the hills. Now what are you going to do?"

"This requires a little thought," Midge said. "I hope you saw where she went."

"Around the back of the little garden house," I said. "I think we've solved a mystery and found her Number One place. My guess is that there is a loose board on the back. It's nailed at the top. She pulls that out and slips inside. When you see the doors locked you don't think about looking inside. That's where she's probably been several times when I couldn't find her."

"I'm going into my act," Midge said.

"I hope she doesn't keep this up much longer," I said. "I'm beginning to feel pretty cramped up here. I never knew maples had such hard branches."

"Belinda, have you disappeared again?" Midge called out in an annoyed voice. "Come back here!"

Naturally Belinda didn't answer. I could picture her, hunched down in the tool house, clutching that crystal ball.

"And it won't do you a bit of good, taking my crystal ball," Midge said sternly. "It can send messages to me for almost a kilometre."

In case Belinda was looking through a crack in the tool house, Midge went through the whole act of putting her head in her hands and concentrating.

"I begin to get a message," she said slowly. "It's very distant and dim but I see a little girl running around in back of a garden tool house carrying a crystal ball. I can't quite make out what she's doing now, but it looks like she is pulling at a loose board and slipping inside the house. That must be it, you're hiding in the garden tool house."

She walked over and opened the door. "Get up off that dirty floor or your clothes will be ruined and your mother will be furious!" Midge said sternly. "And give me back that ball!"

Belinda was beaten. She didn't march out sullenly as she had before, but she walked back very quietly and meekly beside Midge.

"Let's not have any more of this silly hiding," Midge said.

"Can anybody else read your crystal ball?" Belinda asked in a hopeful voice.

"Henry can, and I'm going to advise him to bring it unless you promise me you'll not hide anymore," Midge said. "As a matter of fact, I think I'll send Henry a message through the crystal ball. I'm going to ask him to come nail that board back where it belongs and to take a swim."

For a minute I thought Belinda was going to cry, but she's tough. Midge walked a short distance away from her.

"I'll make some excuse for walking around the house," Midge said into the walkie-talkie. "You get down and appear in a few minutes. We might as well give her the full treatment."

I didn't hear what she told Belinda but a minute later they disappeared around the corner of the house. I got down as fast as I could and went after them. I circled the house behind them until they got back by the pool. Then I strolled in along the drive.

"I got your message," I said. "So I hurried right over."

"You sure did," Midge said. "You must have flown."

"What's this about a board you want nailed?"

"There's a loose board on the garden tool house," Midge said. "Belinda and I think it ought to be nailed down—don't we, Belinda?"

"I guess so," Belinda said, without too much enthusiasm.

I found a hammer and nails in the basement and nailed the board back where it belonged. I'd brought my bathing suit earlier, so I changed and we all went swimming. We had a good time and Belinda behaved herself except once when she thought we weren't looking and kicked the crystal ball into the pool. I doubt if we'll have any more trouble with her. The Henry Reed Baby-Sitting Service is not an outfit to tamper with.

39

Anastasia on the Job

by Lois Lowry

When her best friend went off to camp for the whole summer, Anastasia Krupnik decided to get a job to keep herself busy. She was thrilled when wealthy Mrs. Bellingham answered her ad for a position as a Lady's Companion. But Anastasia soon discovered her new job wasn't quite what she had expected.

Anastasia went directly to the back door. It seemed about five kilometres around the huge house, and it certainly would have been easier to ring the front doorbell. But she had decided, on her way, that it would be appropriate to go to the back on her first day. Later, after she was fully installed as Companion, of course she would enter by the front. Probably she would have her own key.

Later, too, she would call Mrs. Bellingham by her first name, Willa.

From Anastasia At Your Service

But in the beginning she would call her Mrs. Bellingham, she decided. Probably at first Mrs. Bellingham would call her Miss Krupnik. Until they became close friends.

She leaned her bike against a tree and knocked on the back door. After a moment it was opened by a very fat woman. Anastasia was startled. She hadn't expected Mrs. Bellingham to be fat. She hadn't sounded fat on the phone. Also, Willa sounded like a tall, thin name. But names could be deceiving, Anastasia knew. Sam Krupnik, for example, sounded like a tall, bearded man. In reality, Sam Krupnik was a two-and-a-half-year-old brat who still wore Pampers at night. Eventually he would grow into his tall, bearded name; in the meantime, he was a pain in the neck.

"Hello, Mrs. Bellingham," she said politely. "I'm Anas—"

The woman interrupted her. "I'm Edna Fox," she said. "I'm the house-keeper. And you're the girl Mrs. B's taken on. Good thing. We're up to our ears. Come on in."

Mrs. Fox led her into a kitchen that seemed as large as the entire downstairs of the Krupniks' house.

Two women wearing aprons were standing near a large double sink, peeling carrots and potatoes. They looked over and smiled at Anastasia. Anastasia smiled back. It was important for the Companion to stay on good terms with the kitchen help, she knew from the novels she had read.

"Rachel and Gloria," said Mrs. Fox, indicating the two aproned women.

"How do you do," said Anastasia politely.

"Hi, there," said Rachel and Gloria.

"Here's an apron for you," said the housekeeper, handing a flowered apron to Anastasia. "Let's get you started. We are out straight. Two of the help quit last week, without any notice at all. And there's a party tomorrow. You can start on the silverware. The polish is over there."

Anastasia unfolded the apron, puzzled. A Companion wasn't supposed to wear an apron. Especially an apron like this. It was the kind that went on over your head, the kind old ladies wore. Also, it was much too big.

She put it on, tied it behind her back, and stood there, embarrassed.

41

Heaped on a wooden kitchen table that looked roughly the size of a football field was a mound of silverware larger than any mound of silverware Anastasia had ever seen.

"I wonder if there's some mistake," she said timidly to Mrs. Fox. "I thought I was supposed to . . ."

"Mistake isn't the word for it," said Mrs. Fox. "Disaster is what it is. To invite ten people for lunch, with two of the help gone. Madness. Catastrophe. Here are some rags."

Mrs. Fox thrust a handful of cloths into Anastasia's hand and disappeared through a door.

Of course. Anastasia sorted it out in her mind, and she understood. It was an emergency situation. Even the Companion had to pitch in and help in an emergency.

Well, okay. She was a good sport. Companions always were. Anastasia picked up the first of twelve million spoons and began to polish.

She polished.

And polished.

And polished.

"I don't mind doing this kind of thing in an emergency," she said cheerfully to Rachel and Gloria, who continued their peeling silently.

One rag after another turned black as Anastasia polished. After what seemed hours (but it wasn't; she looked at her watch, and only half an hour had passed), there was a large pile of polished spoons and forks beside her on the table. There was a still larger pile of unpolished ones still in the centre. But she made a bundle of the finished ones in her apron and took them over to the sink to wash off the polish.

"Excuse me," she said to Rachel and Gloria, "I'm just going to rinse these off." And she dumped them into the sink.

There was a sudden, deafening crunch.

"Omigod," said Rachel. Or maybe it was Gloria. One of them pushed Anastasia aside and flipped a switch. The crunching noise stopped. The kitchen was very, very silent.

"The garbage disposal was running," said Rachel.

"For the peelings," said Gloria.

"Oh," said Anastasia.

One of them reached into the drain and pulled out a silver spoon. Or what had once been a silver spoon. Now it looked like a piece of abstract sculpture that Anastasia had once seen at the Institute of Contemporary Art.

"I didn't know the disposal was on," she said miserably.

"Obviously," said Mrs. Fox, who suddenly appeared behind her and took the mashed spoon out of her hand.

"It has a kind of interesting shape now," said Anastasia.

Rachel and Gloria turned away and began peeling again. Mrs. Fox didn't say anything.

"Good thing there are a billion more spoons," said Anastasia.

Mrs. Fox left the kitchen again.

Anastasia slowly rinsed and dried the rest of the polished silverware. She arranged it on the table, picked up a clean rag, and began polishing again.

"This is a good way to get in practice," she said after a while, "because I suppose I'll be polishing Mrs. Bellingham's jewellery when I start my regular job."

Rachel and Gloria looked at her curiously and went on peeling carrots and potatoes.

"Of course I won't drop her diamonds down the disposal," said Anastasia. She meant it as a joke. But neither Rachel nor Gloria laughed.

It sure was *boring*, working in a kitchen with people who had no sense of humor. Much as Anastasia hated doing dishes at home, still she and her mother always laughed a lot. If Sam came in the kitchen while they were washing dishes, they put soapsuds on his chin and made him a beard. Sam liked that.

Anastasia began to feel homesick for Sam.

She remembered a silly thing her mother sometimes did. Sometimes her mother picked up a plate, looked into it, and said, "I can *see* myself in this china!"—imitating a TV commercial.

Anastasia picked up a small silver tray she had just polished, looked into it, and said dramatically, "I can *see* myself in this china!"

Rachel and Gloria glanced over at her as if she were crazy. Neither of them laughed.

Anastasia put the tray down and sighed. She *had* seen herself in the tray. She had silver polish on her nose. Her hair was a mess. She looked like a household drudge.

She felt very, very homesick.

She picked up the millionth fork and polished.

And polished.

At four o'clock Mrs. Fox came back into the kitchen. Rachel and Gloria had finished their peeling. They were working silently at something in another corner of the kitchen. The pile of silverware was almost finished.

Mrs. Fox nodded to Anastasia. "Mrs. B wants to see you now," she said.

At last. Anastasia didn't mind being a good sport in an emergency, but two solid hours of silver-polishing was enough. She was ready to get on with her real job.

She took off her apron, wiped the silver polish from her nose with a damp cloth, and smoothed her hair.

She followed Mrs. Fox out of the kitchen. Down a hall. Through a door. Down another hall lined with paintings. Through an oak-panelled room with wall-to-wall bookcases. Across another hall. Into a sunny room filled with plants, where a gray-haired woman sat in a wicker chair, working on a piece of needlepoint.

Mrs. Bellingham. At last. And she was exactly as Anastasia had pictured her. Everything was going to be okay. Starting now, she could forget the drudgery of the emergency silver-polishing, and she and Mrs. Bellingham could get on with the business of Companionship. If she were older, Mrs. Bellingham would offer her a glass of sherry now. Probably she wouldn't offer sherry to someone who was twelve. But that was okay. Anastasia didn't like sherry anyway. She'd settle for some iced tea. Mrs. Fox had disappeared. Probably Mrs. Fox was getting the tea.

Mrs. Bellingham lit a cigarette. Anastasia hoped she wouldn't offer her one. To be polite she would have to take it, but she really hated cigarettes.

But Mrs. Bellingham snapped the silver cigarette case closed and inhaled her cigarette without offering one to Anastasia.

"Well," said Mrs. Bellingham, "we didn't give you much time to break in, did we? Put you right to work!"

Anastasia smiled. "I understand about emergencies, Mrs. Bellingham. Everybody has to pitch in. And I enjoyed getting to know the kitchen staff. That's important, I think." It was sort of a lie—she hadn't enjoyed Rachel and Gloria at all—but it seemed the right thing to say.

"Indeed. Did Mrs. Fox tell you about the luncheon tomorrow?"

"She told me that there was a party tomorrow."

"A family lunch. My granddaughter's birthday."

Anastasia smiled. That was wonderful, she thought. She could just write off the silver-polishing afternoon as a bad beginning. Tomorrow she would get to know the family. She would begin her Companion duties for real. Tonight she would have to think seriously about Conversation Topics. Not politics or religion, she knew. Literature, probably. Tonight she would review in her mind all the books she had ever read. *Gone with the Wind* was one of her favorites. She could talk to people at the luncheon about *Gone with the Wind*. Why Scarlett didn't marry Ashley Wilkes. Stuff like that.

What a terrific job I have, thought Anastasia happily.

"I would like you here promptly at eleven A.M.," said Mrs. Bellingham.

Suddenly Anastasia thought of a problem. She had nothing to wear to a luncheon. She was already wearing her only decent dress, and it had smears of silver polish on it. What she needed was a Basic Black dress. Never in a million years would her mother take her out tonight to buy a Basic Black dress.

She couldn't borrow a dress from Mrs. Bellingham. They weren't the same size. And their taste seemed to be a little different.

"Do you have a dark skirt?" Mrs. Bellingham asked. She had read Anastasia's mind. What a terrific relationship they were going to have, Anastasia thought.

"Yes," she said. "A dark blue denim wraparound."

"Well, that will do, I guess. Wear it with a tailored white blouse. Those sandals you're wearing will be all right."

A denim skirt and a white blouse didn't seem too terrific for an elegant luncheon. Maybe Mrs. Bellingham planned to lend her some jewellery, thought Anastasia.

"Mrs. Fox will give you a white apron," said Mrs. Bellingham.

A *white apron?* Anastasia had been thinking along the lines of a diamond necklace. Suddenly she had a strange feeling that things weren't exactly what she thought they were.

Mrs. Bellingham inhaled her cigarette again. "The luncheon will be buffet," she said, "so you won't have to serve at the table. But be sure to empty ashtrays, keep water glasses filled, that sort of thing."

Anastasia's vision of herself discussing Scarlett O'Hara with the guests at lunch faded and blurred.

I'm the *maid,* she thought in despair, realizing the truth in a horrible sudden flash.

Mrs. Bellingham was making some notes on a pad of paper. Anastasia stood there watching, stricken with disappointment. In her mind she began to compose a letter. She would write it tonight and deliver it in the morning. "Dear Mrs. Bellingham," it would say, "I have decided to go into another profession."

Nam's Journey Begins

by Leo Heaps

This is a true story about Nam, a Vietnamese boy who now lives in Canada. Because of war and poverty in Vietnam, Nam's father decided to send Nam and his sister Ling away to a new life overseas. Nam wanted to go because he hoped that in a new land he would find opportunities to earn money to help his family. With Ling along, he knew he wouldn't be lonely. He could hardly wait for their journey to begin.

from A Boy Called Nam

At last the day came when Nam's father awakened both children before daybreak and said that they must leave within an hour for the coast. Nam was not frightened, only very excited at the prospect of the ocean voyage ahead. When Ling was awakened she dutifully rose and started the morning fire in the small stove to boil some herb tea and cook a pot of rice. It was going to be a long day, and it would be almost nightfall before they reached their destination at the small port where a boat could be found. It was a sad moment as the two oldest children fondly embraced their mother, brothers, and sisters and said goodbye.

Nam, Ling, and their father set out for the coast on foot and finally reached the port before sunset. They found the small town thronged with thousands of refugees and the harbor with countless boats of every description. Some ships were moored alongside the dock and others were anchored some distance from shore. In the harbor, people of all ages, including babes in arms, were packed onto the decks of some of the aged craft. Several overburdened boats, low in the water, were already moving slowly out to sea.

While Nam and Ling waited, their father spoke to one of the sailors working on the wharf, who directed him to a captain in a dirty white cap. The captain had a deep, gruff voice and stood guarding the gangplank of an old wooden ship named the *Ho Chi Minh.* He was busy haggling over the price of passage with a family who carried their few precious possessions on their backs. When they had finished their business, the family went aboard. Then Nam's father approached the captain. The two men argued over the amount of money to be paid until the captain, satisfied with the amount offered, finally agreed to take the children on the long journey, which he said would take two weeks. He told Nam's father that they would have to travel a roundabout route to the south to avoid pirates while at the same time keeping well clear of Chinese waters. The captain promised to bring both children to a safe harbor in the east where there were refugee camps. From here they would eventually be transported to new homes overseas. All their father had to do was to buy passage on this boat and the children had a ticket to freedom. The captain said that there would be many more families aboard by nightfall. The children would surely find a kind grown-up to take care of them.

Nam's father was a simple, trusting man who nonetheless knew from bitter personal experience that nothing in this world went smoothly. There would be difficulties, but he didn't know exactly what they would be. He guessed that the sea held hidden dangers. Certainly the ship was

very old and the planking looked loose and rotten. The hull could not have been more than fifteen metres long and it did not look like a sufficiently sturdy boat to venture upon the high seas. However, the typhoon season was at least a month away, so Nam's father hoped that the sea would remain calm until the voyage was over.

Nam showed no fear of the boat's condition or of the future. He was eager to go aboard and begin the voyage. Already he was comforting Ling, who felt far less confident than her brother. Other people were now lining up behind the Chan family and the captain was eager to do business with them. He quickly reassured the children's father that he had travelled to the refugee camps before and the journey would be routine.

Nam's father could do no more. From his satchel he produced a bag containing two large pots of rice and half a roast duck. Nam's mother had saved the food so that the children would have something to eat on their long voyage. He warmly embraced his children and then, without looking back, quickly vanished into the jostling crowd along the wharf.

When Nam and Ling stepped aboard a few minutes later and joined some of the other refugees huddled on deck, one man rose from the far end of the boat and approached them. He gave a shout of joy at the sight of the two Chan children. It was Kon Ki, a distant cousin, who was twenty-four years old.

"Where did you come from?" Nam asked happily.

"Like you, I came from my village and intend to make the same journey. By good fortune I found passage on this boat."

Kon Ki was grinning, overjoyed to see his young relatives, and when the children realized they would have a friend to accompany them they felt a good deal better. This would make their voyage much less lonely.

The refugee passengers continued to board the boat in ones and twos until well after dark. The captain waited for them from the top of the gangplank and took their gold before allowing them aboard. When he had allowed the last person on deck, he ordered everyone below into the dark and dirty hold. Here they would remain until the vessel was ready to sail early the following morning.

The *Ho Chi Minh* lay quietly moored at that part of the dock no one visited except the poor refugees. When the boat was filled to more than its capacity with passengers, the captain awaited the permission of a gov-

ernment official to depart. The captain only obtained this permission when he had bribed the man with a percentage of the gold the refugees had paid him. As the Chan children and the other refugees descended into the bottom of the ship, they entered a cavern of darkness.

Down in the filthy hold of the *Ho Chi Minh,* Kon Ki and the two children found a small space where they could barely stretch out. The damp, black interior of the boat was dense with people and already the air smelled foul. It was so dark that Nam could barely see Ling and Kon

Ki although they were only centimetres away. It was a while before Nam's eyes grew accustomed to the dark. Never before had he been with so many strangers and crammed into so small a space. From the cries and sobbing around him, he guessed that there were many young children and infants among the men and women aboard.

Every few hours during the night a crew member descended the ladder to where the passengers lay huddled. He warned them to keep quiet and to show no lights, which could be seen between the cracks in the deck planking. Otherwise the vessel might attract the attention of the officials. The government officials had been bribed, but they could always come back and ask for more money and delay the departure even longer.

Ling was frightened of the darkness and their strange surroundings.

"How long must we remain in the dark?" she asked.

"Not much longer," her brother answered. Kon Ki had fallen asleep sitting upright, as he was now unable to find sufficient room to stretch out on the wooden floorboards.

Nam tried to comfort Ling by saying, "In the morning the boat will leave; then we can all go on deck and sit in the warm sunlight and wait for the sight of the new land. There will be plenty of food there and we will all be safe."

Nam was as frightened as Ling was but he pretended that he had no fear. This helped to calm his sister, for she soon fell asleep.

Nam stayed awake peering through the gloom at the troubled faces of the people around him. He saw ordinary men and women who had put their lives into the hands of a captain who had taken all their gold and hidden them in the wet, dirty hold. Sometimes in the night Nam was startled by the cries of small children followed by the soft singing of women rocking their babies to sleep. Although he tried hard not to cry, Nam felt so lonely that tears rose to his eyes as he remembered his loving parents left behind in the village. Deep in his heart he believed he would never see his family again.

He was glad when he felt a small, friendly nudge in his back from Kon Ki, who had suddenly wakened. Kon Ki pointed to a crack in the deck planks above where the first light of day could be seen. Other families soon began to stir and waken as the engines started and the ropes holding the boat were thrown onto the deck. The refugees could feel the gentle rocking as the ship made its slow way through the harbor and into the long ocean swells. Below deck no one was allowed to make any fires, so the passengers ate their food cold and drank water from the small tin containers they had brought with them.

Ling opened their parcel of food and gave a cupful of boiled rice to Nam with a small piece of roast duck. Nam realized that his father had forgotten to give them a canister of water, but Kon Ki had brought a skin bag filled with water, which he hoped would be enough for the three of them until they reached land. For himself, Kon Ki had packets of rice cakes and biscuits and several large bars of chocolate wrapped in a plastic bag.

The gentle swaying of the boat soon changed to a steeper, rhythmic motion and Kon Ki told the children that they were now well out of the harbor and into the great sea itself. He warned them not to be frightened if the boat began to rock violently, since it was a small craft and not designed for a long sea voyage.

As a boy, Kon Ki had gone to sea one summer and he knew that all but the biggest steamships were uncomfortable for passengers on the ocean. He explained to Nam and Ling that the *Ho Chi Minh* was a very old vessel and had not been well maintained. He did not tell them he had noticed that many of the beams were rotten and that already a little water had seeped through the floorboards to wash back and forth in the bilge. Sometimes Nam heard a loud clanking; Kon Ki said this was the motor of the pump that sucked up the water coming in through the leaking planks and tossed it overboard again.

Late in the morning a rough-looking sailor with a scraggly beard and long hair put his head down into the dark hold and ordered everyone up on deck. Nam was pleased to leave the crowded, foul-smelling dungeon, unfit for human beings to live in. He helped Ling up the ladder, followed by Kon Ki, and blinked as he entered the sunlight.

It was a warm day in September and the sea did not look as rough as it had felt when Nam lay at the bottom of the boat. Out in the fresh air and under the warm sun, the world seemed a better place. Even Ling almost smiled. They looked back to watch the dark line of mist-covered shore gradually disappear from sight.

The Ghost Pond

from OWL Magazine

This ghost pond once teemed with life, but now even the animals that live nearby no longer come to it to drink or find food. What happened? Garbage dumped here began seeping poisonous chemicals into the water. For a while the pond still looked healthy, but the underwater plants were dying. Soon many of the pond animals began dying too. They couldn't live without the plants that gave them both food and oxygen to breathe, and they were also absorbing poisons from the garbage into their bodies. When larger predators and scavengers ate these poisoned animals, they started dying also. Strangely enough, however, some life remains in the pond. The sludge worms (1) on the bottom and the insects shown in the magnifying glass—sow bugs (2) and midge larvae (3)—need so little oxygen and can tolerate so much poison that they are able to survive even after everything else is dead.

Can this pond be brought back to life? Turn the page to find out.

The
Rescued
Pond

Do you recognize this scene?
It's the same pond from the previous page, but three years have passed
since the garbage dump was moved
where it would do far less harm. It looks
as if a miracle has taken place, and in a way
it has. Fresh water from the stream feeding the

pond washed away the poisons and brought tiny water plants into the pond. Once the plants started to grow and produce oxygen, animals again made the pond their home. As final proof that all is well, look through the bottom magnifying glass and you'll see the nymphs of the dragonfly (1) and the mayfly (2)—two creatures that never live in polluted water. This pond was lucky because it was not difficult to clean up. But it's not always so easy to repair damage that's been done. This is why so many people now think very carefully before they interfere with nature. It is so often very hard to undo mistakes.

57

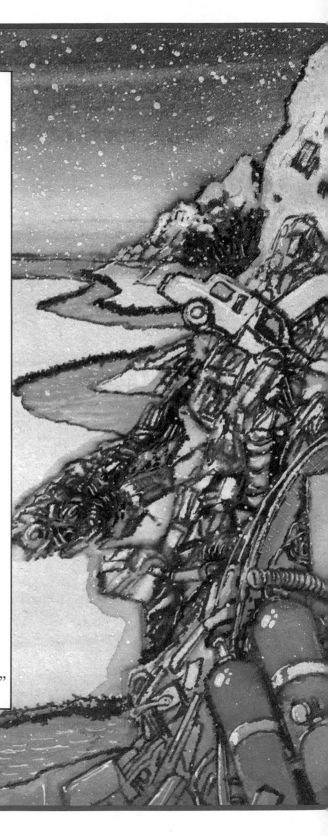

And They Lived Happily Ever After for a While

by John Ciardi

It was down by the Dirty River
   As the Smog was beginning to thin
Because we had been so busy
   Breathing the worst of it in,

That the worst remained inside us
   And whatever we breathed back
Was only—sort of—grayish,
   Or at least not entirely black.

It was down by the Dirty River
   That flows to the Sticky Sea
I gave my heart to my Bonnie,
   And she gave hers to me.

I coughed: "I love you, Bonnie.
   And do you love me true?"
The tears of joy flowed from my eyes
   When she sneezed back: "Yes—Achoo!"

It was high in the Garbage Mountains,
  In Saint Snivens by the Scent,
I married my darling Bonnie
  And we built our Oxygen Tent.

And here till the tanks are empty
  We sit and watch TV
And dream of the Dirty River
  On its way to the Sticky Sea.

Here till the needles quiver
  Shut on the zero mark
We sit hand in hand while the TV screen
  Shines like a moon in the dark.

I cough: "I love you, Bonnie.
  And do you love me true?"
And tears of joy flow from our eyes
  When she sneezes: "Yes—Achoo!"

Consultant: Mark McKenney, Ministry of the Environment. Barry Blitt.

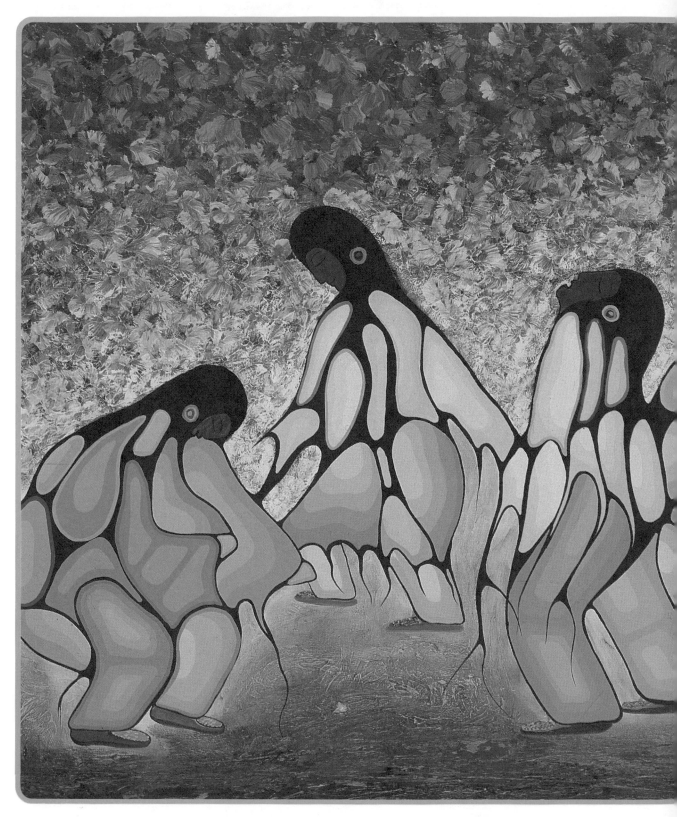

Detail of *Sunset Dancers* by Cecil Youngfox

Say What You Mean and Mean What You Say

The Gift of Grace

by Julia Cunningham

Monsieur Hilaire had been the greatest mime in the world. Now he was old. One morning as he sat down to rest his aching bones after his mime exercises he heard someone clapping. It was Auguste, a poor, mute orphan boy who had been watching outside the window. Hilaire invited the boy in to share a bowl of soup with him.

Auguste lived with Madame Fer, who treated him cruelly. When she came looking for him, Auguste hid upstairs, and Hilaire told her he didn't know where the boy was.

After she had gone out of sight the old man called up the stairwell, "Auguste? You can come down now!" There was no reply. Monsieur Hilaire shrugged at his foolishness. Of

from Burnish Me Bright

course, the boy couldn't answer if he wanted to. Slowly, the backs of his legs aching a little, he ascended the stairs.

The two small whitewashed bedrooms were vacant. The old man sighed at the foot of the steep flight that led to the attic. "Auguste!" he tried again. "The soup is ready! Show yourself, boy, and save my old bones a journey."

But the dark entrance to the loft remained empty.

Monsieur Hilaire smiled to himself. Perhaps if he made a role out of being more ancient than he was the ordeal would be easier. He gave himself a moment to shrink. He curved the fingers of his left hand around the head of an imaginary walking stick. He dropped his head into a slight palsy. A hump seemed to form on his back. Carefully he slid his right foot up and onto the first board. Had anyone been watching they might have believed him incapable of achieving the second. But he did, so painfully, so truly, he knew he would remember this anonymous performance with pleasure.

At last he reached the doorway. He released his body once more into tallness. He stood silent, scanning the familiar outlines of the two costume trunks, the broken harp that had been his mother's, the bookshelf filled with yellowed theatre programs. And then he saw the boy. He was flattened fast against a windowless wall, his arms spread-eagled as though to merge with the beams behind him. His face gleamed with fright.

Monsieur Hilaire stayed where he was. "She is gone, Auguste. I sent her away. You can relax now."

There was no change in the boy's rigidity.

The old man stepped just inside the threshold. He stretched out his own arms in imitation of the boy's and pressed back against the air behind him, making it seem also like a wall. His chest became concave, even his face seemed to revert to youngness, to pinch into fear.

Suddenly the boy's arms fell to his sides and he impulsively ran to the old man, as though to comfort him. He stopped short half a metre away.

Monsieur Hilaire gently resumed himself. "You see how fear looks?" he said. "Come now, help me down to the living room or my slowness will burn the soup."

A few minutes later the two of them sat across from each other at the oak table, spooning up the savory liquid. When they had finished, the

boy's eyes began to take in what surrounded him. Past the paintings and the prints, past the few pieces of worn furniture, past the wall of books, his gaze halted at the ceiling-high mirror.

"Would you like to see my partner?" asked the old man.

The boy frowned.

"Come." Monsieur Hilaire waited until Auguste cautiously followed him to the oblong of glass. "Stand a little to one side, if you please." The man bowed like a courtier, low, with a sweep of his right arm. "May I present Auguste? Auguste, Hilaire." The reflection met the bow. "Step forward," said the mime. The boy obeyed. For an instant he stared at his image. Then he too lowered his body into an answering reverence.

"Now we are four, our partners and ourselves, and by the look of it, very well met." He turned from the mirror. "You have the gift of grace, Auguste," he said solemnly. "Have you also the vision?" He laughed. "But I am indeed a fool. Talk never told it." He faced the mirror again. "Shall I ask my partner to show you a bird?"

Auguste nodded shyly.

"A bird of prey—a hawk? An ostrich? A hummingbird? A crow?"

But, as though a cloak had fallen from his shoulders, he seemed to have removed himself from the presence of the boy, the structure of the room, the boundary of the house. His arms became wings, his feet claws. He was a hawk circling in a dark sky. Then, as he wheeled downward he became smaller, became the victim. He fluttered. He weakened. He alighted on an invisible branch and panted for strength. But the shadow of the hawk still seemed to overcast him. His mouth opened in sound-less terror. It was a beak.

The boy, frozen in this enchantment, suddenly rushed at the helpless-ness of the grounded bird, and spreading himself as wide as he could, became a shield, his back vulnerable to the hawk.

The moment held, then broke.

Monsieur Hilaire let out a long breath. "You believed it and you entered it. What were you, child? A rock? A wind? Or perhaps a descending angel? No matter. You saved him and with great eloquence."

But Auguste appeared not to hear. He was gesturing almost frantically with his hands, pointing first to himself, then toward the mirror, and last, at Monsieur Hilaire.

"What are you trying to tell me, *mon petit?*"

The boy halted in thought. Then, this time quietly, he rose on his toes as tall as he could, assumed a kind of graveness, sucked in his cheeks to hollowness, and began to turn in a circle. With the same calm he became his own size and imitated himself. Then he pointed once more at himself and at the old man, but now at their reflections in the mirror.

"I understand! You want me to teach you."

The boy's two hands joined flat together in front of him and his eyes were very alive.

"You are willing to work? To work very hard? Remember that you must go on with your life on the farm. My years are as limited as my income. I cannot risk taking you in, for your own sake, and you might not have the force to endure two lives."

The boy did not stir from his plea.

"Could you come in the evenings? At first dusk? That way Madame Fer need not know and her ignorance would be a protection for you."

The boy nodded, just once.

The old man glanced down at his arthritically twisted fingers. He felt the pain that was a familiar inhabitant of his joints. Then he looked again at the eagerness before him. "Well, we can try," he said. "We can certainly try."

A quick gaiety livened his voice. "But this is an occasion! Let us toast the contract."

A few moments later, as they clinked glasses, there was a brightness between them that did not come from the lamps or the fire. And they bowed to each other before they drank.

Spotlight: The Famous People Players

by P.K. Purkiss

The lights go out and the theatre is as dark as the inside of your pocket. Around you people hush each other and stop rattling their programs. The show is about to start. You stare ahead into the blackness, wondering what's going to happen next, not knowing what to expect.

Suddenly the stage is alive with color: red and gold and deep blue—colors so bright they hurt your eyes. And music explodes out of the sound system, music you recognize. It's— "Billy Jean." Your eyes adjust to the depth of color and you recognize Michael Jackson on stage, strutting and kicking as he sings. Michael Jackson as large as life, with every sequin visible on the bright jacket, every curl in place, and every movement perfect.

Funny thing, though. There's no spotlight on the stage. What light there is seems to come from Michael himself—as if he were glowing internally, a singing light bulb.

Of course you know it's not Michael Jackson really. It's a puppet, a two-metre-tall combination of plastic and hair and flashy clothes, which is being manipulated by a member of the Famous People Players.

The "Thriller" number is over; Michael Jackson takes a bow and moonwalks off stage as the scene fades once again into dead black.

The music changes dramatically. Now it's racy, pacy, whizz-bang music, flying music—and who should come flying onstage but Superman. As the music builds into the theme from the Superman movies, the Man of Steel flashes across and around the stage, encountering friends and foes of all descriptions, space ships and extra-terrestrial objects, and, finally, the arch villain: Darth Vader himself. The puppets fly at high speeds; they meet in midair and explode into sparks; they disappear and reappear on the other side of the stage. Just like magic.

In fact, it is magic. You watch scene after scene, applauding and laughing with the rest of the audience, but you have no idea how the tricks are done. There's a dragon who loses his head, and a princess who loses her heart. There's a butterfly who disappears in the wave of a wand. There are stars from Hollywood and New York and The Arabian Nights. And the whole show is so dazzlingly, searchingly, gaspingly colorful that when it's over, and the lights come back on, the real world seems dull and washed-out in comparison to the fluorescent black-light world of the Famous People Players.

The idea behind black-light theatre is simple: the puppets are painted in fluorescent colors, and the cast wear dead black outfits, including black hoods and

gloves. Under ultraviolet or "black" stage lighting, the all-black puppeteers fade into invisibility. When they move the giant fluorescent puppets around it looks—even from up close—as if the puppets are moving on their own.

The idea of black-light theatre is simple, but the performance certainly isn't. Good teamwork is absolutely essential. Everyone has to know where everyone else is at all times. For instance, it takes three cast members to manipulate the Elvis puppet; timing and placement have to be perfect so that no one's arm or leg gets between the puppet and the audience. Things get even more difficult in the middle of a complicated routine, with a dozen puppets flying around the stage. And the puppeteers have to make every movement silently and almost blindly, in the dim black light and from under the black velvet hoods that cover their faces. What this means is that the members of the Famous People Players must know their parts blindfolded.

Who are the Famous People Players? No one sees them during the show. You have no idea how they move or sound. To audiences, they are simply thirteen faces that appear momentarily at the end of the shows—suspended in the blackness onstage as they take their bows.

Famous People Players was founded in 1974 by Diane Dupuy, as a project to develop the skills of mentally challenged young people. Her budget was small, and her ideas were all experimental; no one had ever done black-light theatre like this before. No one, including Dupuy, knew what to expect. She designed a few relatively simple routines and taught them to the players—a long and arduous process that required a great deal of repetition to get split-second timing.

The members of the company responded well to Dupuy's teaching and inspiration, and by 1975 they were part of a glittering stage show in Las Vegas. Since then the Famous People Players have appeared on Broadway and toured extensively throughout North America. In 1985 they were invited to perform in China. FPP have been featured in many documentaries and in a TV movie, *Blacklight.*

Today, the operating budget is bigger, the players have more experience, and the routines are longer and more complicated. But the performance still starts with Ms. Dupuy, and every detail is still rehearsed over and over and over again.

For the players themselves, FPP was a big change in lifestyle. Before joining the company, most of them knew only the safe environment of home or a sheltered workshop. Suddenly they had to work fifteen hours a day on details of movements. And they had to get it all perfect. One of the cast remembers spending months learning a ten-second move.

"It was hard at first," he comments. "But really, it's great over here."

Sure, it's great for him over there. He's the one who gets to play Superman.

CHRISTINE'S CRAZY IDEA

by Ken Roberts

Christine just couldn't think of a really original project—and without one she couldn't graduate from junior high school. Then one day she saw a crowd watching a building being knocked down and she got a crazy idea.

Christine rushed up the granite steps of City Hall, stretching to take them two at a time. She stopped at the top to rest. Christine didn't want to look like a sweaty barely-teenager. She wanted to appear as grown-up as possible. Christine held her head high, took a deep breath, and swung open the door.

"May I help you?" asked a middle-aged man as soon as the door closed behind her. The man's hands were clinched together like those of a department store salesman watching a tour of kindergarten students wander through the china section.

"Do you work here?" asked Christine. She had expected to see a long

from Crazy Ideas

counter with signs suspended above it. There had been a counter when she came with her father to renew his business permit.

"Yes," the man sighed.

"What happened to the counter?"

"It's gone. Mayor Barca's idea." The clerk shook his head sadly. "You see, Mayor Barca thought citizens were spending too much time waiting in line. So we work like salespeople now. The more people we help, the more money we make. Let's not waste time. How can I help you?"

"Are there any buildings up for demolition?"

"That's a strange question. Kids who come in here always want to know about summer playground jobs. You're far too young, you know. Besides, summer vacation starts next week. Those jobs were filled months ago."

"I don't want a playground job," Christine said more forcefully. "I want to know if any buildings are about to be demolished."

A thin man with a well-manicured beard swivelled around to listen.

"Hmm," huffed the clerk. "I offered to help so quickly because I could have answered that playground question fast. I do work on commission, you know. Longer questions mean fewer questions."

Christine rolled her eyes. "Look, I'll make you a deal. Find the information I need. I will then walk outside, come back in, and ask about a summer playground job. You can give me an extremely brief answer since I already know I'm too young. The playground question would be a short question and hopefully, since my demolition question will take longer, you would then have two questions of average length. Deal?"

"Deal," agreed the clerk as he scurried away.

The thin man walked casually over to Christine.

"Excuse me," he said with a broad smile. "I couldn't help overhearing your conversation. I happen to know that there's a two-storey brick house on the Patella Traffic Circle due for demolition in a couple of weeks. The city is looking after the contract."

"Thank you."

"My pleasure," said the thin man, touching his hat and bowing gallantly. "Uh . . . Why do you want to know, anyway?"

"Duck!" somebody yelled.

Christine and the thin man quickly covered their heads and stooped.

Christine glanced behind her. Mayor Barca stood in the centre of the room. He was the only person still standing, though he hadn't been the one who'd yelled. Since Christine didn't know who had yelled, she stayed frozen in her protective pose. Everyone in the room stared at Mayor Barca like he was going to explode, or cause an explosion.

Mayor Barca was old now, white-haired and well padded. He always wore the same plaid jacket, the same bow tie, and the same scuffed shoes. And he was always fiddling with some invention. Mayor Barca may have promoted Sceletown as a place that encouraged innovation, but he never seemed able to make machines work for him. The Mayor was inspecting a small black box, and Christine could tell it was the box that was making everyone so nervous.

"Ah, Mr. Hopman," said the Mayor as he noticed the thin man crouched beside Christine. "Come to get your permit, I suppose?"

"Yes, sir, I have," said the thin man as he carefully straightened up.

The Mayor stopped playing with the mysterious black box and walked over to shake hands with Mr. Hopman. Everyone else in the room sighed and returned to whatever they'd been doing. Christine wasn't sure why she'd had to duck so she stood up too.

"Well," said the Mayor, patting Mr. Hopman on the back, "there haven't been any other bids. I'm sure you'll be allowed to demolish that house."

"Excuse me," broke in Christine, "but do you mean the house at the Patella Traffic Circle?"

"Yes, young lady," replied the Mayor. "A new business wants to build there. Going to be great. It's a plant for manufacturing 'Sure Shake,' an antiperspirant for those with sweaty palms. Dynamite idea, eh? Shake. I have some on right now." Mayor Barca held out his hand.

"Sir," said Christine while they shook, "I want to tear down that house too."

Mayor Barca stared at Christine. She only came up to his stomach, so he stepped back for a better look. Christine was painfully aware that her long dark hair was snarled from her run and that she was wearing an old blouse and dirty jeans. But then, she almost always wore old blouses and dirty jeans.

"How old are you?" asked the Mayor.

"Thirteen," said Christine, trying to make the number seem impressive.

Mayor Barca started to say something but stopped suddenly to look down at his hand.

"My hand . . . it's sticky," he muttered. "And it itches too. Have to talk to those 'Sure Shake' people. Does your hand itch?" he asked Christine.

"Uh . . . no," she said truthfully.

"Mayor Barca," interrupted Mr. Hopman. "You just said I could have that contract. You did. Besides, I always get the city's demolition contracts. My bids are the lowest. You know that."

"Calm down," advised the Mayor as he scratched his hand with the gadget he was holding. "Legally I have to accept all bids submitted up to five o'clock. Now," continued the Mayor as he turned to Christine, "what makes you think we should let you have that contract?"

"Because the way I want to tear down that house won't cost the city anything."

"What!" exclaimed Mr. Hopman.

"I'm going to make people pay me so *they* can tear down the house themselves. Three dollars an hour," Christine said as confidently as possible, "is what I plan to charge tense businesspeople, energetic students, and anyone else who wants to ease their frustrations by smashing down walls, ripping out sinks, and poking crowbars through windows."

"You're crazy!" said Mr. Hopman.

"Wait, I'm not finished," declared Christine as she tried her most persuasive, adultlike voice. "I think people would love to smash down part of a building, and I think other people would gladly pay to watch, especially since the wreckers will be neighbors and friends. So, we'll set up bleachers and charge admission to spectators. We'll install a portable shower too, so the workers won't have to go away dirty and sweaty. And we'll provide coveralls so their clothes . . ."

"But what if somebody gets hurt?" asked Mr. Hopman, almost shouting.

Christine looked up at Mayor Barca to see what he was thinking. After all, he was the person she had to convince. It didn't look like the Mayor was even listening. He was carefully inspecting tiny little red

bumps on his hand. Christine was sorry she'd shaken hands with the Mayor now. She wanted him to listen.

"We'll keep checking, of course, to make sure wreckers take off the roof before they start on the walls. We'll have them sign releases too. Our grandfather will supervise. He's worked on houses before. And we'll assign each worker a specific area so nobody collapses a wall on somebody else. We might even put in a loudspeaker system so that . . ."

"By gosh, I love it!" exclaimed Mayor Barca as he accidentally hit every button on his little black box.

"Duck!" screamed a clerk.

The Mayor, Christine, Mr. Hopman, and everyone else in the room dropped to the floor. Christine peeked through her fingers to see what was happening.

Each filing cabinet and desk drawer flew open and spit paper into the

air. The place looked like a snowstorm was passing through. Clerks jumped up and ran around catching and clutching sheets of paper as though they were prizes.

"Oops, I get carried away with this thing," said Mayor Barca as he stood up. "It's supposed to work like a remote control for a television set or a garage door. See, you push a button and a filing cabinet opens up and lifts the file you want. Great idea, eh? But as you can see, it opens all the files at once and throws everything all around the place. Still, I rather like the blasted thing. It just needs a little work. I . . ."

"Mayor Barca," prompted Christine.

"Oh, oh yes. I love your idea, young lady. Hopman? How come you never come up with innovative ideas like that?"

Mr. Hopman glared at Christine.

"See," said the Mayor with a broad grin, "I told you the future belongs to the young. They're educating them to be imaginative at my junior high. Tell you what, young lady, let's call the newspaper! Let's phone the television station and the radio stations! I may have been mayor for twenty-seven years now, but I still *love* to get my picture in the paper and on the news. How'd you like your picture in there with me?"

"Excuse me," broke in the clerk who'd rushed off to help Christine, "but I was helping this girl here and don't want to waste any more time. There's a house on the Patella Traffic . . ."

"I know," said Christine calmly.

"She knows!" whined the clerk to Mayor Barca.

Jingle Jangle

by Richard Scrimger

"Cheese, please!"
This catchy little phrase is a jingle.
Cheese sellers hope that the words

"Cheese, please!" will make people think
about cheese when they go shopping.
And if people *think* about cheese,

chances are more likely that they will actually *buy* cheese. In the same way, pork sellers hope that their jingle "Put pork on your fork!" will make people think about buying pork.

Jingles are just a modern version of the street sellers' cries of long ago. Vendors sold their goods on the street or in market stalls, calling their jingles to attract buyers:

"Lace, lace, penny a pair boot-lace!"

"Two bundles a penny, primroses!"

"Here's your *nice* gingerbread
Your *spiced* gingerbread!"

Today, jingles are part of advertisements. You see and hear them every day—on television and radio, in newspapers and on billboards.

So jingles are simple catchy phrases that advertisers use to sell products because they are easy to remember. But what makes them memorable, what makes them "jingle" in the mind? You probably noticed that the cheese and pork jingles both rhyme. Rhyming is one way to make a jingle easy to remember, but it isn't the only way. "Coke is it!" doesn't rhyme. Neither does "Get cracking!" or "Black's is photography!" These jingles are successful not just because they are simple, but because they are parts of songs.

It may seem strange, but words with music are easier to remember than words alone. Try it for yourself: How many popular songs do you know? And how many poems do you know? If you're like most people, you probably remember many more song lyrics than poems or any other kind of writing—except one. (Which one? You'll find out shortly, if you haven't already guessed.) People who write advertisements know how memorable songs are, so they use music to make their jingles ring in your head—and stick in your mind.

Jingles sound easy to make up, but a lot of work goes into creating them. People who write jingles often start with one idea, or one picture, and work from that. A dry, dusty landscape transformed by a sudden shower of rain will not sell cheese or mattresses or computers, but it will sell 7-Up—with the jingle "Feels so good coming down!"

The reason advertisers take so much time and trouble over a few words and perhaps a catchy tune is that jingles can be used and reused in so many ways. Most big advertising campaigns begin with television, because TV commercials reach more people than any other kind of advertisement, and they can tell a whole story, with words and music and pictures, in just thirty seconds. And it is at the end of that thirty-second commercial that most TV advertisers put

Client:	Dairy Bureau	Job No.	DBC-85	Date:
Product:	Cheese	Commercial No.		
Title:	Scott & Joey & Cheese 'lunch'	Length:	T30-6	Page:

VIDEO

Open on a wide shot. Schoolyard front steps. Scott & Joey talking to each other as they begin lunch.

SCOTT & JOEY & CHEESE.

Medium shot - quick cuts back & forth of boys talking to each other.

Soft focus - pan tabletop beauty shot of cheeses & assorted fruits, crackers, etc.

Medium shot - Scott & Joey giggling.

SUPER -
CHEESE, PLEASE.

CHEESE, PLEASE.

AUDIO

Scott - What ya got for lunch, Joey?

Joey - Ham sandwich, an apple, & cheese

Scott - Cheese?

Scott - Trade ya my cookie for cheese.

Joey - No.

Scott - For half a sandwich?

Joey - No. But ... I kinda always liked your bike, Scott.

Scott - mmm ...

(Woman's voice over) -

Cheddar cheese for Scott & Joey & you. It's always the answer.

It's practically indispensable ... so always have enough.

Scott & Joey - Cheese, please!

their jingle. So the last thing you hear, the last thing you see on the screen—and the last thing you remember—is the jingle, "You can count on the Commerce!" or "Have you driven a Ford lately?"

Once you've seen a commercial on TV, wherever you hear or see the jingle—on a billboard, in a newspaper or magazine, over the radio—you think back to the commercial. The jingle is a kind of shorthand: it is a quick (and less expensive) way of rerunning the whole thirty seconds. Wherever you see or hear the words "Goodyear, take me home!" you remember the commercial you saw.

If a jingle is not memorable and does not become popular, the commercial is not successful, and it isn't used very often. The old jingle for cheddar cheese was "Show your cheddar more warmth; take it out of the fridge more often!" It didn't catch on because it was too long to be memorable, so the advertising campaign switched to the shorter, catchier "Cheese, please!"

Surprisingly, the most common problem for jingles is their very success. They are too memorable. People get tired of them. A jingle is supposed to catch a trendy, fashionable moment in time and fasten a product onto it. As times change, fashions change, and commercials and jingles must change with them. If a jingle lasts more than a year

or two, it is considered very successful—and very old. By then everybody knows it. Everybody. Because the most popular kind of writing in the world today—more popular than the most popular songs—is advertising jingles.

Test yourself. How many titles of songs, or books, or movies do you remember? How many jingles do you remember?

Get cracking!

Hugga Mugga Max.

Quality is Job 1.

Milk makes it.

Get a handle on good soup.

Reach out and touch someone.

When you've got the munchies nothing else will do.

"You got it, Pontiac!"

Confusion in the Marketplace

by Norton Juster

When Milo drove his small electric car through a mysterious turnpike tollbooth that had appeared in his room, he found himself in The Lands Beyond. With his companion, the ticking watchdog Tock, he travelled to the great city of Dictionopolis. In the city square they found lines of stalls heaped with merchandise. Overhead a large banner proclaimed: WELCOME TO THE WORD MARKET.

As they approached, Milo could see crowds of people pushing and shouting their way among the stalls, buying and selling, trading and bargaining. Huge wooden-wheeled carts streamed into the market square from the orchards, and long caravans bound for the four corners of the kingdom made ready to leave. Sacks and boxes were piled high waiting to be delivered to the ships that sailed the Sea of Knowledge, and off to one side a group of minstrels sang songs to the delight of those either too young or too old to engage in trade. But above all the noise and tumult of the crowd could be heard the merchants' voices loudly advertising their products.

"Get your fresh-picked ifs, ands, and buts."

"Hey-yaa, hey-yaa, hey-yaa, nice ripe wheres and whens."

"Juicy, tempting words for sale."

So many words and so many people! They were from every place imaginable and some places even beyond that, and they were all busy sorting, choosing, and stuffing things into cases. As soon as one was filled, another was begun. There seemed to be no end to the bustle and activity.

Milo and Tock wandered up and down the aisles looking at the wonderful assortment of words for sale. There were short ones and easy ones for everyday use, and long and very important ones for special occasions, and even some marvellously fancy ones packed in individual gift boxes for use in royal decrees and pronouncements.

"Step right up, step right up—fancy, best-quality words right here," announced one man in a booming voice. "Step right up—ah, what can I do for you, little boy? How about a nice bagful of pronouns—or maybe you'd like our special assortment of names?"

Milo had never thought much about words before, but these looked so good that he longed to have some.

"Look, Tock," he cried, "aren't they wonderful?"

"They're fine, if you have something to say," replied Tock in a tired voice, for he was much more interested in finding a bone than in shop-

from The Phantom Tollbooth

ping for new words.

"Maybe if I buy some I can learn how to use them," said Milo eagerly as he began to pick through the words in the stall. Finally he chose three that looked particularly good to him—"quagmire," "flabbergast," and "upholstery." He had no idea what they meant, but they looked very grand and elegant.

"How much are these?" he inquired, and when the man whispered the answer he quickly put them back on the shelf and started to walk on.

"Why not take a few kilograms of 'happys'?" advised the salesman. "They're much more practical—and very useful for Happy Birthday, Happy New Year, happy days, and happy-go-lucky."

"I'd like to very much," began Milo, "but—"

"Or perhaps you'd be interested in a package of 'goods'—always handy for good morning, good afternoon, good evening, and goodbye," he suggested.

Milo did want to buy something, but the only money he had was the coin he needed to get back through the tollbooth, and Tock, of course, had nothing but the time.

"No, thank you," replied Milo. "We're just looking." And they continued on through the market.

As they turned down the last aisle of stalls, Milo noticed a wagon that seemed different from the rest. On its side was a small neatly lettered sign that said "DO IT YOURSELF," and inside were twenty-six bins filled with all the letters of the alphabet from *A* to *Z*.

"These are for people who like to make their own words," the man in charge informed him. "You can pick any assortment you like or buy a special box complete with all letters, punctuation marks, and a book of instructions. Here, taste an *A;* they're very good."

Milo nibbled carefully at the letter and discovered that it was quite sweet and delicious—just the way you'd expect an *A* to taste.

"I knew you'd like it," laughed the letter man, popping two *G*'s and an *R* into his mouth and letting the juice drip down his chin. "*A*'s are one of our most popular letters. All of them aren't that good," he confided in a low voice. "Take the *Z*, for instance—very dry and sawdusty. And the *X*? Why, it tastes like a trunkful of stale air. That's why people hardly ever use them. But most of the others are quite tasty.

Try some more."

He gave Milo an *I*, which was icy and refreshing, and Tock a crisp, crunchy *C*.

"Most people are just too lazy to make their own words," he continued, "but it's much more fun."

"Is it difficult? I'm not much good at making words," admitted Milo, spitting the pits from a *P*.

"Perhaps I can be of some assistance—a-s-s-i-s-t-a-n-c-e," buzzed an unfamiliar voice, and when Milo looked up he saw an enormous bee, at least twice his size, sitting on top of the wagon.

"I am the Spelling Bee," announced the Spelling Bee. "Don't be alarmed—a-l-a-r-m-e-d."

Tock ducked under the wagon, and Milo, who was not overly fond of normal-sized bees, began to back away slowly.

"I can spell anything—a-n-y-t-h-i-n-g," he boasted, testing his wings. "Try me, try me!"

"Can you spell goodbye?" suggested Milo as he continued to back away.

The bee gently lifted himself into the air and circled lazily over Milo's head.

"Perhaps—p-e-r-h-a-p-s—you are under the misapprehension—m-i-s-a-p-p-r-e-h-e-n-s-i-o-n—that I am dangerous," he said, turning a smart loop to the left. "Let me assure—a-s-s-u-r-e—you that my intentions are peaceful—p-e-a-c-e-f-u-l." And with that he settled back on top of the wagon and fanned himself with one wing. "Now," he panted, "think of the most difficult word you can and I'll spell it. Hurry up, hurry up!" And he jumped up and down impatiently.

He looks friendly enough, thought Milo, not sure just how friendly a friendly bumblebee should be, and tried to think of a very difficult word. "Spell 'vegetable,' " he suggested, for it was one that always troubled him at school.

"That is a difficult one," said the bee, winking at the letter man. "Let me see now . . . hmmmmmm . . ." He frowned and wiped his brow and paced slowly back and forth on top of the wagon. "How much time do I have?"

"Just ten seconds," cried Milo excitedly. "Count them off, Tock."

"Oh dear, oh dear, oh dear, oh dear," the bee repeated, continuing to pace nervously. Then, just as the time ran out, he spelled as fast as he could—"v-e-g-e-t-a-b-l-e."

"Correct," shouted the letter man, and everyone cheered.

"Can you spell everything?" asked Milo admiringly.

"Just about," replied the bee with a hint of pride in his voice. "You see, years ago I was just an ordinary bee minding my own business, smelling flowers all day, and occasionally picking up part-time work in people's bonnets. Then one day I realized that I'd never amount to anything without an education and, being naturally adept at spelling, I decided that—"

"BALDERDASH!" shouted a booming voice. And from around the wagon stepped a large beetlelike insect dressed in a lavish coat, striped pants, checked vest, spats, and a derby hat. "Let me repeat—BALDER-DASH!" he shouted again, swinging his cane and clicking his heels in midair. "Come now, don't be ill-mannered. Isn't someone going to introduce me to the little boy?"

"This," said the bee with complete disdain, "is the Humbug. A very dislikable fellow."

"NONSENSE! Everyone loves a Humbug," shouted the Humbug. "As I was saying to the king just the other day—"

"You've never met the king," accused the bee angrily. Then, turning to Milo, he said, "Don't believe a thing this old fraud says."

"BOSH!" replied the Humbug. "We're an old and noble family, honorable to the core—*Insecticus Humbugium,* if I may use the Latin. Why, we fought in the crusades with Richard the Lion Heart, crossed the Atlantic with Columbus, blazed trails with the pioneers, and today many members of the family hold prominent government positions throughout the world. History is full of Humbugs."

"A very pretty speech—s-p-e-e-c-h," sneered the bee. "Now why don't you go away? I was just advising the lad of the importance of proper spelling."

"BAH!" said the bug, putting an arm around Milo.

"As soon as you learn to spell one word, they ask you to spell another. You can never catch up—so why bother? Take my advice, my boy, and forget about it. As my great-great-great-grandfather George Washington Humbug used to say—"

"You, sir," shouted the bee very excitedly, "are an impostor—i-m-p-o-s-t-o-r—who can't even spell his own name."

"A slavish concern for the composition of words is the sign of a bankrupt intellect," roared the Humbug, waving his cane furiously.

Milo didn't have any idea what this meant, but it seemed to infuriate the Spelling Bee, who flew down and knocked off the Humbug's hat with his wing.

"Be careful," shouted Milo as the bug swung his cane again, catching the bee on the foot and knocking over the box of *W*'s.

"My foot!" shouted the bee.

"My hat!" shouted the bug—and the fight was on.

The Spelling Bee buzzed dangerously in and out of range of the Humbug's wildly swinging cane as they menaced and threatened each other, and the crowd stepped back out of danger.

"There must be some other way to—" began Milo. And then he yelled, "WATCH OUT," but it was too late.

There was a tremendous crash as the Humbug in his great fury tripped into one of the stalls, knocking it into another, then another, then another, then another, until every stall in the marketplace had been upset and the words lay scrambled in great confusion all over the square.

The bee, who had tangled himself in some bunting, toppled to the ground, knocking Milo over on top of him, and lay there shouting, "Help! Help! There's a little boy on me."

The bug sprawled untidily on a mound of squashed letters and Tock, his alarm ringing persistently, was buried under a pile of words.

Take Sky

by David McCord

Now think of words. Take *sky*
And ask yourself just why—
Like sun, moon, star, and cloud—
It sounds so well out loud,
And pleases so the sight
When printed black on white.
Take syllable and thimble:
The sound of *them* is nimble.
Take bucket, spring, and dip
Cold water to your lip.
Take balsam, fir, and pine:
Your woodland smell and mine.
Take kindle, blaze, and flicker—
What lights the hearth fire quicker?

Three words we fear but form:
Gale, twister, thunderstorm;
Others that simply shake
Are tremble, temblor, quake.
But granite, stone, and rock:
Too solid, they, to shock.
Put honey, bee, and flower
With sunny, shade, and shower;
Put *wild* with bird and wing,
Put *bird* with song and sing.
Aren't paddle, trail, and camp
The cabin and the lamp?
Now look at words of rest—
Sleep, quiet, calm, and blest;

At words we learn in youth—
Grace, skill, ambition, truth;
At words of lifelong need—
Grit, courage, strength, and deed;
Deep-rooted words that say
Love, hope, dream, yearn, and pray;
Light-hearted words—girl, boy,
Live, laugh, play, share, enjoy.
October, April, June—
Come late and gone too soon.
Remember, words are life:
Child, husband, mother, wife;
Remember, and I'm done:
Words taken one by one

Are poems as they stand—
Shore, beacon, harbor, land;
Brook, river, mountain, vale,
Crow, rabbit, otter, quail;
Faith, freedom, water, snow,
Wind, weather, flood, and floe.
Like light across the lawn
Are morning, sea, and dawn;
Words of the green earth growing—
Seed, soil, and farmer sowing.
Like wind upon the mouth
Sad, summer, rain, and south.
Amen. Put not asunder
Man's *first* word: wonder. . . wonder. . .

91

Augustus Gloop Goes Up the Pipe

by
Roald Dahl

Charlie Bucket and four other children have found the fabulous Golden Tickets that entitle them to a lifetime supply of the world's most wonderful candy—plus a trip to the Willy Wonka factory to see how the candy is made. In the Chocolate Room they discover a great brown river of warm chocolate, and see Willy Wonka's tiny workers, the Oompa-Loompas. While everyone is watching the Oompa-Loompas, greedy Augustus Gloop makes a terrible mistake. He sneaks down to the edge of the river and begins to scoop hot melted chocolate into his mouth as quickly as he can.

When Mr. Wonka turned round and saw what Augustus Gloop was doing, he cried out, "Oh, no! *Please,* Augustus, *please!* I beg of you not to do that. My chocolate must be untouched by human hands!"

"Augustus!" called out Mrs. Gloop. "Didn't you hear what the man said? Come away from that river at once!"

"This stuff is *tee*-riffic!" said Augustus, taking not the slightest notice of his mother or Mr. Wonka. "Oh boy, I need a bucket to drink it properly!"

"Augustus," cried Mr. Wonka, hopping up and down and waggling his stick in the air, "you *must* come away. You are dirtying my chocolate!"

"Augustus!" cried Mrs. Gloop.

from Charlie and the Chocolate Factory

92

"Augustus!" cried Mr. Gloop.

But Augustus was deaf to everything except the call of his enormous stomach. He was now lying full length on the ground with his head far out over the river, lapping up the chocolate like a dog.

"Augustus!" shouted Mrs. Gloop. "You'll be giving that nasty cold of yours to about a million people all over the country!"

"Be careful, Augustus!" shouted Mr. Gloop. "You're leaning too far out!"

Mr. Gloop was absolutely right. For suddenly there was a shriek, and then a splash, and into the river went Augustus Gloop, and in one second he had disappeared under the brown surface.

"Save him!" screamed Mrs. Gloop, going white in the face, and waving her umbrella about. "He'll drown! He can't swim a yard! Save him! Save him!"

"Good heavens, woman," said Mr. Gloop, "I'm not diving in there! I've got my best suit on!"

Augustus Gloop's face came up again to the surface, painted brown with chocolate. "Help! Help! Help!" he yelled. "Fish me out!"

"Don't just *stand* there!" Mrs. Gloop screamed at Mr. Gloop. "*Do* something!"

"I *am* doing something!" said Mr. Gloop, who was now taking off his jacket and getting ready to dive into the chocolate. But while he was doing this, the wretched boy was being sucked closer and closer toward the mouth of one of the great pipes that was dangling down into the river. Then all at once, the powerful suction took hold of him completely, and he was pulled under the surface and then into the mouth of the pipe.

The crowd on the riverbank waited breathlessly to see where he would come out.

"*There he goes!*" somebody shouted, pointing upwards.

And sure enough, because the pipe was made of glass, Augustus Gloop could be clearly seen shooting up inside it, head first, like a torpedo.

"Help! Murder! Police!" screamed Mrs. Gloop. "Augustus, come back at once! Where are you going?"

"It's a wonder to me," said Mr. Gloop, "how that pipe is big enough for him to go through it."

"It *isn't* big enough!" said Charlie Bucket. "Oh dear, look! He's slowing down!"

"So he is!" said Grandpa Joe.

"He's going to stick!" said Charlie.

"I think he is!" said Grandpa Joe.

"By golly, he *has* stuck!" said Charlie.

"It's his stomach that's done it!" said Mr. Gloop.

"He's blocked the whole pipe!" said Grandpa Joe.

"Smash the pipe!" yelled Mrs. Gloop, still waving her umbrella. "Augustus, come out of there at once!"

The watchers below could see the chocolate swishing around the boy in the pipe, and they could see it building up behind him in a solid mass, pushing against the blockage. The pressure was terrific. Something had to give. Something did give, and that something was Augustus. *WHOOF!* Up he shot again like a bullet in the barrel of a gun.

"He's disappeared!" yelled Mrs. Gloop. "Where does that pipe go to? Quick! Call the fire brigade!"

"Keep calm!" cried Mr. Wonka. "Keep calm, my dear lady, keep calm. There is no danger! No danger whatsoever! Augustus has gone on a little journey, that's all. A most interesting little journey. But he'll come out of it just fine,
     you wait and see."

"How can he possibly come out just fine!" snapped Mrs. Gloop. "He'll be made into marshmallows in five seconds!"

"Impossible!" cried Mr. Wonka. "Unthinkable! Inconceivable! Absurd! He could never be made into marshmallows!"

"And why not, may I ask?" shouted Mrs. Gloop.

"Because that pipe doesn't *go* to the Marshmallow Room!" Mr. Wonka answered. "It doesn't go anywhere near it! That pipe—the one Augustus went up—happens to lead directly to the room where I make a most delicious kind of strawberry-flavored chocolate-coated fudge. . . ."

"Then he'll be made into strawberry-flavored chocolate-coated fudge!" screamed Mrs. Gloop. "My poor Augustus! They'll be selling him by the pound all over the country tomorrow morning!"

"Quite right," said Mr. Gloop.

"I *know* I'm right," said Mrs. Gloop.

"It's beyond a joke," said Mr. Gloop.

"Mr. Wonka doesn't seem to think so!" cried Mrs. Gloop. "Just look at him! He's laughing his head off! How *dare* you laugh like that when my boy's just gone up the pipe! You monster!" she shrieked, pointing her umbrella at Mr. Wonka as though she were going to run him through. "You think it's a joke, do you? You think that sucking my boy up into your Fudge Room like that is just one great big colossal joke?"

"He'll be perfectly safe," said Mr. Wonka, giggling slightly.

"He'll be chocolate fudge!" shrieked Mrs. Gloop.

"Never!" cried Mr. Wonka.

"Of course he will!" shrieked Mrs. Gloop.

"I wouldn't allow it!" cried Mr. Wonka.

"And why not?" shrieked Mrs. Gloop.

"Because the taste would be terrible," said Mr. Wonka. "Just imagine it! Augustus-flavored chocolate-coated Gloop! No one would buy it."

"They most certainly would!" cried Mr. Gloop indignantly.

"I don't want to think about it!" shrieked Mrs. Gloop.

"Nor do I," said Mr. Wonka. "And I do promise you, madam, that your darling boy is perfectly safe."

"If he's perfectly safe, then where is he?" snapped Mrs. Gloop. "Lead me to him this instant!"

Mr. Wonka turned around and clicked his fingers sharply, *click, click, click,* three times. Immediately, an Oompa-Loompa appeared, as if from nowhere, and stood beside him.

The Oompa-Loompa bowed and smiled, showing beautiful white teeth. His skin was rosy-white, his long hair was golden-brown, and the top of his head came just above the height of Mr. Wonka's knee. He wore the usual deerskin slung over his shoulder.

"Now listen to me!" said Mr. Wonka, looking down at the tiny man, "I want you to take Mr. and Mrs. Gloop up to the Fudge Room and help them to find their son, Augustus. He's just gone up the pipe."

The Oompa-Loompa took one look at Mrs. Gloop and exploded into peals of laughter.

"Oh, do be quiet!" said Mr. Wonka. "Control yourself! Pull yourself together! Mrs. Gloop doesn't think it's at all funny!"

"You can say that again!" said Mrs. Gloop.

"Go straight to the Fudge Room," Mr. Wonka said to the Oompa-Loompa, "and when you get there, take a long stick and start poking around inside the big chocolate-mixing barrel. I'm almost certain you'll find him in there. But you'd better look sharp! You'll have to hurry! If you leave him in the chocolate-mixing barrel too long, he's liable to get poured out into the fudge boiler, and that really *would* be a disaster, wouldn't it? My fudge would become *quite* uneatable!"

Mrs. Gloop let out a shriek of fury.

"I'm joking," said Mr. Wonka, giggling madly behind his beard. "I didn't mean it. Forgive me. I'm so sorry. Goodbye, Mrs. Gloop! And Mr. Gloop! Goodbye! Goodbye! I'll see you later. . . ."

As Mr. and Mrs. Gloop and their tiny escort hurried away, the five Oompa-Loompas on the far side of the river suddenly began hopping and dancing about and beating wildly upon a number of very small drums. "Augustus Gloop!" they chanted. "Augustus Gloop! Augustus Gloop! Augustus Gloop!"

"Grandpa!" cried Charlie. "Listen to them, Grandpa! What *are* they doing?"

"Ssshh!" whispered Grandpa Joe. "I think they're going to sing us a song!"

"*Augustus Gloop!*" chanted the Oompa-Loompas.
"*Augustus Gloop! Augustus Gloop!*
The great big greedy nincompoop!
How long could we allow this beast
To gorge and guzzle, feed and feast
On everything he wanted to?
Great Scott! It simply wouldn't do!
However long this pig might live,
We're positive he'd never give
Even the smallest bit of fun
Or happiness to anyone.
So what we do in cases such
As this, we use the gentle touch,
And carefully we take the brat
And turn him into something that
Will give great pleasure to us all—
A doll, for instance, or a ball,
Or marbles or a rocking horse.
But this revolting boy, of course,
Was so unutterably vile,
So greedy, foul, and infantile,
He left a most disgusting taste
Inside our mouths, and so in haste
We chose a thing that, come what may,
Would take the nasty taste away.
'Come on!' we cried, 'The time is ripe
To send him shooting up the pipe!
He has to go! It has to be!'
And very soon, he's going to see
Inside the room to which he's gone
Some funny things are going on.

But don't, dear children, be alarmed;
Augustus Gloop will not be harmed,
Although, of course, we must admit
He will be altered quite a bit.
He'll be quite changed from what he's been,
When he goes through the fudge machine:
Slowly, the wheels go round and round,
The cogs begin to grind and pound;
A hundred knives go slice, slice, slice;
We add some sugar, cream, and spice;
We boil him for a minute more,
Until we're absolutely sure
That all the greed and all the gall
Is boiled away for once and all.
Then out he comes! And now! By grace!
A miracle has taken place!
This boy, who only just before
Was loathed by men from shore to shore,
This greedy brute, this louse's ear,
Is loved by people everywhere!
For who could hate or bear a grudge
Against a luscious bit of fudge?"

"I *told* you they loved singing!" cried Mr. Wonka. "Aren't they delightful? Aren't they charming? But you mustn't believe a word they said. It's all nonsense, every bit of it!"

"Are the Oompa-Loompas really joking, Grandpa!" asked Charlie.

"Of course they're joking," answered Grandpa Joe. "They *must* be joking. At least, I hope they're joking. Don't you?"

Tea and Advice

by Bernice Thurman Hunter

Beatrice liked to write stories, so she was delighted when she found out that her new friend, Gloria, lived right next door to L.M. Montgomery. She was even more thrilled when the famous author of Anne of Green Gables *invited her to tea.*

At exactly one o'clock on Saturday I met Gloria on the corner of Jane and Bloor. She looked gorgeous in her new tunic with the razor-sharp pleats and her red velvet jacket. Her stylish outfit made me acutely aware of my old navy pleatless skirt and blue sweater, neatly darned at the elbows. But Mum had painstakingly turned the collar and cuffs of my white blouse, so it looked almost as good as new.

The night before I had done up my fine hair in pin curls and it had combed out kind of frizzy, but not too bad. I had wet my eyelashes with vaseline, which made them look thicker and longer, and put on two layers of lip rouge. (Willa said not to use too much or I might look

from As Ever, Booky

cheap.) I couldn't do a thing about the shape of my nose, but on the whole I was quite pleased with myself.

Under my arm I carried a grammar-school workbook with my latest story penned carefully inside. The title was "Victoria, the Girl Who Never Told a Lie in Her Life." I was sure it was the best thing I'd ever written.

Veering left off Bloor Street we walked along a tree-lined avenue, called Riverside Drive, on the banks of the Humber. It was a beautiful, winding road with rolling lawns and weeping willows, and no sidewalks. The houses were big and far apart. Glittering stone driveways curved up to wide, two-car garages.

On Veeny Street in Swansea, the little village on the western outskirts of Toronto where I lived, we didn't have garages. Our houses were so tightly packed together there was barely enough room for alleyways between. But it didn't matter because nobody on Veeny Street owned a car anyway.

Gloria stopped in front of a magnificent mansion where a man was busy raking up a pile of red and gold leaves. "That's my house," she said, a bit smugly I thought.

"Is that your father?" I asked innocently.

"No! That's Willy, the gardener."

Willy the gardener tipped his cap to Gloria, then stared me up and down as if I was an oddity on Riverside Drive.

Gloria pointed to the house next door. "That's where the Macdonalds live," she said matter-of-factly.

I gazed, speechless, at a white stone house with gabled windows, all hemmed in by shrubs and trees and flowers. A rustic sign nailed to a fence post read *Journey's End.*

At that moment the dark wooden door swung open and out stepped a regal lady who looked for all the world like Queen Mary, the king's mother, even to the long string of pearls looped twice around her neck. She smiled and beckoned to us and my heart did somersaults.

"She looks like a genius!" I whispered.

"She is!" my friend agreed knowingly.

Gloria introduced us. "Mrs. Macdonald, this is my friend Bee-triss." (She had wonderful manners, but terrible pronunciation. The way she said my name made it sound like a vegetable!)

"I'm pleased to meet you, Beatrice." It sounded entirely different coming from *her*. She reached out and took my hand, and my legs turned to jelly.

Completely forgetting Dad's well-meant advice, I started to babble. "Oh, Miss Montgomery, I love all your books and I've read every one at least twice, some of them three times, and I especially love *Emily Climbs* and *Anne of Avonlea*. My mother loves *Pat of Silver Bush* best and she told me to tell you if I got the chance that she greatly admires Judy Plum. But I personally adore *The Story Girl* and *Kilmeny of the Orchard* and *The Blue Castle*—oh, Barney was so romantic—and I hope you have time to write a hundred more books because I think you're the greatest writer the world has ever known."

Luckily, I ran out of breath.

"That's very kind of you, Beatrice, and do thank your mother for her compliment about Judy Plum." She spoke just as if I'd said something perfectly sensible. "Gloria tells me that you're a story girl too. Come into the garden and we'll talk about it."

We followed her down a white gravel path that led to a backyard filled with daisies and chrysanthemums and evergreens. At the foot of one big pine tree was a smooth granite rock with the word *Lucky* painted on it.

"That stone was shipped up to me from my home in Prince Edward Island," the author explained softly, "and under it my dear little pussycat lies sleeping. He was my inseparable companion for fourteen years and I miss him sorely."

Suddenly I was consumed with jealousy over the bones of that old dead cat.

As we sat down on red cedar chairs, I felt a splinter snag my silk stocking—or I should say Willa's. I had no silk stockings, just lisle, and I had borrowed Willa's best pair. Only she didn't know it yet.

I was trying desperately to think of something intelligent to say when the back door was pushed open by a woman's behind. Out she came with a loaded tray and set the table with china dishes, silver spoons, and a fancy teapot with little legs on it. Then she set two glass plates within easy reach. One held sandwiches and the other teacakes.

"Thank you, Marny,"
Mrs. Macdonald said,
then to me, "Cream
and sugar, Beatrice?"

"Yes, please." We
never had real cream
at home, just milk.

She put the cream and
sugar in the cup first, then
poured the tea. Mum never did that.

"Help yourselves, girls," she said.
Then she leaned back, casually sipping
her tea as if she had nothing better to do
than entertain two schoolgirls, when all the
time I knew there was another great novel
churning around in her head just dying to get out.

I watched Gloria surreptitiously and copied everything
she did. She spread a linen napkin on her lap, so I did too.
She took two sandwiches, so I did too—a three-cornered egg-salad
with the crusts cut off and a green-cheese pinwheel. Green cheese!
Imagine!

I had never tasted anything so delectable. We ate six sandwiches.
When Mrs. Macdonald offered us more Gloria politely refused. So
I did too, even though I could easily have eaten the whole works
in two minutes flat. Then we each had another cup of tea and a
teacake. The pink icing cracked when you bit into it. Inside, it was
soft and white as a marshmallow.

Finally Marny came and cleared it all away.

"May I see your work, Beatrice?" asked Mrs. Macdonald suddenly.
My work? At first I didn't know what she meant. Then I followed
her eyes to my notebook. My hand shook as I passed it to her.

The pages rustled as she turned them. Sunlight filtered through
the leaves and glinted on her silver hair. Gloria and I slanted glances
at each other, but we didn't say a word. A bluebird flashed by
almost close enough to touch.

Presently Mrs. Macdonald closed the book and removed her gold-rimmed glasses. "Your story is lovely, Beatrice." Her voice was gentle and kind, but I didn't like the word "lovely." I had hoped to hear "brilliant" or "witty" or just plain "excellent."

"My dear"—now her tone had become very serious—"allow me to give you some advice from my own experience. *Do* keep writing. You have a lively imagination and your characters ring true. But do not, I repeat, *do not* expect to publish at your tender age. The inevitable rejections would surely defeat you. Instead, channel your energies into your studies."

My heart sank. "But—but—it's more fun to write stories than do homework!" The stupid words were out before I could stop them.

"True. But your first priority must be your school work, because no one needs higher education more than a journalist. Will you remember that, Beatrice?"

"Yes, Miss Montgomery," I said, but I was already defeated. The thought of all that higher education struck terror in my heart. And besides, I was dying to be done with school so I could go out to work and make money to buy nice clothes like Gloria's.

We said goodbye, promising to come back soon. But I never did go back. And I'd even forgotten to get her autograph.

"Well, you dumb-bell, you wasted your whole Saturday afternoon," jeered Arthur. For once I agreed with him.

"Don't fret, Bea," Mum consoled me. "When you write Miss Montgomery your bread-and-butter note you can ask for her signature then."

So that's what I did. About three days later back came her reply in her own handwriting, which was so hard to read that I had to ask Willa to decipher it for me. In it she repeated her solemn advice and her compliment about my "lovely" story. The letter was signed *Sincerely, L.M. Montgomery Macdonald.*

I put it and my story far back on the closet shelf and didn't look at them again for years.

The Cremation of Sam McGee

by Robert W. Service

There are strange things done in the midnight sun
* By the men who moil for gold;*
The Arctic trails have their secret tales
* That would make your blood run cold;*
The Northern Lights have seen queer sights,
* But the queerest they ever did see*
Was that night on the marge of Lake Lebarge
* I cremated Sam McGee.*

Now Sam McGee was from Tennessee, where the cotton
  blooms and blows.
Why he left his home in the South to roam 'round the Pole,
  God only knows.
He was always cold, but the land of gold seemed to hold him
  like a spell;
Though he'd often say in his homely way that "he'd sooner live
  in hell."

On a Christmas Day we were mushing our way over the
  Dawson trail.
Talk of your cold! through the parka's fold it stabbed like a
  driven nail.
If our eyes we'd close, then the lashes froze till sometimes we
  couldn't see;
It wasn't much fun, but the only one to whimper was Sam
  McGee.

And that very night, as we lay packed tight in our robes
 beneath the snow,
And the dogs were fed, and the stars o'erhead were dancing
 heel and toe,
He turned to me, and "Cap," says he, "I'll cash in this trip, I
 guess;
And if I do, I'm asking that you won't refuse my last request."

Well, he seemed so low that I couldn't say no; then he says
 with a sort of moan:
"It's the cursèd cold, and it's got right hold till I'm chilled clean
 through to the bone.
Yet 'tain't being dead—it's my awful dread of the icy grave that
 pains;
So I want you to swear that, foul or fair, you'll cremate my
 last remains."

A pal's last need is a thing to heed, so I swore I would not fail;
And we started on at the streak of dawn; but God! he looked
 ghastly pale.
He crouched on the sleigh, and he raved all day of his home
 in Tennessee;
And before nightfall a corpse was all that was left of Sam
 McGee.

There wasn't a breath in that land of death, and I hurried,
 horror driven,
With a corpse half hid that I couldn't get rid, because of a
 promise given;
It was lashed to the sleigh, and it seemed to say: "You may tax
 your brawn and brains,
But you promised true, and it's up to you to cremate those last
 remains."

Now a promise made is a debt unpaid, and the trail has its
  own stern code.
In the days to come, though my lips were dumb, in my heart
  how I cursed that load.
In the long, long night, by the lone firelight, while the huskies,
  round in a ring,
Howled out their woes to the homeless snows—O God! how
  I loathed the thing.

And every day that quiet clay seemed to heavy and heavier
  grow;
And on I went, though the dogs were spent and the grub
  was getting low;
The trail was bad, and I felt half mad, but I swore I would not
  give in;
And I'd often sing to the hateful thing, and it hearkened with
  a grin.

Till I came to the marge of Lake Lebarge, and a derelict there
  lay;
It was jammed in the ice, but I saw in a trice it was called
  the "Alice May."
And I looked at it, and I thought a bit, and I looked at my
  frozen chum;
Then "Here," said I, with a sudden cry, "is my cre-ma-tor-eum."

Some planks I tore from the cabin floor, and I lit the boiler
  fire;
Some coal I found that was lying around, and I heaped the
  fuel higher;
The flames just soared, and the furnace roared—such a blaze
  you seldom see;
And I burrowed a hole in the glowing coal, and I stuffed in
  Sam McGee.

108

Then I made a hike, for I didn't like to hear him sizzle so;
And the heavens scowled, and the huskies howled, and the
   wind began to blow.
It was icy cold, but the hot sweat rolled down my cheeks, and
   I don't know why;
And the greasy smoke in an inky cloak went streaking down
   the sky.

I do not know how long in the snow I wrestled with grisly
   fear;
But the stars came out and they danced about ere again I
   ventured near;
I was sick with dread, but I bravely said: "I'll just take a peep
   inside.
I guess he's cooked, and it's time I looked," . . . then the door
   I opened wide.

And there sat Sam, looking cool and calm, in the heart of the
   furnace roar;
And he wore a smile you could see a mile, and he said: "Please
   close that door.
It's fine in here, but I greatly fear you'll let in the cold and
   storm—
Since I left Plumtree, down in Tennessee, it's the first time I've
   been warm."

There are strange things done in the midnight sun
   By the men who moil for gold;
The Arctic trails have their secret tales
   That would make your blood run cold;
The Northern Lights have seen queer sights,
   But the queerest they ever did see
Was that night on the marge of Lake Lebarge
   I cremated Sam McGee.

Silverspot

by Ernest Thompson Seton

Silverspot was a wise old crow; his name was given because of the silvery white spot that was like a nickel, stuck on his right side, between the eye and the bill, and it was owing to this spot that I was able to know him from the other crows, and put together the parts of his history that came to my knowledge.

Crows are, as you must know, our most intelligent birds—"Wise as an old crow" did not become a saying without good reason. Crows know the value of organization, and are as well drilled as soldiers—very much better than some soldiers, in fact, for crows are always on duty, always at war, and always dependent on each other for life and safety. Their leaders not only are the oldest and wisest of the band, but also the strongest and bravest, for they must be ready at any time with sheer force to put down an upstart or a rebel. The rank and file are the youngsters and the crows without special gifts.

from Wild Animals I Have Known

Old Silverspot was the leader of a large band of crows that made their headquarters near Toronto, Canada, in Castle Frank, which is a pine-clad hill on the northeast edge of the city. This band numbered about two hundred, and for reasons that I never understood did not increase. In mild winters they stayed along the Niagara River; in cold winters they went much farther south. But each year in the last week of February Old Silverspot would muster his followers and boldly cross the forty miles of open water that lies between Toronto and Niagara; not, how-ever, in a straight line would he go, but always in a curve to the west, whereby he kept in sight of the familiar landmark of Dundas Mountain, until the pine-clad hill itself came in view. Each year he came with his troop, and for about six weeks took up his abode on the hill. Each morning thereafter the crows set out in three bands to forage. One band went southeast to Ashbridge's Bay. One went north up the Don, and one, the largest, went northwestward up the ravine. The last Silverspot led in person. Who led the others I never found out.

On calm mornings they flew high and straight away. But when it was windy the band flew low, and followed the ravine for shelter. My win-dows overlooked the ravine, and it was thus that in 1885 I first noticed this old crow. I was a newcomer in the neighborhood, but an old resi-dent said to me then "that there old crow has been a-flying up and down this ravine for more than twenty years." My chances to watch were in the ravine, and Silverspot doggedly clinging to the old route, though now it was edged with houses and spanned by bridges, became a very familiar acquaintance. Twice each day in March and part of April, then again in the late summer and the fall, he passed and repassed, and gave me chances to see his movements, and hear his orders to his bands, and so, little by little, opened my eyes to the fact that the crows, though a little people, are of great wit, a race of birds with a language and a social system that is wonderfully human in many of its chief points, and in some is better carried out than our own.

One windy day I stood on the high bridge across the ravine, as the old crow, heading his long, straggling troop, came flying down homeward. Half a mile away I could hear the contented *"All's well, come right along!"* as we should say, or as he put it, and as also his lieutenant echoed it at the rear of the band. They were flying very low to be out of the wind, and would have to rise a little to clear the bridge on which I was. Silverspot

saw me standing there, and as I was closely watching him he didn't like it. He checked his flight and called out, *"Be on your guard,"* or

and rose much higher in the air. Then seeing that I was not armed he flew over my head about twenty feet, and his followers in turn did the same, dipping again to the old level when past the bridge.

Next day I was at the same place, and as the crows came near I raised my walking stick and pointed it at them. The old

112

fellow at once cried out *"Danger,"* and rose fifty feet higher than before.

Ca

Seeing that it was not a gun, he ventured to fly over.

But on the third day I took with me a gun, and at once he cried out, *"Great danger—a gun."* His lieutenant repeated the cry, and every crow in the troop began to tower and scatter from the rest, till they were far above gunshot, and so passed safely over, coming down again to the shelter of the valley when well beyond reach. Another time, as the long, straggling troop came down the valley, a red-tailed hawk alighted on a tree close by their intended route. The leader cried out, *"Hawk, hawk,"* and stayed his flight, as did each crow on nearing him, until all were massed in a solid body. Then, no longer fearing the hawk, they passed on. But a quarter of a mile farther on a man with a gun appeared below, and the cry, *"Great danger—a gun,"* at once caused them to scatter widely and tower till far beyond range. Many others of his words of command I learned in the course of my long acquaintance, and found that sometimes a very little difference in the sound makes a very great difference in meaning.

ca ca ca ca   Caw

Caw   Caw

The Ways of Living Things

by Jack Prelutsky

There is wonder past all wonder
in the ways of living things,
in a worm's intrepid wriggling,
in the song a blackbird sings,

In the grandeur of an eagle
and the fury of a shark,
in the calmness of a tortoise
on a meadow in the dark,

In the splendor of a sea gull
as it plummets from the sky,
in the incandescent shimmer
of a noisy dragonfly,

In a heron, still and silent
underneath a crescent moon,
in a butterfly emerging
from its silver-spun cocoon.

In a fish's joyful splashing,
in a snake that makes no sound,
in the smallest salamander
there is wonder to be found.

What the Wind Said

by Russell Hoban

"Far away is where I've come from," said the wind.
"Guess what I've brought you."
   "What?" I asked.
"Shadows dancing on a brown road by an old
Stone fence," the wind said. "Do you like that?"
   "Yes," I said. "What else?"
"Daisies nodding, and the drone of one small airplane
In a sleepy sky," the wind continued.
   "I like the airplane, and the daisies too," I said.
   "What else?"
"That's not enough?" the wind complained.
   "No," I said. "I want the song that you were singing.
   Give me that."
"That's mine," the wind said. "Find your own." And left.

Detail of *Wave Silent* by Ron Bolt

Ride the Wave

The Elusive Secret
of Oak Island

by Jean Booker

The underwater camera is lowered down a seventy-metre shaft. Nearby a man watches on a closed-circuit monitor. Suddenly, what seems to be a human hand appears on the screen. The scene changes and three wooden chests come into view, followed by a picture of a human body propped against a wall of the underground cavern.

Sounds like a hair-raising adventure tale? It is. It's part of the story of a search for hidden treasure on Oak Island, a search that has been going on for almost two hundred years.

Oak Island is about sixty-five kilometres southwest of Halifax and is one of a group of over three hundred islands in Mahone Bay on the Atlantic coast of Nova Scotia. The island is one and a half kilometres long and three-quarters of a kilometre across at its widest point.

In the summer of 1795 a teenage boy was exploring uninhabited Oak Island when he noticed something unusual. In the middle of a clearing there was a huge oak tree with a branch about five metres up that was cut off a metre from the trunk. Beneath this branch was a depression four metres in diameter. The next day the boy went back to the island with two friends. Using picks and shovels, they dug below the tree and discovered the soil was loose. At a depth of half a metre the young men found a layer of flagstones and, on removing them, realized they were digging in a round shaft more than two metres wide. It looked as if the sawed-off oak branch above could have been used originally to help remove the earth from this shaft.

The young men continued digging for several days and were surprised to find snugly fitting platforms of oak logs across the pit every three metres to a depth of nine metres. They felt sure that pirate treasure was buried there, but when it wasn't discovered at the nine-metre level, they gave up their search. However, two of them bought land lots on Oak Island and all three kept looking for many more years.

Seven years later—in 1802—another try was made to find the treasure, this time by a Truro company. Machinery was brought to Oak Island and the original pit was re-excavated to a depth of twenty-seven metres. Oak platforms were again found every three metres and quantities of charcoal, putty, and coconut fibre. The presence of coconut fibre was interesting because, while Oak Island is about twenty-five hundred kilometres away from the closest coconut tree, ships in the sixteenth century used the fibre as packing round cargo to prevent water damage.

A replica of the stone found in the original pit.

Twenty-seven metres down the workers found a big flat stone with strange carvings on the bottom. These carvings were later deciphered to read, "Ten feet below are two million pounds buried." But where is this stone now? Unfortunately it has disappeared.

That evening, after removing the stone, the workers were sure they were about to find the treasure. But on returning early the following morning, they found instead eighteen metres of water in the shaft! Efforts to bail out the water failed, and the men eventually gave up as some of them had farms to look after and couldn't neglect them any longer.

The next year the company returned and this time dug a new shaft four metres southeast of the original one. From this shaft they hoped to tunnel through to the first one and reach the treasure. They got to a depth of thirty-three and a half metres and were within half a metre of the first shaft when the water flooded in. Two hours later the water in the new shaft measured twenty metres. The water was salty and seemed to rise and fall with the ocean tides. Somehow the sea was getting into the shafts, but how?

Water continued to foil other explorations over the years. It was discovered that Smith's Cove Beach, which was about 150 metres east of the original shaft, was not a natural beach, but was composed of tonnes of coconut fibre several centimetres deep, underneath the sand between the low and high tide lines. Beneath the coconut fibre was eel grass and a layer of beach rocks packed tightly together. Efforts to build a stone and clay cofferdam to hold back the tides failed, but led to the discovery of five fan-shaped drains under the beach. These drains were even-

An aerial view of Oak Island.

tually thought to be part of a huge feeder system that allowed sea water to enter the original shaft at a rate of twenty-seven hundred litres per minute.

Who constructed these underground tunnels and why? The answers to these questions have still to be found. Most theories centre around buried pirate treasure. It is estimated that the original work on Oak Island must have taken about 100 000 hours! It was obviously an important project, yet to date no one has come up with any concrete answers or any real signs of buried treasure. Could the treasure have been removed years ago, or is it still there? Or was there ever any treasure at all?

A company called Triton Alliance Ltd. is trying to solve the Oak Island mystery. They were the ones who lowered the underwater camera into Borehole 10-X in August 1971 and took photographs of the mysterious human hand. Unfortunately these photographs are not clear, but a Montreal physiologist felt that one of the pictures taken off the monitor could have been that of a human body, and a Halifax pathologist stated that human flesh could be preserved in a damp airless place.

Further exploration of Borehole 10-X by professional divers revealed a large cave at the bottom of the hole, but visibility was very bad. It was too dangerous for the divers to explore it fully, and in November 1976 the shaft caved in.

So far, since 1795, approximately $2 000 000 have been spent trying to discover the elusive secret of Oak Island—but the mystery remains.

The Pirates Attack

by Avi

Kidnapped by pirates, Kevin at first defied the pirate captain. However, he soon real-ized that only by appearing to co-operate could he ever make his escape. So he agreed to learn seamanship and gunnery from Jacob Small, the master gunner. It wasn't long before Kevin figured out how the pirates preyed on passing ships. Warned by rocket when a ship was approaching, they would tow a floating battery of heavy guns out to intercept and sink the vessel.

One day, just as he had feared, Kevin was forced to go along when the pirates attacked.

. . . we tumbled down on the beach toward the boats, which were already beginning to leave the shore.

It was one of those balmy late-summer days, not a cloud in the sky, and the sun feeling hot no matter where one stood, a day on which the birds appeared to float more than fly, a day on which there were all kinds of excuses for doing nothing.

But the men who pulled on their oars were of no such mind. As the boats passed the cannon platform, ropes were flung out and some of the men, led by Jacob Small, leaped upon its deck and began to work the anchor. In moments, the floating battery was in tow.

from Captain Grey

Another rocket, shooting from the hill, exploded with a single report, telling us which direction to go out of the bay's mouth. The tide pouring out, we moved along with great speed, as though racing down a flowing river.

Throughout, Captain Grey, sitting tall, spyglass in hand, constantly shouted orders now to this boat, now to that, calling men by name, urging one faster, another slower, pointing out the slacker at the oars, praising the efforts of someone else. Seeing all, he let everybody know what he saw.

The men, dressed in their strange uniforms, were all armed with weapons: pistols, swords, muskets, and daggers of every kind, shape, and age, from the best Spanish steel to Jersey pig-iron bayonets. It was a crowd of clowns gone mad.

At the mouth of the bay I saw Sand Island close up for the first time. It was as it had been described, long, low, with nothing but sun and rock on its high spine. A few small trees, twisted and bent double,

marked the futility of life there.

Once we shot out from behind the protection of the island, smooth water was behind us. The ocean, rolling with high and heavy waves, marked a rhythm that was at one with my beating heart.

"There she is!" cried a voice before us. My eyes turned toward the open sea, then down the coast.

Captain Grey stood. "A merchant marine!" he cried. "Fat and slow!"

"What colors?" cried a man.

"French," replied the captain.

The men, as one, cheered.

The captain, scowling, gave his orders. "Custer! Porter! Take the lee!" Oars shifted. The battle plan was laid, as two of the longboats swept out to sea to outflank any escape by the ship. The floating battery, pulled by the four longboats, continued its straight course toward the ship, rising and falling in the sea with ponderous motion. Because the wind tended to blow toward the coast at that point, it was difficult for ships to find their way out of the trap so carefully set.

The merchant ship, fully rigged, was a big one, but it was easy to see why she had been marked for attack. She was not fast, she was un-armed, and she was alone—the last was the most crucial point of all.

I had no idea how many crew she carried, but I quickly counted our force. There were seven boats in all, each with six men. Forty-two. There was the floating battery, three men to each cannon plus Jacob Small. I counted thirteen. By my reckoning we had set to sea with close to sixty men.

Slowly, the French approached, a wonder to my eye. Her staysails had long been in view. Now the main topgallant staysail and the foresail bil-lowed forward before her bloated hull, giving her the appearance of a mountain crowned with clouds gliding upon the sea and summer air, pushing forward without fear. . . .

The pirates, plunging forward, worked in silence, the oars alone sound-ing as they cut the sea. From long experience, all knew what to do.

The hardest part was waiting for the floating battery to come up, for she was slower than the rest, and the captain's men had to be careful, lest they or their cannons be swept off by a sudden toss of waves. As it was, they kept the cannons covered, waiting to load only at the last possible moment, lest the powder get wet and misfire. The first shots were the crucial ones.

The French ship loomed larger and larger. As we drew closer we observed sailors begin to climb the riggings, arms waving, as if to greet us. It was their last opportunity to show their faith and trust in man.

Two of the longboats were now on the far side of the ship and were waiting for the cannons to creep closer, which they did, the four towing boats straining at the lines.

At last the crucial moment was reached.

The captain, suddenly standing erect, waved an arm. Someone on the ship actually waved back. But that was not the captain's intent. In more deadly response the four towing boats moved so that each corner of the raft was pulled in different ways, which had the effect of steadying the platform. At that point the canvas covers were swept off and the men leaped to load the guns. They could not have been twenty yards from the prancing ship, which still did not perceive its peril.

It was too late.

The first cannon shot forth with an enormous crash. The tightness of the lines, the steadiness of the platform, made the ball go true. I saw the fire from the cannon first, then the shot itself leap across the short water gap and slam against the ship's hull with a wrenching, splintering crush.

The mountain shivered.

I watched, amazed, as those who pulled the cannon raft swung about ninety degrees, presenting the second corner of the battery, and another cannon, to the ship. It too fired. Once more I saw the great ship shake.

And that is the way it went. Spun about like a turret, the raft presented one cannon after another, spitting load after load directly against the ship's lower hull. I could hear the terror and confusion on the ship's decks.

Twelve shots were fired. Twelve shots were true. Upon the twelfth explosion, the longboats that were not pulling the raft hurled themselves against the merchant ship from the other side. The men, dropping their oars, tied themselves to the ship, then sprang upon her with murderous intent.

Moments later, the towing boats joined them, but from the other side. The captain's boat shot forward with such speed that I was sent flying from my seat to the bottom of the boat. Momentarily stunned, I scrambled up and saw the ship loom over us.

To my astonishment I was left alone, as members of the crew and the captain himself climbed up to the ship. I was too frightened to follow, but I could hear well enough what was happening: the shots, the scraping of blades, the screams.

The struggle did not take long. The ship, having been taken completely by surprise, crushed with cannonading, boarded instantly by men who cared little for what they faced, gave way quickly. A sudden silence told me the fight was over. All I heard was the licking, lapping breath of sea against the empty boats.

My legs weak, I climbed aboard the helpless ship. When my head cleared the railing, all that I feared lay visible before me.

That it was dreadful you might already have guessed, for no words of mine would be able to express the calculated cruelty of the whole affair. We had taken the ship by surprise, and the defense of her crew was but poor. Far from showing any mercy, Captain Grey and his men had made the crew suffer for their innocence. The only men alive on the deck were the captain's men. Those from the French ship's crew who had resisted lay dead upon the decks.

A quick glance informed me that at least twenty of the Frenchmen had died on deck. Those who remained alive were pushed below. The ship was rendered useless too: the deadeyes split, the rigging hung idle. The sails whipped and fluttered without command.

Under the captain's direction, his men were hauling up boxes and chests, anything of value. Goods were quickly piled in a great heap. Hardly pausing, the men began to load the stolen goods into the boats that lay below. The captain did not interfere other than to make sure that necessities were taken first—food and the like—after which the men were allowed to loot at will.

From beneath the deck I could hear cries, calls, and curses, but no one from the captain's "nation" paid them any mind. They went about their thievery in silence.

All things considered, not much was taken, though what was removed was surely the best cargo. Some twenty-five cases altogether, a small portion, no doubt, of what the ship held. Nonetheless, the captain and his men seemed satisfied.

Meanwhile, I wandered about the ship with no one paying attention to me, or saying a word. At one point I asked a man whose name I knew what was to become of the ship's crew, but he would not answer other than to point to the captain if I wanted my question answered. I did not dare ask him.

Once the loading was done, Captain Grey surveyed the deck for the last time, then gave sharp orders to reboard the longboats. I was struck with the sudden notion that I could hide someplace, so that when the ship sailed off, I would be able to go with it. I would gain my freedom and inform on the gang. But before I could find a place to hide, the captain, observing me, ordered me back into the boat. My heart sinking, I had no choice but to comply.

As we began to push away I turned to the captain. "What about the ship?" I asked.

"You'll see soon enough," he replied, calling on the boats to hurry.

I had no understanding what was to happen until, with a sudden, sickening dread, I discovered their intent. Jacob Small, once more on the floating battery, but now closer to the ship than before, began to load the guns.

"You'll not sink her!" I cried.

"Why not?" was his curt answer. "Doesn't France sink what ships she wills? Does not the United States?"

"But you've put men into the hold!"

"Let them appeal to their parliaments, kings, and congresses," he said. "They can form a committee and pass some laws."

Even as he spoke the first cannon went off. Such was its closeness and power that a gaping hole, splintered and torn, flowered upon the boat's hull. Water poured in.

The raft, slowly turning, began a casual bombardment. Above the smashing of the shot rose the cries, shrieks, and prayers of the men trapped on the doomed ship.

Their prayers went unanswered. As the captain called away his boats, the great merchant ship went over on her side, then slid beneath the waters, a great foaming bubble rolling over the spot as if to mark the place. Then the sea itself mercifully hid the shame. Soon there was nothing left of the dreadful act but the shrill cries of gulls who had joined us and, like scavengers without souls, plucked through the flotsam on the waves.

The Ships of Yule

by Bliss Carman

When I was just a little boy,
Before I went to school,
I had a fleet of forty sail
I called the Ships of Yule;

Of every rig, from rakish brig
And gallant barkentine,
To little Fundy fishing boats
With gunwales painted green.

They used to go on trading trips
Around the world for me,
For though I had to stay on shore
My heart was on the sea.

They stopped at every port to call
From Babylon to Rome,
To load with all the lovely things
We never had at home;

With elephants and ivory
Bought from the King of Tyre,
And shells and silks and sandal-wood
That sailor men admire;

With figs and dates from Samarcand,
And squatty ginger-jars,
And scented silver amulets
From Indian bazaars;

With sugar-cane from Port of Spain,
And monkeys from Ceylon,
And paper lanterns from Pekin
With painted dragons on;

With cocoanuts from Zanzibar,
And pines from Singapore;
And when they had unloaded these
They could go back for more.

And even after I was big
And had to go to school,
My mind was often far away
Aboard the Ships of Yule.

Ghost Ship

by Seymour Simon

There are many stories of ghost ships at sea. Most of them are just made-up tales. Even those stories that are based on fact are usually easily explained. But there is at least one account of a ghost ship that is factual and yet very mysterious. The story concerns a sailing ship named the *Mary Celeste.*

The mystery began on the afternoon of December 4, 1872. The British sailing ship *Dei Gratia* was about one thousand kilometres off the coast of Portugal. The lookout reported spotting a sail on the horizon.

As the two ships drew closer, Captain David Morehouse of the *Dei Gratia* observed the other ship through his telescope and recognized it as the *Mary Celeste.* But something was clearly wrong. Part of the *Mary Celeste*'s sails were missing and the ship was wallowing from side to side in the heavy seas. Captain Morehouse could see no one at the wheel and nobody on deck.

Morehouse hailed the ship again and again. No one answered his calls. He decided to investigate and ordered a small boat launched with a crew of three. A few minutes later the three sailors stood on the deck of the

Mary Celeste. They stamped their feet on the deck and shouted. No answer.

The seamen went below deck and looked into the cabins, the galley, and the cargo hold. Finally they had searched the entire ship. There wasn't a person on board. The ship was drifting along without her crew.

The ship itself seemed to be in good condition. The pumps were working below deck, there were no leaks, and even the sails were in fairly good shape. The cargo, seventeen hundred casks of industrial alcohol, was still lashed in place.

A small yawl carried on the deck of the *Mary Celeste* and used as a lifeboat was gone. Also missing were some navigational instruments and some of the ship's papers. But the logbook was still in the captain's cabin. The last entry was dated November 24, two weeks earlier. It gave no hint of any trouble.

The crew must have abandoned the *Mary Celeste* in a great hurry. The captain had left the logbook and his clothing. The crew had left not only their clothing and other personal belongings, but had even left behind their pipes and tobacco. It was common knowledge that sailors would leave their tobacco behind only if they were in great danger.

But what could that danger have been? The boarders could find absolutely nothing wrong with the ship. There was plenty of food and drinking water on board. It's true that sailors abandon burning or sinking ships at sea. But why abandon an undamaged ship?

Even if the *Mary Celeste* had been caught in a storm, the large ship would still have been safer than the smaller lifeboat. And there was no sign of a fire on board or any other damage. In fact, the boarding party of three seamen was able to sail the *Mary Celeste* one thousand kilometres to Gibralter all by themselves.

Could pirates have boarded the ship and done away with the crew? Could there have been a mutiny? Neither seemed likely. In either case there should have been signs of a struggle. But there were none. Pirates would have taken more than just a few instruments. Mutineers would certainly have taken their clothing and tobacco along with them. There just seemed to be no reason for the crew to be gone.

Even before the *Mary Celeste* was found abandoned, the ship seemed to be unlucky. She had been built in Nova Scotia and launched in 1861.

Her original name was the *Amazon*. Her first captain died two days after he took command. On her first voyage, she suffered damage to her hull. While the damage was being repaired, fire broke out aboard ship. Her second captain lost his job because of these misfortunes.

Her third captain sailed her across the Atlantic—and promptly ran into another ship in the Straits of Dover. She was repaired once again, and sailed home with still another captain. A few years later, the *Amazon* ran aground on Cape Breton Island and was badly damaged.

This time the *Amazon* was completely rebuilt and sold to new owners. They renamed her the *Mary Celeste* and planned to sail her under an American flag. Her new captain was Benjamin Spooner Briggs. He was just thirty-eight years old, but had spent most of those years at sea. He had been captain of three previous ships and had the reputation of being a good sailor.

Briggs and Captain Morehouse of the *Dei Gratia* were good friends. They dined together the night before the *Mary Celeste* was to sail. Briggs took his wife and infant daughter along with him on the newly rebuilt ship's first voyage. He certainly did not seem nervous or sense anything wrong.

Weeks later, when Captain Morehouse found the abandoned *Mary Celeste* he may have felt sorry for his friend Captain Briggs. But Morehouse knew that the *Mary Celeste* would bring him a good profit. Under the laws of the sea, Morehouse could claim a part of the value of the abandoned ship and its cargo.

Morehouse's friendship with Briggs seemed suspicious to the attorney general of Gibralter. He decided to try to prove that Morehouse was responsible for whatever happened to the *Mary Celeste*. But there was very little evidence of that. In fact, the attorney general could only come up with three bits of possible foul play. First, there was a small cut in the ship's railing. Second, Briggs's sword, found beneath his bunk, had a few rust spots that might have been blood. And third, the last log entry had been made hundreds of kilometres from where the *Mary Celeste* had been found.

The members of the naval court of inquiry were not impressed by the supposed evidence. The cut railing could have been an accident. The spots on the sword did not even look like blood. And ships' logs were

often made out days later than they should have been. Besides, there was no sign of any struggle at all. Captain Morehouse and his crew were quickly cleared of any wrongdoing.

The naval court was also supposed to come up with an opinion on what really happened to the *Mary Celeste*. But after three months of investigations they could find no evidence of any kind. They admitted that they could find no explanation for the disappearance of Captain Briggs and his crew.

In the years that followed, all kinds of explanations were offered as to what happened to the *Mary Celeste*. Some said that the ship was attacked by monsters from the depths of the sea, such as giant squids or whales or even more fearsome creatures. Others thought that sickness aboard ship or pirates of one kind or another were responsible. More recent explanations involve the crew being abducted by UFOs or visitors from outer space.

About the time of the trial, the *Mary Celeste*'s owner came up with an explanation that at least seems possible. He suggested that some of the alcohol in the cargo may have leaked. Hot weather might have evaporated the alcohol and built up enough gas pressure to blow open the hatch cover.

Captain Briggs may have mistakenly thought that a fire caused the explosion. He might have ordered the crew to abandon ship at once. The small lifeboat could have been swamped in the rough seas. This would leave the ship empty and yet perfectly sound.

But any explosion could not have been a large one because there was no evidence of any damage. In fact, there is nothing to prove that any part of this explanation is correct. No one has ever been able to come up with a satisfactory explanation. To this day, the disappearance of the crew of the *Mary Celeste* remains one of the most puzzling sea mysteries of all time.

The Voyage of Dove

by Robin Lee Graham with Derek L.T. Gill

On July 27, 1965, sixteen-year-old Robin Graham and his cats Suzette and Joliette set sail on his boat Dove from San Pedro, California. Thus began an odyssey that would last for over five years and bring Robin all the way around the world—by sea—alone. At times fearful, at times elated, Robin tape-recorded his thoughts throughout the journey.

The Beginning
July 27, 1965

The morning of July 27, 1965, was a marvellous one, with the sun burning off the mist in the outer harbor. Excitement killed my appetite, but I sat down with Jud Croft and ate a bowl of breakfast cereal. Jill Gibson, a girl-friend who had come up from Newport, delighted the photographers by giving me a kiss.

Then my father came aboard. He looked ill at ease, uptight, and when he put out his hand I noticed it was trembling. He said something about seeing me in Hawaii. Then, at exactly ten o'clock, I started up *Dove's* inboard engine.

That was the beginning of it all.

I wonder now if I had been able to see the future whether I would have sailed at all. Supposing at that moment I had been able to sense the loneliness that drove me to within a breath of madness, supposing I had seen my demastings or that huge storm in the Indian Ocean—would I have left the slipway at San Pedro?

August 10, 1965

When I'd been out sixteen days I picked up a Hawaiian radio station and introduced the cats to Hawaiian music. I complained into the recorder: *They don't seem to appreciate the music as much as I do. The Honolulu station has just spoken about me. The announcer read a letter from my father, who's asked all ships to look out for me. That's me they're talking about! They talked for five minutes, really weird! But I haven't seen any ships anyway. The only way I know that there are other people somewhere is by a jet trail. I'm trying to picture a guy sailing along in a small boat in the mid-Pacific. And that guy's me!*

All along my route I was to find out that the first or the second question a news reporter asked me was what I did all the time at sea. It sounds strange, but I was hardly ever without something to do—usually small things like cleaning up the boat, or mending something, or cooking. If there wasn't anything to do I'd read or make work, like painting the inside of the cabin or cleaning up the stove.

I would make quite a big deal out of writing a note and putting it into a bottle. The first time I did this was when I was on my way to Hawaii. The note read:

"My name is Robin Lee Graham. I am sixteen years old and sailing a 24-foot sailboat to Honolulu. My position is 127°W; 22°N. If you find this note please write to me and tell me where you found it. Thanks a lot." I added my uncle's California address. I never did receive a reply to my bottled notes. Perhaps they are still bobbling about in the Pacific or yellowing in the sun on some distant shore.

August 16, 1965

Easily the best moments of ocean sailing are those when land is first sighted. I saw Oahu at dawn on my twenty-second day at sea and whooped so loudly that the cats arched their backs.

At noon on September 14, 1965, Robin left Hawaii and headed again across the Pacific Ocean for Fanning Island and from there to American Samoa.

September 20, 1965

Only four days out of Hawaii I saw the most beautiful sunset of the whole five years of my voyage. At least that is the one I best remember. I took a picture of it, but it doesn't really show up well. There was no one to point it out to except the cats, and they weren't interested, so I told the tape: *The reds and the pinks are sort of coming toward me from the horizon and then the greens and the yellows are moving in and out like they're being woven.*

I needed something like this to cheer me up because I was still so homesick. Loneliness slowed me down. When my morale was low I spent much longer calculating my position and making entries in my logbook.

On days when the cats irritated me I complained into the tape recorder: *Suzette and Joliette are so dumb. Why can't they talk to me? All they can do is chase their tails and go to sleep. . . . I don't know what's wrong. I don't even want to eat. Even that fruitcake tastes like warm water. You know what I mean?*

September 26, 1965

It was weird how when I was on the skids of self-pity something would turn up to distract me. The sunset was one example, and another was when I was in the doldrums under flopping sails, twelve days out from Hawaii: I saw my first school of porpoises.

I recorded: *The porpoises are now all around* Dove. *I can hear their squeaks. It's amazing how loud they can talk. I guess I can hear them so well because my hull is so thin. I wonder if they're trying to talk to me. Maybe one porpoise hit the keel, because I heard a thumping and she was squeaking real loud. It was nerve-wracking but exciting. It has been so long since I heard any voice, and it's almost as though someone was trying to answer me.*

To celebrate the visit of the porpoises I gave the cats a sardine supper.

October 20, 1965

Perhaps it was because I was too pleased with myself on this occasion or because I was pushing *Dove* a little too hard that the accident happened. *Dove* was closing on Samoa when a squall hit, not a heavy squall but blustery enough to be taken seriously. The upshot was that the lower aft shroud broke. Within an eyeblink the mast buckled and fell overboard, carrying with it the mainsail and the *jib*. Although the wind was perhaps twenty knots, *Dove* stopped like a duck full of buckshot.

I told the tape: *Here I was within fifteen miles of Tutuila after five hundred hours of sailing and now I'm not going to make it.*

It took me twenty minutes to heave the sodden sails and broken mast aboard and two hours to raise the boom and set a jury rig with half the mainsail. I was in no great danger, but it seemed a good idea to put out the brilliant orange distress

signal. When an aircraft headed my way I lit a flare, but aimed it at my bare right foot. The steam came off my toes as the aircraft headed out to sea.

Now, with the jury rig I could only sail downwind. A look at the chart and I saw that my only hope of an early landfall was to make for Apia on Upolu Island, fifty-two miles distant.

A jet pilot once told me that he was trained for emergencies. A child, he claimed, could fly an airliner but what separated the experts from the beginners in the cockpit was the moment that might never happen in a long career—the moment when all the red lights start blinking. It's the same with sailing. Anyone can learn in half an afternoon to sail around a harbor, but an emergency like a demasting calls for seamanship. I was wondering just how good my seamanship was as the wind drove crippled *Dove* under her clumsy shortened sail toward Upolu's jagged lee shore.

Due more to a lucky shift of wind than to my sailing skill, *Dove* nosed past Danger Point. At dawn next morning sandy beaches were on my beam and green hills beyond. I celebrated with a breakfast of canned asparagus. By noon I had anchored in the lovely harbor of Apia, right opposite Aggie's Hotel.

One of my first expeditions at Apia was to visit the tomb of Robert Louis Stevenson, who, like Gauguin in Tahiti, had become a legend in his time. The tomb is quite high up on Mount Vaea, overlooking the town. I could have driven there by way of the treelined "Road of Loving Hearts" built by the people of Samoa for their beloved Tusitala ("Teller of Tales"), but I preferred to climb the five-hundred-foot trail up the face of the hill. In the early morning light I read the Requiem carved on the stone tomb:

> Home is the sailor, home from the sea,
> And the hunter home from the hill.

The sailor Robin was not yet home. Two-thirds of the globe was left to circle. After waiting months at Apia for repairs, Robin continued his voyage. He navigated—sometimes reluctantly—the Indian and South Atlantic Oceans. When he went through the Panama Canal, he was back again in the Pacific Ocean . . . on his way home.

The Way Home
April 1, 1970

April Fool's Day and I'm the fool. This is my ninth day out and I'm only 525 miles from the Galapagos.

I ran into a flat calm yesterday and it's still calm this morning. I started the engine at three forty-five, and ran all the time. I take saltwater showers as often as I can, but when it's hot it's hard to keep clean. I got a breeze in the midafternoon, and for a while I was scooting along at better than six knots. But before midnight it was flat calm again.

It was really awful. I had a sort of breakdown at the end of the day. I had trouble taking down the main. Then I found the boom van so tightly tied I couldn't undo it. I was working with a flashlight, and I got so mad I went below and threw the flashlight against the bulkhead and broke it. I grabbed a diving knife and went back to cut the jammed line, and I almost slashed the sail up too. Thank goodness I stopped short of doing that because I have no spare sails.

But on April 4, I was awakened by an unusual sound—waves beating against the hull. I leaped through the companionway and hoisted the main and genoa. *Dove* heeled over and I taped: *This is the best day. It's so beautiful. I'm right on course 307 degrees. Wind! Wind! It has to be the trades!*

141

April 29, 1970

That last night at sea I sat on deck with a quilt wrapped around me to keep out the cold. Occasionally I spoke into the tape recorder: *Okay, boy! I'm now off Pyramid Head. . . . Those must be the lights of Santa Catalina, good old romantic Catalina. . . . Two o'clock and the moon's just risen. Looks like the moon the cow jumped over. . . . Wind is gentle now. . . . My provisions and supplies have just made it. Same for my endurance. . . . Thirty-eight days! Oh, boy!*

Mostly I just thought to myself of the five-year voyage and what it had all added up to.

I'd learned so many things at sea—like kindness has got nothing to do with money and happiness has got nothing to do with rank or race. There were some pretty awful memories, like the time I was nearly run down by a ship at night and the big storm off Malagasy. I thought of the good things too, like the time in the Yasawas and the howl of jackals on the African veld, the thrill of making Mauritius on time under a jury rig and of mending a pelican's beak in the Galapagos.

Little flashes of memory darted through my mind as I sat on deck. I thought how you feel beautiful things deep inside you so that they become part of you.

At sea I had learned how little a person needs, not how much. I wondered why people hold on to life as if the universe depended on them. It seemed to me that so many people hold back from doing the things they really want to do because of fear. Being alone had made me realize that people are pretty insignificant in the universe, like specks of dust.

Karana's Sea Journey

by Scott O'Dell

Island of the Blue Dolphins *is based on a true story of an Indian girl who spent eighteen years alone on an island 120 km off the coast of California.*

For many years Karana's people lived peacefully on their island, called Ghalas-at. But after the Aleuts came and killed many of the people, the survivors decided to leave their island home. Just after leaving the island, Karana discovered that her younger brother had accidentally been left behind. The ship could not turn back and so Karana jumped overboard to join her brother on the island. Shortly afterward her brother was killed by the wild dogs that roamed the island and Karana was left alone.

from Island of the Blue Dolphins

I had decided during the days of the storm, when I had given up hope of seeing the ship, that I would take one of the canoes and go to the country that lay toward the east. I remembered how Kimki, before he had gone, had asked the advice of his ancestors who had lived many ages in the past, who had come to the island from that country, and likewise the advice of Zuma, the medicine man who held power over the wind and the seas. But these things I could not do, for Zuma had been killed by the Aleuts, and in all my life I had never been able to speak with the dead, though many times I had tried.

Yet I cannot say that I was really afraid as I stood there on the shore. I knew that my ancestors had crossed the sea in their canoes, coming from that place which lay beyond. Kimki, too, had crossed the sea. I was not nearly so skilled with a canoe as these men, but I must say that whatever might befall me on the endless waters did not trouble me. It meant far less than the thought of staying on the island alone, without a home or companions, pursued by wild dogs, where everything reminded me of those who were dead and those who had gone away.

Of the four canoes stored there against the cliff, I chose the smallest, which was still very heavy because it could carry six people. The task that faced me was to push it down the rocky shore and into the water, a distance four or five times its length.

This I did by first removing all the large rocks in front of the canoe. I then filled in all these holes with pebbles and along this path laid down long strips of kelp, making a slippery bed. The shore was steep and once I got the canoe to move with its own weight, it slid down the path and into the water.

The sun was in the west when I left the shore. The sea was calm behind the high cliffs. Using the two-bladed paddle I quickly skirted the south part of the island. As I reached the sandspit the wind struck. I was paddling from the back of the canoe because you can go faster kneeling there, but I could not handle it in the wind.

Kneeling in the middle of the canoe, I paddled hard and did not pause until I had gone through the tides that run fast around the sandspit. There were many small waves and I was soon wet, but as I came out from behind the spit the spray lessened and the waves grew long and rolling. Though it would have been easier to go the way they slanted, this would have taken me in the wrong direction. I therefore kept them on my left hand, as well as the island, which grew smaller and smaller, behind me.

At dusk I looked back. The Island of the Blue Dolphins had disappeared. This was the first time that I felt afraid.

There were only hills and valleys of water around me now. When I was in a valley I could see nothing and when the canoe rose out of it, only the ocean stretching away and away.

Night fell and I drank from the basket. The water cooled my throat.

The sea was black and there was no difference between it and the sky. The waves made no sound among themselves, only faint noises as they went under the canoe or struck against it. Sometimes the noises seemed angry and at other times like people laughing. I was not hungry because of my fear.

The first star made me feel less afraid. It came out low in the sky and it was in front of me, toward the east. Other stars began to appear all around, but it was this one I kept my gaze upon. It was in the figure that we call a serpent, a star that shone green and that I knew. Now and then it was hidden by mist, yet it always came out brightly again.

Without this star I would have been lost, for the waves never changed. They came always from the same direction and in a manner that kept pushing me away from the place I wanted to reach. For this reason the canoe made a path in the black water like a snake. But somehow I kept moving toward the star that shone in the east.

This star rose high and then I kept the North Star on my left hand, the one we call "the star that does not move." The wind grew quiet. Since it always died down when the night was half over, I knew how long I had been travelling and how far away the dawn was.

About this time I found that the canoe was leaking. Before dark I had emptied one of the baskets in which food was stored and used it to dip out the water that came over the sides. The water that now moved around my knees was not from the waves.

I stopped paddling and worked with the basket until the bottom of the canoe was almost dry. Then I searched around, feeling in the dark along the smooth planks, and found the place near the bow where the water was seeping through a crack as long as my hand and the width of a finger. Most of the time it was out of the sea, but it leaked whenever the canoe dipped forward in the waves.

The places between the planks were filled with black pitch, which we gather along the shore. Lacking this, I tore a piece of fibre from my skirt and pressed it into the crack, which held back the water.

Dawn broke in a clear sky and as the sun came out of the waves I saw that it was far off on my left. During the night I had drifted south of the place I wished to go, so I changed my direction and paddled along the path made by the rising sun.

There was no wind on this morning and the long waves went quietly under the canoe. I therefore moved faster than during the night.

I was very tired, but more hopeful than I had been since I left the island. If the good weather did not change I would cover many leagues before dark. Another night and another day might bring me within sight of the shore toward which I was going.

Not long after dawn, while I was thinking of this strange place and what it would look like, the canoe began to leak again. This crack was between the same planks, but was a larger one and close to where I was kneeling.

The fibre I tore from my skirt and pushed into the crack held back most of the water that seeped in whenever the canoe rose and fell with the waves. Yet I could see that the planks were weak from one end to the other, probably from the canoe being stored so long in the sun, and that they might open along their whole length if the waves grew rougher.

It was suddenly clear to me that it was dangerous to go on. The voyage would take two more days, perhaps longer. By turning back to the island I would not have nearly so far to travel.

Still I could not make up my mind to do so. The sea was calm and I had come far. The thought of turning back after all this labor was more than I could bear. Even greater was the thought of the deserted island I would return to, of living there alone and forgotten. For how many suns and how many moons?

The canoe drifted idly on the calm sea while these thoughts went over and over in my mind, but when I saw the water seeping through the crack again, I picked up the paddle. There was no choice except to turn back toward the island.

I knew that only by the best of fortune would I ever reach it.

The wind did not blow until the sun was overhead. Before that time I covered a good distance, pausing only when it was necessary to dip water from the canoe. With the wind I went more slowly and had to stop more often because of the water spilling over the sides, but the leak did not grow worse.

This was my first good fortune. The next was when a swarm of dolphins appeared. They came swimming out of the west, but as they saw the canoe they turned around in a great circle and began to follow me. They swam up slowly and so close that I could see their eyes, which are large and the color of the ocean. Then they swam on ahead of the canoe, crossing back and forth in front of it, diving in and out, as if they were weaving a piece of cloth with their broad snouts.

Dolphins are animals of good omen. It made me happy to have them swimming around the canoe, and though my hands had begun to bleed from the chafing of the paddle, just watching them made me forget the pain. I was very lonely before they appeared, but now I felt that I had friends with me and did not feel the same.

The blue dolphins left me shortly before dusk. They left as quickly as they had come, going on into the west, but for a long time I could see the last of the sun shining on them. After night fell I could still see them in my thoughts and it was because of this that I kept on paddling when I wanted to lie down and sleep.

More than anything, it was the blue dolphins that took me back home.

Fog came with the night, yet from time to time I could see the star that stands high in the west, the red star called Magat, which is part of the figure that looks like a crawfish and is known by that name. The crack in the planks grew wider so I had to stop often to fill it with fibre and to dip out the water.

The night was very long, longer than the night before. Twice I dozed kneeling there in the canoe, though I was more afraid than I had ever been. But the morning broke clear and in front of me lay the dim line of the island like a great fish sunning itself on the sea.

I reached it before the sun was high, the sandspit and its tides that bore me into the shore. My legs were stiff from kneeling and as the canoe struck the sand I fell when I rose to climb out. I crawled through the shallow water and up the beach. There I lay for a long time, hugging the sand in happiness.

I was too tired to think of the wild dogs. Soon I fell asleep.

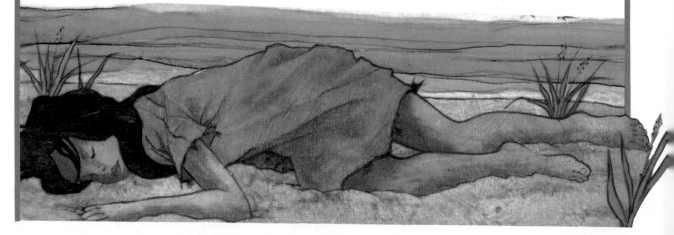

My Friend the Grouper

by Jacques Cousteau

On his first dive near Assumption Island in the Indian Ocean, Luis Marden met a rather friendly fish. It was a grouper of about thirty kilograms. Its coat was brown with a pale marbled pattern that changed from time to time. The big fish strolled right up to Marden, who prepared to take its picture. When the grouper nudged the flashbulb bag with its nose, Luis had to back away to get proper focus. But the fish followed. By a series of retreats, Marden finally shot the fish in focus and swam away to find others. The grouper tagged along, nuzzling the photographer. As Luis lined up another subject, the big fish pushed itself into the picture. The diver had to dodge aside to make his shot. When Luis took the used bulb off the camera, the fish tried to eat it.

After Marden brought up this tale, Delmas and Dumas, two crew members, went down with a canvas bag full of chopped meat. The big fish came up to them. As the divers released some food in the water, the grouper's cavernous mouth opened. Meat scraps vanished into its belly. The men cautiously tried hand-feeding it, and the big fish plucked meat out of their hands without harming them. In that first session Dumas and Delmas taught the grouper several tricks. They named the clever beast Ulysses.

Ulysses became a close friend. He followed us about like a pet, sometimes nibbling our fins. After deep dives, when we were waiting ten metres down to decompress, the boredom was relieved by Ulysses' horsing around with us. When we left he would hang around just under the surface like a boy sadly watching his playmates being called in to lunch. Ulysses quickly learned our schedule. Early in the morning we would find him waiting for us under the ladder. Then he would go down with us for a round of clumsy mischief and meals from the canvas bag.

When he was in a good mood, Ulysses would let any of us pet him and scratch his head. But the big fish had a temper, too. Sometimes he bungled into camera set-ups, and the men shoved him away. Then he would leave, slamming the door behind him: when he stormed off, his first tail stroke was so powerful that it made an audible boom. He also resented us when we forgot the meat bag. When angry, he would hang ten metres off, keeping that distance whether we went toward him or away from him. However, next morning he would be under the diving ladder, his anger a thing of the past.

Delmas was cautious when feeding Ulysses. No sooner was a piece of meat out of the bag than the huge gaping mouth was flying at it. A grouper has no real teeth, but his mouth and throat have rows of grinders that would not improve the use of your arm if you placed it inside. One morning Ulysses tore the sack out of Delmas's hand and swallowed it whole. Defiantly he swam away, well aware that there was no more food to be had.

The next morning there was no Ulysses under the ladder. He did not appear down in our work area. In the afternoon divers spread out to look for him. We found him lying on the sand in front of his den. His gills were pulsing like the panting of a sick person. He had no interest in us. The next morning he was still in bed with a bad case of indigestion caused by swallowing the food bag. Dr. Martin-Laval advised us to keep an eye on our friend. Ulysses, he said, was in danger of a fatal stomach obstruction. On the third day, we found the fish fallen flat on his side. He seemed dangerously ill. I asked the doctor to do something. Martin-Laval was faced with his most unusual case. Since he could not bring the fish to his surgery, he prepared to operate in the patient's bedroom. It was sundown before everything was ready. All equipment had been assembled, and three divers had been briefed as assistants. We went to sleep hoping that Ulysses would last through the night.

At first light a scouting team plunged. Ulysses was gone. The divers roamed about, looking for him. Suddenly, Falco felt something pulling at

his gear. It was Ulysses, announcing that all was well. He was happy and hungry. He had managed to rid his body of the meat sack.

There came a time when we had to take a four-day trip to the island of Aldabra. In leaving we came across a boat containing one of the four inhabitants of Assumption Island. He held up a large fish. It was a thirty-kilogram grouper. We were sure it was Ulysses. Our passage to Aldabra was full of mourning and disgust. We spoke a lot about the effect man has on nature. We knew Ulysses would never have grown so large had he not learned to avoid hooks. We had made him feel comfortable around humans. We had baited him with finger morsels and led him to bite the fatal hook.

We returned to Assumption in a bleak mood. With Ulysses gone, the reef would not be the same. While I brought the *Calypso* into her anchorage, Falco eagerly jumped over the side. In a minute he popped up, leaping out of the water like a joyful porpoise. "Ulysses is alive!" Falco bellowed. As soon as the diving ladder was down, our friend was there waiting for the fun to resume.

We tried feeding other citizens of the reef, and all responded heartily. We swam along throwing out chopped meat from a bag the way a farmer would scatter seeds. This brought out fish by the thousands. But watching us

feed them put Ulysses in a rage. He would crash into the sack, bite our fins, tug on our bathing trunks, and whip his tail to scatter the smallest fish.

We wanted to film this feeding scene, but Ulysses kept breaking it up. He would not get out of the way and often bumped the camera or the flood lamps. Finally, Falco thought of a way to get rid of Ulysses without banging his snout and hurting his sense of dignity. First we lowered the antishark cage to the bottom. Ulysses supervised the placing of the cage and the opening of the door. Then Delmas waved his feeding arm toward the opening and the grouper swam in. The door clanked shut, and Ulysses was a problem no more.

We kept the fish caged for three days while we shot the film. When we opened the cage the grouper made no move to depart. It seems the food was so plentiful in the cage that Ulysses preferred to stay there! Falco went in and pushed him through the door. Ulysses swam off in a sulk, at a much slower pace than usual. He was fat and out of shape.

After six weeks at Assumption Reef, it was time to leave.

"Let's take Ulysses with us," said Delmas.

The idea was favored by all. However, I had to oppose the notion. In France, Ulysses would face a life as a prisoner in an aquarium or would have to be set free in the sea. We had to realize he was not used to colder water. On top of that he was so friendly that the first spearman he met would have an easy kill. No, as much as we did not like the idea, we had to say good-bye to our friend.

Four years later, after Ulysses had become a star in our film, *The Silent World,* a boat made a special call at Assumption Bay and sent divers down to look for the tame grouper. The sailors reported, "Ulysses is doing fine. He was easy to recognize. He swam up immediately to the divers."

Perhaps we will go back someday and see him again. He's a fish worth going halfway round the earth to meet.

The Vigil

by Jan Andrews

aitlin Roberts and her brother, Kevin, dashed along the dirt road that led through their small, Newfoundland village. They went past the church and down onto the beach and for a moment they stood together, throwing pebbles through the mist and drizzle out into the calm, flat, grayness of the sea, drinking in the quiet and freedom of an early Saturday morning. Then they were off again, heading for the high, rough arm of land that led on into the next cove in the coastline of Bonavista Bay. They scrambled to the top, two slight, wiry figures of about the same height, both ruggedly dressed in windbeakers, blue jeans, and rubber boots.

A lock of Caitlin's long, black hair fell across her face. As she pushed it back, her gray eyes widened.

"Kev," she cried, pointing ahead. "Look!"

What she had seen sped them on. Within seconds they were running, hard as they could, down to where a huge, black shape lay stranded on the beach.

"A whale," Kevin called. As he spoke, his boot kicked at a broad line of small, dead fish, thrown up along the high-water mark. "Must have come after the capelin," he panted.

The two of them were close to the great creature now. Their coming had alarmed it. It began to thrash and churn about. Stones and sand and spray were flung up from where the outgoing tide lapped around its tail. Its body

153

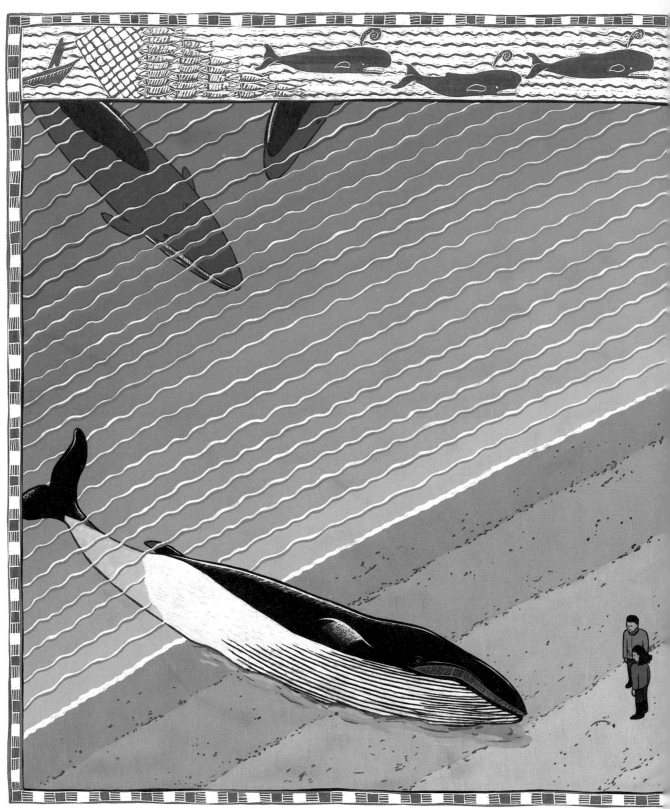

154

writhed and twisted, carving deep into the seabed. Its fins flapped as if, in some dreadful way, it was trying to walk. They stood back, watching in horror.

"Won't get off, will it?" Caitlin said bleakly, so the words made a statement rather than a question.

Kevin shook his dark, curly head. "No," he answered. "Remember, up by Twillingate, last year. There was one there. It was on TV. Folks came from St. John's even, trying to push it off. Weren't no good."

He bent, picked up a stone, weighed it in his hand, and let it drop. The whale thrashed still more desperately. Air came sighing and steaming out of its blowhole. A long, shuddering, heaving breath was sucked back in.

"Let's go somewhere else," Caitlin suggested.

Kevin nodded in agreement. They moved on up the beach, walking quickly at first, their boots clumping against the shift and rattle of the pebbles, their hands thrust deep into their jacket pockets. Then gradually, their steps slowed. They stopped here and there to poke in pretended interest at driftwood and shells and seaweed. A glance passed between them. Kevin looked over his shoulder and, with one accord, they turned back.

"Go gentle, this time, eh?" Caitlin whispered.

Again Kevin took up a stone and again he let it drop. The whale seemed exhausted. It was eyeing them warily through its tiny, deep-set eyes but, though its body almost quivered with tension, it lay still. They moved quietly nearer.

They had almost reached the place where they had stood before when they realized that, out between the rocks on the cove's mouth, other whales were appearing. A steam-spout thrust upwards and then another. Four dark, enormous shapes rose magnificently from the water, arched through the mist, and plunged.

"They come to be with it," Kevin said. "I heard of that."

"Shh," Caitlin commanded. "Listen!" From the blowhole of the whale on the beach a strange, high sound soared. It was answered by a succession of wavering notes, and again the four shapes rose, this time closer in to the shore. Squeaks and cries and long drawn whistles thrilled electric onto the gray, cold morning air.

"Like they're talking to each other," Caitlin said in awe.

Suddenly, she realized her cheeks were wet with tears. She looked at the creature on the beach and then out into the cove. Beside her, there came a small, choked-back sob. Turning, she saw that Kevin was crying too. He wiped his hand slowly across his eyes.

"They'll stay now till it's dead, won't they?" Caitlin asked through the lump in her throat.

"Yes! Yes, 'course!"

As the communication between the whales went on, Kevin perched himself against a rock.

"Will you mind, Cat?" he said, at last.

"Mind what?"

"When it's dead and Dad and the men come to cut it. I seen that on TV too. There's a wonderful lot of meat on a whale."

Caitlin hung her head to let her black hair shut out her vision for a while. "Sort of," she answered. "But . . . but it'd only rot and stink otherwise, like the capelin."

"What if . . . ?"

The harshness in her brother's voice made her glance up quickly. His round, usually cheerful, face was pale and strained.

"What if what, now?" she asked.

"Well, well if there'd been a gang of us, say. See . . . see it'd have been different. We'd have yelled and laughed and someone would've thrown a stone. Someone would've, sure to! Then we'd all have done it. T'wouldn't have been like it is now. T'wouldn't, would it? Not at all! No way!"

The worry in Caitlin's gray eyes acknowledged the truth of his statement. He looked at his watch.

"Some other kid's bound to come here before long," he said. "Soon as one knows, they all will."

"We'll have to stay here then."

"We'll have to guard it, all day if need be."

"But . . ."

"Cat, we're not enough. Say, like the Riley boys! There's five and they're all so big. They won't take no mind of us."

"We need help, a grown-up."

"Yeah, but . . . well, everyone's got something going Saturdays and . . ."

"We can't both go, Cat."

"I'll stay then. OK, Kev?"

"And I'll go. OK?"

"OK."

Kevin hesitated. "Cat," he said. "We're not being daft, are we? I mean . . . I mean it's only an old whale and it's going to die, for sure, anyway."

Doubt crept into Caitlin's mind. Already the drizzle was soaking through her jeans and running down her neck. She could feel the beginnings of cold and hunger, and fear of what the other kids in the village would say.

"I dunno," she muttered.

The whale on the beach let out another of its high, strange cries. Once more the cry was answered. Brother and sister looked at one another. They knew then that, just as they had not been able to walk away before, so they would not be able to walk away now.

"We got to, haven't we?" Caitlin whispered.

Kevin nodded. Resolutely, he made for the worn track back to the village; resolutely Caitlin squared her thin shoulders and planted her feet and took up her position at the whale's side. It breathed, shuddered, breathed again.

"We got to," Caitlin told herself. "And . . . and we will!"

So it was with the watching of Caitlin and Kevin Roberts and the help and authority of Mr. Jones on land, and with the companionship of its fellows waiting and calling to it from the sea, the whale on the beach came to the moment of its death with peace. Gentle then was its passing, gentle and calm, like a cloud moving across the sun and breaking up and disappearing on a summer's day certain as the tide that rose to wash healing and salt and

cold around it. For the first time, Caitlin put out a hand to touch the great body.

"The men'll come tomorrow, won't they?" she said softly. "They'll cut it. It'll be all a mess, then nothing."

Kevin reached over and touched the dead mammal, too.

"I won't be sorry we stayed," he said. "Not ever."

Caitlin took a last look out into the cove. Somehow she could feel that already the other whales were swimming past the rocks and out into the open and away.

"No more won't I," she said firmly. "No more won't neither of us."

The Singing Float

by Monica Hughes

The singing woke Melissa, high, clear notes like those of a violin, at the very edge of hearing. She sat up in bed. The cabin was silent, the only light a strip of pure white between the not-quite-closed curtains across the window.

She slipped out of bed and padded to the window, her toes curling away from the chill of the floor. She pushed the drape aside and looked out. Beyond the fringe of pines the land dropped abruptly to the beach, and she could see, framed by the dark strokes of the trees, a line of silver stretching clear to the horizon.

It rippled like a bolt of silk flung down from the sky toward her feet. She stood, frozen in its magic, until the moon sailed out from behind an obscuring pine and the silken path became only its reflection on the still surface of the sea. She shivered, scampered back to bed, and lay in a ball, warming her feet with her hands, until she fell asleep.

When Melissa woke, the sun was shining in an ordinary sort of way.

The tide was out and the memory of the singing and of the white moon's path was like a dream. She pulled on shorts and a T-shirt, made her bed neatly, and dusted her collection of shells with a tissue. That did not take long. She had collected only five, but each of them was perfect, without a flaw or a chip.

When everything was in order she ran into the living room, which was really living and dining room and kitchen all in one, with a fireplace where you could roast marshmallows and a big window overlooking the Pacific.

"Good morning, Half Pint."

"Morning, Daddy." She gave him a kiss and got her special hug in return. "Good morning, Mom. What's for breakfast?"

"Sausages and scrambled eggs. If you and Dad do the dishes."

"Worth it. I'm starving." She stood by the stove and carried the plates to the table as Mom filled them.

"Full moon last night. Extra high tide. Good pickings on the shore today, Lissa."

"Oh, I do hope so. Do you realize that we've only got two more days? Only *two*. I can't believe it."

"Me neither."

When breakfast was eaten and the dishes put away, Melissa picked her way carefully down the path to the beach. There were steps roughly carved between tree roots, and at the bottom was a tangle of weather-whitened timbers, painful to bare feet. She crossed it with care and then did what she did every morning: raced as fast as she could across the sand to the very edge of the sea.

Only then, standing with her toes dug into the wet sand, the sea foaming at her insteps, did she turn and look back along the beach. This was the magic moment. The moment of choice. Where shall I look today? Where is the best shell hiding? Above all, *will* there at last be a glass float?

Glass floats were as rare as hens' teeth, Daddy said, now that the Japanese fisherfolk had started using plastic floats of gaudy green and pink to hold up their gill nets and mark their traps, instead of the smoky iridescent globes of blown glass the size of a large grapefruit.

"Only two more days," she said as she stood with the water dragging at her toes. "Only *two* more days." She looked at the rocky headland to the north and along the white beach that curved around to the southern headland.

"Where, oh where, do I begin today?"

Into her mind came the high, clear note she had heard in the night. Slowly she followed the sound, walking over strands of shining brown kelp and pale half-buried logs and tree roots smoothed by the sea. She walked without thought toward a tangle of seaweed at the uppermost limit of last night's tide.

There, among fat cords and shiny ribbons and air bladders, was the faint glint of a rainbow. She dropped to her knees and gently loosened the strands one by one. There it was, perfect, like a huge frozen soap bubble. She lifted it out and cradled it in the palms of her hands. The singing in her head had stopped, and the whole morning was still.

"You beauty, oh you beauty," she whispered. For a brief second it seemed that something flickered in the depths of the glass globe. Then the sun dazzled on its curve and she blinked. When she looked again she could see nothing inside.

She got to her feet and began to walk slowly back toward their cabin, holding the float carefully in both hands.

"What have you got?" Mom turned as the screen door banged.

"Just look!"

"Oh, what a beauty."

"Clever girl."

Was I? she wondered. It had been more like being led than finding. She wadded some tissues in the centre of the table and set the float down upon them. "Isn't it the most perfect thing in the whole world? I don't care if we have to go home in two days. I wouldn't care if we had to go tomorrow. Right now, even."

"Well, I would." Mom laughed. "I'm counting on two more days' fun with you and Dad. What's the plan, Phil, now Melissa has done her beachcombing?"

"I thought we might drive up to Tofino and take the boat out to look at the seals. Maybe even get a peek at a whale."

"Great idea. I've already packed lunch. Lissa, get your shoes and socks on. And better take a jacket. It might be cool on the water."

"But . . ." Melissa looked longingly at her float. Like a rainbow, she thought. Of my very own.

"Dear girl, you can't sit in here all day. The sun's shining. Go get your shoes, quick!"

"But . . ." she said as she went.

"*And* your jacket. Phil, have you got the thermos? And I've got the basket. Oh, Lissa, *do* wake up!"

Melissa followed them reluctantly out of the cabin. In the shadowy living room the globe glowed.

"Oh, I forgot to lock the door!" she cried out, halfway to Tofino. "Dad, we have to go back. My float . . ."

"It won't walk away. And I did check the door. My goodness, Lissa, I think you must be bewitched."

Perhaps I am, she thought, and kneeled on the back seat of the car, watching the road unwind between the pines, taking them farther and farther away from the cabin.

At any other time the boat ride to the seal rocks and beyond, almost out to the salmon fishing grounds, would have been the high point of the holidays. Indeed, part of Melissa enjoyed every moment. But the other part of her kept looking back to the low line of the shore and thinking: There is the bay. And there must be our cabin, and in it, on the table . . .

She gripped the aft railing so tightly that her knuckles went white. For one crazy minute she'd actually wanted to dive into the water and swim ashore, *she* who could barely make it across the school pool.

She jumped when Mom touched her shoulder.

"Melissa, Mrs. White would like to talk to you. She owns a gift shop in town. She's very interested in your float."

Melissa turned, her face lighting up. "It's so perfect," she said. "About *this* big. And like a rainbow."

"Will you sell it to me?" Mrs. White said abruptly.

"Huh?"

"I'll give you . . . ten dollars."

Melissa shook her head.

"You can buy a lot of candy with ten dollars."

"Candy's bad for your teeth."

"Books then. Whatever." The woman smiled. Melissa didn't like her smile. It wasn't quite real. She shook her head again.

"Twenty dollars. My last word. That's a lot of money for a young girl."

Melissa looked at Mom, but for once she was no help at all. "It's your find, love. Your decision." She walked away and left the two of them together.

"N-no," Melissa stammered. "Thank you."

The smile became fixed. "Thirty dollars," the woman snapped. "Oh, come on now. If it's as good as you say I'll make it thirty-five. Think what you could do with thirty-five dollars!"

Melissa went on shaking her head dumbly.

"They're fragile things, these floats. You might not even get it home in one piece. Suppose you drop it? What have you got then? Nothing. Better take my offer."

Melissa was no longer listening. The boat had turned for shore, and she could hear the singing once again, high, sweet, piercing.

On the drive home Mom suddenly said, "That woman, what's-her-name, Mrs. White, said you were rude to her, Melissa."

"Was I?" said Melissa vaguely. "I didn't think I was."

As soon as Dad had parked she ran along the path. "Oh, hurry, where's the key?"

"My goodness, but you're jumpy." Mom unlocked the door with maddening slowness.

Melissa rushed into the living room. "It's still there."

"Of course it is, Silly Billy. Tell me, how much *did* that woman offer you for the float?"

"Thirty-five dollars." Melissa dropped into a chair and, elbows on the table, chin on hands, stared into the iridescent glass. She didn't notice the expression on her parents' faces.

"Thirty-five dollars!"

Dad whistled. "Which I suppose means she could sell it for twice that. That's an expensive bauble, Melissa. You'd better take care of it!"

They all stared at the float. Then . . . "I almost thought—but that's ridiculous." Mom shook her head as if to clear it. "Look, let's have a proper bake-out on the beach. That salmon we bought in Tofino. Will you get a fire started, Phil? I'll make a salad. Melissa, that thing's making me nervous. Will you please put it safely in your room?"

Melissa lifted the float from its bed of tissues and gasped.

"Hey, careful! You nearly dropped it then. Want me to look after it for you?"

"No, thanks, Dad. It's fine." Melissa walked quickly out of the room. The glass float was suddenly as hot as a baked potato. She put it safely down on her dressing table and rubbed her hands. The palms were pink and puffy. She stared at the float. Deep inside it something glittered and moved. She ran out of the room, her heart thumping, and went to help Mom dry the lettuce.

Sitting with her back against a log, Melissa licked the last of the salmon off her fingers and stared vaguely out to sea. The sun had set, and the dark was creeping up the beach with the incoming tide. Far out past their headland she could see the rhythmic flash-flash of a lighthouse. The wind rose and she shivered suddenly.

"Time to go in. Hot chocolate by the fire and then bed."

"Our last day tomorrow. I wish we could come back here for ever and ever."

"I second that." Dad kissed the top of her head. He began to pick up the remains of their meal, and Mom shook out the rug. Melissa followed them up to the cabin, suddenly reluctant to face whatever it was that moved within the float.

Mom lit the fire, and Dad stirred chocolate on the stove. Beyond the uncurtained window the blackness was broken only by the comforting lighthouse signal. Melissa drank her chocolate in very small sips. It was almost cold by the time she got to the bottom.

"Enough hanging around," Mom said at last. "Teeth and bed. Off you go." And she had to kiss them good night and go into her room.

She walked over to the dressing table and touched the float with a fingertip. It was as cool as . . . as cool as glass. In the semidarkness it was just a smoky glass globe, so fragile she could crush it just like *that*. She found she was holding it in the palm of her hand, her fingers closed tightly about it. She hadn't even remembered deciding to pick it up. She put it down with a gasp, tore into her pyjamas, and jumped into bed.

She fell asleep and into a muddled dream in which she was a princess, imprisoned by a magic spell in a tiny spherical house. Each day she grew weaker and weaker. One day she would be too weak to shine anymore and would cease to be. . . .

The singing woke her and she sat up, shivering, still in the sadness of her dream. From the dressing table came a faint rosy glow. She could see its reflection in the mirror. Surely she wouldn't have imagined *that*?

"What is it?" she whispered desperately. "What do you *want*?"

Freedom. The word slid into her mind, and it was the right word, the word behind the singing and the dream.

"How?"

You know how. In her mind was the picture of her hand holding the

165

float, her fingers tight about it, crushing.

"Break it? I couldn't. Not possibly." She buried her head in the pillow and pulled the covers over her ears to muffle the sound of singing. Or was it weeping?

Next morning, after making her bed and dusting her shells—she didn't feel up to touching the float—Melissa had breakfast and ran down the beach until the sea seethed around her bare toes and the tide tugged at her ankles. Then she turned to look along the shore. The very last day. Where shall I go? What shall I find?

But the magic was quite gone. Suddenly it didn't matter whether she walked south or north. It wasn't important to find another perfect shell. Nothing mattered.

In the end she walked south along the creamy edge of the sea, scuffing the wet sand with her toes, her hands in her pockets. She trudged all the way to the southern headland, which was covered with barnacles and mussels and great red and purple starfish. Then she turned and trudged slowly back.

All the colors seemed to have drained out of the sea and the sand. Melissa shivered and looked up at the sky. The sun was shining steadily, and there wasn't a cloud in sight. Then the singing began again, very faintly, as if whoever it was had moved farther away. Or was, perhaps, becoming weaker.

She sat on a log with her head in her hands. "What am I to do? Oh, I wish I'd sold it to that horrid woman. Then I'd have the thirty-five dollars and none of this worry." But she knew, as soon as she said it, that her wish wasn't true. Mrs. White wasn't the kind of person to pay attention to the singing, even if she could hear it. And she would *never* let the float go.

Neither can I, thought Melissa desperately.

Then she heard Dad calling her and she had to run along the beach with a happy smile on her face and be very excited about a trip down the coast to Ucluelet.

They had a splendid dinner out, to celebrate the last night of the holidays, and for whole minutes at a time Melissa was able to forget. But eventually they drove up the dark winding road to the cabin, and Melissa had to open her bedroom door and go in.

There was no color at all in the globe tonight, and the singing was fainter than the sound of the sea. "If I just hang on," she told herself, "it'll stop altogether and then I'll just have a beautiful float."

No you won't, a small voice inside said coldly. It'll be a coffin. For something. For someone.

She sighed heavily, got into her pyjamas and brushed her teeth, and kissed Mom and Dad good night. Then she sat up in bed with the pillow at her back and her arms tightly around her knees, waiting. She knew exactly what had to be done.

The quiet voices of Mom and Dad stopped at last. A long time later a silveriness at her window told Melissa that the moon must be high over the sea. She got out of bed and put on her slippers. Then she picked up the float and quietly opened the front door.

The path to the beach was striped with moonshine and shadow. She held the float in both hands until she was safely down on the sand. The tide had reached the high mark. There was no wind, and the water was almost still, with just a faint swell like the breathing of a giant. The silken path of the moon lay from the horizon almost to her feet.

It was the right time and the right place. She held the float with a tissue around it to protect her hand. Then she shut her eyes and squeezed.

It took much more pressure than she had expected. I can't, she thought. I can't. Then, quite suddenly, it collapsed. She had a flash of intense happiness and opened her eyes in time to see something dart into the moon's white path.

For an instant she saw clearly a beautiful face, small and pale as carved ivory. The lips smiled and the dark eyes glowed with joy. "Wait!" Melissa called, and her voice was shockingly loud in the stillness of the turning of the tide. "Tell me who you are."

The figure paused on its upward flight, and the gossamer robes curved about it in a prism flash of rainbow colors. You are a princess, Melissa found herself thinking, imprisoned by a Japanese ogre. How many years ago? She imagined her bobbing helplessly across the ocean, singing her sad song, until the day when at last wind and tide brought her to this beach and drew Melissa to her.

I set her free. Melissa drew a deep breath and savored the happiness

that tingled through her whole body, making her feel more alive than she had ever felt before, so that she could understand the voice of the sea and the breeze, and smell each separate scent of salt and iodine, seaweed and pine tree, moonlight and night.

Then a small cloud slid for a moment across the moon. At once the white path was gone and with it the fairy princess. Melissa was alone, shivering and sad, with her hands full of shards of rainbow-shot glass. She wrapped the pieces carefully in the tissue and walked slowly back to the cabin and put them in the wastebasket in her room. She got into bed and turned her back on the moonlit stripe that lay between the not-quite-shut curtains.

Melissa woke to the bustle of packing. Breakfast was cereal and rolls, so as to dirty no more dishes than necessary.

" . . . and give me your glass float, Lissa, and I'll pack it among all our soiled clothes. It'll be as safe as houses there."

Melissa tried to swallow a piece of roll that had turned into a lump of concrete as all the misery of the night before came flooding back. "It's broken. I broke it."

"Oh, Lissa . . ." Mom began, then stopped. "Never mind, love. Bring me your other treasures, and I'll see they get home safely."

It began to rain as they started out. By the time they had reached the main road, the wipers were going full speed. Melissa sat in the back surrounded by bags and leaned her forehead against the seat in front. She tried to recapture that tiny moment of joy, but she couldn't. All that was left was this black heaviness.

I don't have my float, and I'll never find another. I don't even have the thirty-five dollars. I've got nothing.

She shut her eyes and tried to remember the rainbow colors that appeared and vanished as you turned the float in the light. Maybe she should have saved the pieces. Maybe in them would have been a tiny memory . . .

"Oh, look, Melissa!" Mom suddenly cried. "Did you ever see anything so beautiful!"

She looked up. The rain clouds had been torn apart and the sun had appeared in the gap. Directly ahead of them, arching from the headland to the sea, was a perfect double rainbow.

Detail of *The Night Visitor* by Jean-Paul Lemieux

A Shiver of Mysteries

It's a Mystery

by Rex Montague

Imelda was behaving oddly. She was trotting around in circles with her head down. And she was crying. I walked over.

"Imelda," I said. "Why are you crying? What's wrong?"

"My new school bag," she replied, "the one grampa made for me from different strips of leather. With my wallet inside. I was waiting for the bus and I just left it for a minute to go to the corner to see if the bus was coming and now it's gone. Someone must have stolen it!"

There is lots of variety in mystery stories. They exist in many forms: short stories and novels, stage plays, comic books, TV shows, movies. They are set in many places: cities, villages, castles, mountain cabins. Some mystery stories are about lords and ladies and billionaires; some are about down-and-outs and gangsters. But *all* mystery stories have some characteristics in common.

The most important of these characteristics is the mystery itself. Every mystery story contains a riddle to be solved, a puzzle to be explained. Usually this riddle involves a crime, and the question is: who has done it? In fact, mystery stories are often called *whodunits.*

Whatever the crime is—murder, theft, kidnapping, blackmail—it generally takes place early on in the story, and the person who solves the crime is the detective. Every mystery story has a detective. Some detectives work for the police. Others, like Sherlock Holmes, work for themselves. They're private detectives—sometimes called *private eyes* or *private investigators,* like Magnum P.I. Still others, like Nancy Drew or the Hardy

Boys, are amateur detectives. They just happen to be around when a crime is discovered.

"Don't worry, Imelda, kid," I said. Actually, Imelda is my sister, just one year younger than me, but detectives always talk like this. "I'll find your bag. Now, when did you first notice that it was missing?"

"Just a few minutes ago," she sniffed.

The trail was still warm. I looked at my watch. 4:15.

"Where were you while you were waiting for the bus?" I asked.

She sniffed again. "I was . . . sitting down . . . over there." She pointed to a bench, set back from the sidewalk on the grass.

The detective's first action is to examine the *scene of the crime*. Often there are clues that identify who was there when the crime was committed. Perhaps someone dropped a handkerchief or glove at the scene of the crime. Perhaps there are footprints or fingerprints. The detective follows up these clues in the investigation.

I approached the bench slowly, head down, my eyes searching the ground for clues. Fortunately it was a wet day; the ground around the bench was soft. "You were alone, weren't you?" I said over my shoulder.

"Yes," Imelda answered. "But—how did you know that?"

I pointed. "Only one set of footprints." Hmmm. If there was only one set of footprints, how had the thief got to the bench? I was puzzled. Then I saw them. Lines on the damp grass, parallel lines approaching the bench and then curving round and heading off again toward the wet sidewalk, where they disappeared.

"Imelda," I said. "The bag thief is in a wheelchair!"

Apart from the detective, mystery stories always have three other kinds of characters: *victims, suspects,* and *villains*. Victims are people that crimes happen to. They get robbed or kidnapped or murdered. (In murder mysteries, the victims don't usually play a big part because they are dead.) Suspects are possible villains: people who might have done the crime. One of the rules of mystery story writing is that anyone can be a suspect. Any character that is mentioned in the story, any character that appears on the screen or the stage, might be the villain.

"The only person I know in a wheelchair," whispered Imelda, "is grampa. He wouldn't take my bag."

"What about the new school librarian?" I said. "She's in a wheelchair. Maybe she was taking the shortcut from school across the park to get to the corner bookstore and saw your bag on the bench and took it."

Imelda's eyes widened. "The librarian?" she gasped. "Why?"

"Well, maybe she liked it. It's a unique bag, and grampa used real good leather. And then again, maybe it *was* grampa. He did say he was sorry he gave you the bag because you don't take good care of it. Maybe he stole it to punish you. Or to give it to somebody else."

Imelda shook her head. "Grampa wouldn't do that."

I decided to pursue my investigation at the corner bookstore.

"Did you see anyone around here in a wheelchair about ten minutes ago?" I asked the lady behind the counter.

"Why—yes!" she said. "An old man went speeding by with a funny grin on his face. He went that way." She pointed. "I remember him because he was wearing a bright red track suit."

"A red track suit!" Imelda wailed. "That sounds like—"

"Quiet," I said. We left the store.

The villain in a mystery story generally has a *motive,* a reason for committing the crime. But in most mysteries there are several suspects and they each have a motive. So in addition to motive, the villain must also have had the *opportunity* to commit the crime. That narrows down the number of suspects. Who was there when the crime happened?

"Grampa wears a red track suit!" Imelda wailed. "He must be the one who took my bag." I nodded tightly. It sure looked like it.

"We'll have to find out where he was at 4:00," I said. "He might have an alibi."

Mystery writers love *alibis.* An alibi is proof that a suspect was *somewhere else* when the crime was committed. If the alibi is real—if a suspect really was in Australia or in a hospital having an operation at the moment of the crime—then that suspect cannot be the villain.

By eliminating suspects one by one, until only one suspect is left, the detective clears up the mystery.

When we got home we saw sinister signs on the dry driveway: two lines of parallel tire tracks! I scratched my head: what could they mean?

Mother opened the front door. "Imelda! You careless child! You left your school bag on the bench near the bus stop. If grampa hadn't found it and come all the way over here to give it back, someone might have stolen it!"

The mystery seemed to be solved. The case didn't rank among my greatest successes as a detective, so I didn't bother doing what the detective does at the end of every mystery story: go over the case from the beginning, to explain how the crime was committed and identify which clues were important and which were red herrings.

If Imelda's smart she won't say anything either.

Susan Super Sleuth
and the
Diamond Dilemma

by William Ettridge

Susan's Uncle Ted was a police detective, and Susan liked nothing better than discussing cases with him. When she saw him coming out of a jewellery store looking preoccupied, she was sure he was deep in another mystery. She just couldn't let him be until she found out all about it.

"**W**hy don't we go and have a cup of tea and talk about it?" Susan coaxed Uncle Ted along the sidewalk to a small restaurant in the next building. "You know that discussing a problem often helps to bring it into focus."

"Very well." He capitulated with a smile. "In you go." She led the way to a corner booth, isolated from the few other customers.

She drained her cup and, pushing it and the saucer to one side, leaned across the table with a conspiratorial air. Screwing up her features to what she fondly imagined to be a gangsterlike scowl, she demanded, "Okay, Uncle. Spill the beans!"

He smiled at her antics as he lifted his briefcase from the floor, placed it on the table between them, and opened the lid.

"This is an unusual case of theft." He spoke in a low voice, but immediately broke into a peal of laughter joined by Susan. "No pun intended, of course." When they had regained their composure he went on. "A number of uncut diamonds worth about thirty thousand dollars were taken from a locked safe. There are no signs of forced entry or tampering, and only two people have keys." Susan stared at him intently as he spoke. "The keys are held by the partners, Mr. Hodge and Mr. Sims, and they are both quite sure that at no time have the keys left their possession."

"You're suggesting that nobody took an impression and had a duplicate key cut." It was more of a statement than a question, and her uncle nodded his agreement. "When was the theft discovered?"

"This morning, but let me give you the facts in a chronological sequence." He opened his notebook. "Wednesday morning, December the third, Mr. Hodge returned from California with the diamonds in the box." He took a small cardboard box from his case and offered it to Susan. She quickly drew back her hands. "It's all right; the surface is too rough to take fingerprints," he assured her.

She picked it up and, removing the lid, looked inside; it was empty except for a bed of cotton batting. She poked it with her finger, grimacing. "It's damp!" She looked closely at the outside of the box. "The box is water-stained. Did someone try to flush away the evidence?"

"No, no," he answered with a chuckle. "Just before Mr. Hodge put the box away in the safe, he accidentally spilled water over it; his secretary saw it happen. She offered to replace the box, but he was in a hurry to leave for Montreal, and he locked it away, leaving immediately."

Susan looked at the box once more, a puzzled frown wrinkling her forehead. She placed it carefully on the table before cupping her chin in her hands. "Carry on, Uncle."

"Thursday afternoon, the next day, the other partner, Mr. Sims, visited the office for about two hours before leaving for Amsterdam." He paused as Susan raised her eyebrows. Then she shook her head.

"No. It's too obvious. He can't be the thief."

"You're quite right; as usual. Sims was ill at home on Tuesday and Wednesday with a very bad cold. He left his bed against doctor's orders on Thursday because he considered the Amsterdam trip to be very important. As it was, he collapsed in the taxi on the way to the airport and is now in hospital with pneumonia. As you may imagine, the taxi driver was questioned; Mr. Sims had left nothing in the cab. He certainly does not have the diamonds with him in hospital." Her uncle referred again to his notes. "We have investigated the secretary, and I'm sure that she is completely innocent. I can't believe that even a top-flight actress could fake her emotional condition; she is quite distraught."

"Did the secretary actually see the diamonds?"

"She saw them."

"Did she actually handle them?" Susan persisted with the line of questioning, "Or was she close enough to touch them?"

"Hm-m-m," her uncle pondered as he recalled the interview with the secretary. He again looked at his notes. "Ah yes! She had just entered the office as Mr. Hodge was about to replace the lid on the box. It was as he picked up the lid that he accidentally knocked over the glass of water, some of it spilling into the box. Obviously, you suspicious little devil, you suspect Mr. Hodge of placing an empty box in the safe." His eyes twinkled.

"Well, you taught me the first rule of detection," she accused. "Assume nothing, and question everything." She picked up her empty cup, but replaced it with a shake of the head at her uncle's offer of another pot of tea. "When was the theft discovered?"

"This morning, and by both Mr. Hodge and his secretary. But first, let me outline the usual morning precedure at Hodge and Sims. Every morning the secretary arrives at nine o'clock. She collects the mail from the post office box on her way to the office, placing it on Mr. Hodge's desk ready for his attention. Mr. Hodge usually arrives before nine-fifteen, closely followed by Mr. Sims when he is in town. As soon as Mr. Hodge arrives, it is his practice to open the mail, while the secretary sits ready to take dictation as he replies to the letters."

Susan listened intently, her computerlike mind storing the information ready for instant retrieval as needed. She stared unblinkingly as he continued.

"This morning Mr. Hodge found this envelope in his mail." He reached into the case and passed her an ordinary foolscap envelope. "It contained nothing but this Polaroid photograph." He passed it to her. "It carried no fingerprints, but there is a crudely printed message on the back."

Susan examined the envelope closely. The typewriter used to print the address appeared to have no irregularities, but an expert would no doubt be able to identify the machine, should it ever be located. The envelope had been slit open with a letter opener, Susan noticed.

Uncle Ted spoke as Susan continued to examine the envelope. "Immediately he saw the photograph with its message, Mr. Hodge showed it to his secretary, and together they went to the safe. He opened it, but it was she who removed the box. She wasted no time in calling the police; in fact, I was on the premises before nine-thirty."

Suddenly taking a nail file from her pocket, Susan raised her eyebrows at her uncle for permission, and at his nod carefully peeled away the severed flap of the envelope, frequently breathing on it to loosen the glue. Borrowing her uncle's magnifying glass, she peered at the uncovered surfaces of the back of the envelope and the flap. With a satisfied little chuckle, she passed the envelope to her uncle, pointing to a distinct smudge close to the right-hand edge on that part of the back which she had uncovered.

"Got something, eh?" He reached into his case and extracted a small bottle of gray powder and a camel's-hair brush. Gently he brushed powder over the area, then taking the magnifying glass in his hand, peered at the thumblike print revealed. Shaking his head he passed the envelope back to Susan. "Definitely a print there, but it is too smudged to be of any value."

"Just a minute!" Susan examined the print closely. "Look! That definitely looks like an impression of a scar."

Uncle Ted leaned forward for a closer look. "I do believe it is."

Susan next turned her attention to the photograph, looking firstly at the crudely printed message on the back: "HAVE DIAMONDS—WILL SELL BACK $15 000—WAIT FOR CONTACT." Turning it over she concentrated on the picture. It was black and white, and showed several large, rough, uncut stones scattered on a sheet of what appeared to be plain white paper. This paper was in turn on a sheet of newspaper, portions of which were visible at the upper and right-hand edges of the picture. Again Susan lifted the glass to her eye for closer scrutiny. After two or three minutes she placed it carefully on the table and, sitting back, closed her eyes as she concentrated. Her uncle waited patiently; he had witnessed a similar performance many times. He was not surprised when eventually her eyes opened and she rattled off a number of questions.

"Are Mr. Hodge, Mr. Sims, or the secretary left-handed? Does one of them have a scar on the right thumb? Were the offices searched? Is there a refrigerator in the office? Where—"

"Whoa! Whoa!" Uncle Ted laughed as he held up his hand as if to stop a runaway horse. "One question at a time, please. Yes, the secretary is left-handed; I noticed that when she signed her statement. In the same way I know that the partners are both right-handed. As to the scar, I cannot tell you, but certainly I'll find out. What was the next question?"

"Refrigerator."

"No, I did not see a refrigerator on the premises, but both partners have cocktail cabinets in their offices, and they may well contain refrigeration units. Lastly; yes, the premises were searched, but without result."

"One more question. When did Mr. Hodge return from Montreal?"

"He came back on the midnight flight, last night."

Susan sat in thought, then coming to a decision, she said, "If Mr. Hodge does have a scar on his right thumb, I suggest that you obtain a search warrant and check his house, especially the garbage."

"And what shall I be searching for?"

"The negative of the photograph, of course."

"What if Mr. Sims has a scar on his thumb? Should I also search his residence?" Uncle Ted rose as he spoke, replacing the items of evidence in the briefcase. Together they moved to the door as Susan explained her theories.

That evening she could hardly contain her impatience. Frequently she walked across to the window to watch for Uncle Ted's car. She barely touched her dinner. At last her mother complained.

"Stop playing with your food, Susan."

Her father smiled; Susan's restlessness was an obvious indication that she was once again involved in her favorite hobby—detection. There was a certain, unmistakable way that she moved about when working on a case with her uncle, and he knew the sign well.

"Relax, Susan. He'll be here shortly, I'm sure." He chuckled at her look of surprise. "You don't have to tell me; you're into another case with your Uncle Ted." She grinned her confirmation.

Suddenly she jumped up and rushed to the door as she spotted a car pulling to a stop in the roadway outside. "Was I right? Was I right?" she called to her uncle, not waiting for him to reach the house.

"Yes, you were quite right." The two stood talking together for a minute. Then Susan sighed with pleasure. "Mr. Hodge is in custody," her uncle added. "Now perhaps I may have a cup of coffee, while you tell your mother and father all about it?"

Ten minutes later they were seated around the dining room table as Susan told her parents about the conversation in the restaurant.

"But why were you so sure it was Mr. Hodge?" her mother asked.

"There were a number of clues, but the most important was the photograph." Uncle Ted took it from his briefcase and passed it to Susan's mother.

"If you look closely, Mom, you can see part of a newspaper at the top of the picture." She leaned over and pointed with her finger. "Under a magnifying glass you can see the letters 'ER, 5, 1987.' Then, lower down, and on the right"—she again pointed with her finger—"you can see the last few words of a line, '17 DAYS TO—', and the next line, '—SHOPPERS WILL—'. I think that the date of the paper is December 5, 1987, because there are seventeen shopping days to Christmas."

"Why, that's today!" Her mother voiced her surprise. "The photograph could only have been taken this morning. But the boy doesn't bring the newspaper until seven o'clock. How could anyone take a photograph of today's paper and have it delivered through the mail before nine o'clock?"

"That's the point, you see. The letter would have to be in the post office before the last sort at seven o'clock. I checked, and that is not the same paper as ours; the type is different. I suspected that it is an early edition of a newspaper that may be found at Montreal airport before midnight."

"And, indeed it is," Uncle Ted interjected. "As Susan saw it, Hodge had the opportunity to buy the newspaper, take it home, take the photograph, and mail the letter, all before seven this morning."

"How silly of him to use that newspaper," her mother sniffed.

"I'm glad he was silly." Susan smiled at her.

"And from that clue, you figured Mr. Hodge as the thief?" her father asked.

"Oh, no! There were other clues. Look at the printing." She turned over the photograph. "At first it looks like that of a small child, but the words used and the use of 'HAVE' rather than 'GOT' suggests that it is an adult, one who is capable of far neater work. The letters slope backward, and usually one would think, 'Ah! Left-handed!' but because of the poor way in which the letters are formed, I thought it more likely that a right-handed person had used his left hand to disguise his writing. Uncle Ted told me that the secretary is left-handed, and that while Mr. Sims is right-handed, he is, and was, in hospital, and had no opportunity to mail the letter in time. Thus, I dismissed them from my suspicions."

"Perhaps the scar print was the conclusive piece of evidence," Uncle Ted said. "Apart from finding the negative in Hodge's garbage. After leaving Susan at the restaurant, I returned to the office of Hodge and Sims and, while asking Mr. Hodge a few questions, I managed to get a glimpse of his right thumb, and it is scarred. So from there I went and obtained a search warrant, and the rest you know."

"Well, I never . . . Susan Super Sleuth strikes again!" Her father smiled at her proudly.

"But how did he remove the diamonds without his secretary's knowledge? I thought he left for Montreal immediately after he locked the safe?" Susan's mother was puzzled.

"Hah! That's the clever part, you see? There were no diamonds in the safe in the first place," Uncle Ted answered.

"No diamonds? But, the secretary saw them."

"No she didn't, mother," Susan contradicted. "What she saw were pieces of broken ice cube, which, of course, melted in a few hours. Mr. Hodge carefully staged the accident with the glass of water to provide a logical explanation for the wet cotton batting when the empty box was discovered."

"Then there really was no theft at all?" Susan's father asked.

"What did he hope to gain by the charade?" The mother's brow climbed in question.

"Insurance," Susan explained. "He expected the photograph to establish automatically the existence of the diamonds so that when nothing further was heard from the thief, the insurance company would pay up."

"So, it's more a case of swindle than of theft," Uncle Ted explained.

"Right," Susan agreed. "Except Hodge not only planned to collect from the insurance company; he also meant to cheat his partner. You see, he really had purchased diamonds with thirty thousand dollars that he withdrew from the partners' account; he has a signed receipt from a reputable Californian dealer to prove it. Presumably he planned to dispose of them later and pocket the proceeds."

"Cool customer!" Her father exclaimed.

"Yes, and he might well have pulled it off if poor Mr. Sims had gone to Amsterdam as planned," Susan observed.

"Well, I guess Mr. Hodge has learned something from this; you should take nothing for granted." Uncle Ted wagged his finger at Susan with a grin.

"I know what I've learned." Susan's mother paused, ensuring that she had their undivided attention before continuing with a suppressed laugh. "I've often wondered why underworld slang for diamonds is 'ice.' Now I know!"

Solving the Case of the Kidnapped Nephew

by Sue Alexander

Characters

COURT CLERK

JUDGE ALEXANDRA FAIRMAN

TIMOTHY CRANE

MS. GARFIELD, attorney for the accused

MR. BRADBURY, prosecuting attorney

PAMELA MADISON

EDITH ALLWELL

JONATHAN SLOTE

BRIAN FARLEY

JONATHAN SLOTE   MR. BRADBURY   BRIAN FARLEY   EDITH ALLWELL   PAMELA MADISON   TIMOTHY CRANE   MS. GARFIELD

The scene is a courtroom. There are three tables and ten chairs. A gavel is on the Judge's table. Pamela Madison walks with the aid of a cane (or stick) and carries a purse containing a letter in an envelope and a folded piece of yellow paper. Brian is wearing one green sock and one red sock. Each attorney has a folder of papers. The attorneys stand while they are questioning witnesses.

The Judge's chambers are to the audience's left, the doorway is to the audience's right. The Court Clerk and the Judge enter and exit from the Judge's chambers. All others enter and exit on the doorway side.

Act Two

As the act begins, everyone except the judge and the clerk returns to the courtroom. They don't all come at once—they straggle in. When everyone is in his or her seat the clerk comes in and faces them all.

CLERK: All rise!
(Everyone stands up. The judge comes in and takes her seat.)

CLERK: Be seated.
(Everyone, including the clerk, sits down.)

JUDGE: Mr. Bradbury, call your witness.

BRADBURY: *(He rises.)* Mr. Brian Farley.
(Brian comes to the witness chair and stands in front of it.)

CLERK: *(The clerk stands.)* Do you swear to tell the truth, the whole truth, and nothing but the truth?

BRIAN: I do. *(He sits down. So does the clerk.)*

BRADBURY: Mr. Farley, please tell the court what happened to you on May 22nd.

BRIAN: Yes, sir. Just before my plane landed, the airflight attendant told me that I'd got a message not to go to my aunt's house. I was to meet her at a different address. I took a cab there. No sooner had I rung the bell, when the door opened and somebody grabbed me. I never did see the man's face. Before I knew what was happening, I was bound, gagged, and blindfolded. Then I heard the man go out. He came back some time later, pushed me out the door, and into a car. We drove for quite some time. Then he stopped the car, untied my hands, and pushed me out. He drove away before I could get the blindfold off. When I finally managed to remove it, I found that I was back at the airport. I hailed a cab and went to my aunt's house.

BRADBURY: Thank you, Mr. Farley. Your witness, Ms. Garfield. *(He sits down.)*

GARFIELD: *(She is talking to herself in a loud whisper.)* Something isn't . . . but what is it? *(She rises.)* I would like to reserve my cross-examination until later, Your Honor. *(She sits down.)*

JUDGE: Very well. Call another witness, Mr. Bradbury.

(Brian returns to his seat.)

BRADBURY: *(He rises.)* The prosecution has no other witnesses, Your Honor. *(He sits down.)*

JUDGE: Then we will hear from the defence. Ms. Garfield.

GARFIELD: *(She rises.)* The defence calls Timothy Crane.

(Timothy goes to the witness chair and stands in front of it.)

CLERK: *(The clerk stands.)* Do you swear to tell the truth, the whole truth, and nothing but the truth?

TIMOTHY: I do. *(He sits down. So does the clerk.)*

GARFIELD: Mr. Crane, please tell the court what you did on the day in question.

TIMOTHY: I left the house a little after nine in the morning and went to the racetrack. I was to meet a guy I know. He'd promised to give me a good solid tip on the sixth race. And I needed that tip. I'd lost a lot of money, including most of what I'd borrowed from my friend, Jon Slote. I figured that with a good tip, I could make back what I'd lost—and maybe more. But the guy never showed up. I hunted all over for him. Then the races started. I bet—and lost. I felt sick so I went home, back to Mrs. Madison's.

GARFIELD: Did you see anyone you knew at the racetrack?

TIMOTHY: No. If it had been my regular day off, I probably would have—the same people seem to be there all the time. But this was a different day. Besides, I was busy looking for the guy I was supposed to meet. I didn't pay any attention to who was there.

GARFIELD: Were you aware that it was the day that Mrs. Madison's nephew was to arrive?

TIMOTHY: Yes. His telegram had come just before I left the house.

GARFIELD: *(She walks back and forth for a moment, thinking. Then she stops.)* Mr. Crane, did you read the telegram?

TIMOTHY: Yes. I open all the mail. As soon as I read it, I gave it to

Mrs. Madison.

GARFIELD: Do you happen to know what she did with it?

TIMOTHY: Hmmm. I think she put it in her purse.

GARFIELD: *(She turns toward the judge.)* Your Honor, if Mrs. Madison still has the telegram in her purse, perhaps we might see it?

JUDGE: *(She nods, then turns and looks at Pamela.)* Mrs. Madison, do you have that telegram?

PAMELA: I'll see, Your Honor. *(She opens her purse and searches through it. After a second or two she pulls out a folded piece of yellow paper.)* Yes. Here it is.

JUDGE: Give it to the clerk, please.
(The clerk takes the telegram and brings it to Ms. Garfield.)

GARFIELD Thank you. *(She takes it from the clerk and reads aloud.)* It says: "Arriving 1:30 P.M. Do not meet me. Will take a cab." And it's signed Brian. *(She hands it to Timothy.)* Is this the telegram you saw?

TIMOTHY: *(He looks at it.)* Yes, it is. *(He hands it back to Garfield.)*

GARFIELD: Thank you, Mr. Crane. I have no further questions. Your witness, Mr. Bradbury. *(She returns to her seat and puts the telegram on the table in front of her.)*

BRADBURY: Your testimony was very interesting, Mr. Crane. But do you really expect us to believe that you saw no one you knew at the racetrack? After all, it is a place you go often.

TIMOTHY: Yes, but I didn't see anyone I knew that day.

BRADBURY: Of course, you didn't. Because you weren't there! You never went to the racetrack. Instead, you were holding Brian Farley prisoner! You knew your employer had a great deal of cash on hand and that she would gladly exchange it for the safe return of her nephew.

TIMOTHY: No! That's not true! I didn't do it! I didn't!

BRADBURY: I submit that you did, Mr. Crane. No further questions. *(He returns to his seat.)*

JUDGE: You may step down, Mr. Crane. Ms. Garfield, call your next witness. *(Crane returns to his seat.)*

GARFIELD: *(She rises.)* I have no other witnesses, Your Honor. But at this time I'd like to have Brian Farley recalled to the stand for cross-examination.

JUDGE: Very well. Brian Farley, take the stand.
(Brian goes to the witness chair and sits down.)

JUDGE: Remember, Mr. Farley, you are still under oath.

BRIAN: Yes, Your Honor.

GARFIELD: Mr. Farley, before you left England, you sent a telegram to your aunt not to meet your plane. Why was that?

BRIAN: I wanted to save her a trip to the airport.

GARFIELD: That was very considerate of you. By the way, what time did your plane arrive?

BRIAN: One-thirty in the afternoon.

GARFIELD: And it was a direct, non-stop flight from England?

BRIAN: Yes.

GARFIELD: *(She walks over to the table and picks up the telegram.)* Can you tell me then, Mr. Farley, how your aunt received this *telegram* from you and not a cablegram? Telegrams are *land* wires, not overseas wires.

BRIAN: Why—uhhh . . .

GARFIELD: Mr. Farley, how long have you been out of work?

BRIAN: About six months. But I don't see what that has to do with anything.

GARFIELD: Let's let the court decide that. Tell me, if you've not worked in six months, where did you get the money for the trip?

BRIAN: I—I—borrowed it. I'm to pay it back within a month.

GARFIELD: I see. Mr. Farley, what would you say if I contended that you were never kidnapped at all? That you, in fact, landed in the United States in the morning, saw the newspaper report of your aunt's sale of a racehorse to Admiral Denay, guessed that she had a lot of cash on hand—and cooked up this scheme to rob her?

BRIAN: That's ridiculous!

GARFIELD: Is it? Tell me, Mr. Farley, what color socks are you wearing?

BRIAN: What . . .? *(He pulls up both legs of his pants so that his socks show and looks down at them.)* They're green. But I don't see . . .

GARFIELD: No, *you* don't. But perhaps the court will. You are not wearing two green socks, Mr. Farley. Only one is green. The other is red. You can't tell the difference because you are color-blind.

BRIAN: So what?

GARFIELD: Isn't it strange that the messenger who brought the ransom note also wore one red sock and one green

one? Perhaps he, too, is color-blind. Or perhaps, Mr. Farley, *you* were the messenger!

BRIAN: I—I—oh, what's the use! Yes, I did it. Just the way you said. I thought no one would find out! *(He covers his face with his hands.)* I'll give the money back!

JUDGE: *(She pounds the gavel.)* Mr. Bradbury, I think a motion to dismiss the case against Mr. Crane is in order.

BRADBURY: *(He rises.)* I so move, Your Honor.

JUDGE: Motion granted. Case dismissed! *(She pounds the gavel once.)* The clerk will escort Mr. Farley to the bailiff where he will be advised of his rights and then removed to the jail.

(The clerk goes over to the witness stand and takes Brian's arm and escorts him out the doorway side.)

JUDGE: Court is adjourned. *(She gets up and goes out.)*

(Everyone, except Timothy and Garfield, rises and heads for the doorway, talking among themselves.)

TIMOTHY: *(He turns to Garfield.)* I don't know how to thank you . . .

(On her way to the door, Pamela has stopped next to Timothy's chair. She puts her hand on his shoulder and faces Garfield.)

PAMELA: Let me add my thanks, too. Though it hurts to know that my own nephew tried to rob me, it makes me feel better to know that my trust in Tim all these years hasn't been misplaced.

GARFIELD: No thanks are necessary. Tim's telling me that Brian is color-blind was what gave me the answer. The path to truth, in this case, was marked in red and green.

(Garfield and Timothy rise. Timothy takes Pamela's arm and all three go out together.)

190

The Village over the Mountain

by Julia L. Sauer

All her life Greta had loved the fog. Her mother said it was unnatural. She herself hated the great gray clouds blowing in from the sea. But somehow in every generation of Addingtons a child was born who understood the fog—no one knew why, not even Greta, until the day on the old Post Road when the surrey came by with a woman whose plum-colored dress rustled "like a three-master coming up in the wind." Greta drove with her to Blue Cove, suddenly sure that there, where no house had stood for a hundred years, she would find what she was seeking. "Go on," said the woman. "In the second house you'll find Retha Morrill. You two will pull well together."

from Fog Magic

Greta watched the surrey disappear into the thicker mists below. Then, with a pounding heart, she stepped through the arch of spruces.

Her feet crunched on gravel. She was walking on a neat path. At her right loomed a big barn. Beyond she traced the outlines of a house—small, neat, gray-shingled,—and another, and another. A smell of wood smoke was in the air. Something brushed against her ankle. She looked down. A gray cat, the largest she had ever seen, was looking at her pleasantly.

"You beauty," Greta said to her and stooped to stroke the long hair. But it was one thing to greet a guest and quite another to be touched. Without loss of dignity, without haste, the gray cat was simply beyond reach. But she was leading the way, her plume of a tail erect. Where the second neat path turned off toward a house the cat looked back to be sure that Greta was following. Suddenly a door banged. Around the side of the house and down the path a little girl came running. She stopped when she saw Greta and gathered the cat into her arms. The two girls stood looking at each other.

"I'm Retha Morrill," said the Blue Cove child slowly, "and I think that Princess must have brought you." She smiled and took Greta's hand. "I'm glad you've come. Let's—let's go in to Mother."

Greta could think of nothing to say. She could only smile back and follow. But she knew, and Retha knew, that as the woman had said, they would pull well together. At the doorway Retha dropped Princess on the wide stone before the steps.

"Please wait here," she said. "I'll find Mother."

Greta nodded. She still wasn't sure of her voice. She watched Princess curl into a graceful heap on the stone—gray stone, gray fur, gray mist, gray shingles, all softly blending and blurring before her eyes. She knew that stone well. It had strange markings on it. She had often traced them with her finger where it lay in the empty pasture beside her favorite cellar hole.

There was a brisk step inside the house and a tall woman stood in the doorway.

"Come in, child, come in," she began. Then she stopped and looked long at her visitor. And Greta looked up at her. She had never seen such blue eyes in all her life before—nor such *seeing* eyes. They were eyes that would always see through and beyond—even through the close mist of the fog itself. The woman put out her hand and drew Greta inside before she spoke again. Her voice was a little unsteady but very gentle.

"You are from over the mountain," she said. "I can tell. And I'd know it even if this were the sunniest day in the year."

Greta didn't quite know what the words meant but she knew somehow in her heart that she and this strange woman would understand each other without words. In just the flash of a moment they had travelled the longest road in the world—the road that leads from eye to eye.

"I am Laura Morrill," Retha's mother continued quietly. "Retha shouldn't have left you standing outside—not such a welcome guest.

Now turn toward the light and let me look at you. Humph! Yes. You *must* be an Addington. Would your name be Greta, now? Yes?" She laughed. "So I guessed it right the very first time! Well, you have the Addington look and the Addington eyes, and there's always a Greta among the Addingtons! Yes, and there's always a child among the Addingtons that loves the fog it was born to. You're that child, I take it, in your generation." Her laughing face grew sober and she gave Greta a long, steady look. Then she smiled again quickly and smoothed back Greta's hair with a quick stroke of her hand.

"It's the things you were born to that give you satisfaction in this world, Greta. Leastwise, that's what I think. And maybe the fog's one of them. Not happiness, mind! Satisfaction isn't always happiness by a long sight; then again, it isn't sorrow either. But the rocks and the spruces and the fogs of your own land are things that nourish you. You can always have them, no matter what else you find or what else you lose. Now run along and let Retha show you the village. You two must get acquainted."

"May I leave my pail here?" Greta asked her. "I picked quite a few berries for Mother, coming over."

"Of course you may," Laura Morrill told her. "But that reminds me! You must be hungry. We're through our dinner long since but I'll get you something. I dare say you left home early."

"I brought a sandwich to eat on the way," Greta told her. "Only there hasn't been time."

"Sit right down and eat it here, then. Retha, you fetch a glass of milk and I'll get you a piece of strawberry pie. Retha went berrying early this morning, too, and I made my first wild strawberry pie of the season."

After Greta had eaten she and Retha went out to explore the village. Its single street followed the curve of the shoreline. There were houses on only one side, with patches of gardens behind white fences. Across the road in a narrow stretch of meadow, cows were grazing. Thick spruces hedged the meadow in at the lower side where there was a sharp drop, almost a precipice, to the shore. But the street was high enough so that Greta knew on a clear day you could look from the houses straight out to the open sea.

It was pleasant walking slowly up the street with Retha, but Greta couldn't find anything to say. To ask questions might break the spell. She might find herself back again in the empty clearing. And Retha knew that it would be impolite to question a stranger. They reached the end of the street before either spoke.

"There's our school, and there's our church," Retha said. She pointed out the little white building across the end of the street next to the neat church with its steeple.

"The shore curves in here, and there's another bay down there where you can find all sorts of things to play with. Our church is nice. Sometime maybe you'll be here on a Sunday so you can see it inside. There isn't any burying ground," she added. "It's all rock here and we can't have our own. When folks die they have to go over the mountain to be buried. Now let's go back to the Post Road and I'll show you the shore and the wharf and the fish houses and the stores."

In one of the dooryards two very small children were playing. As they came near Greta saw that there was a man seated on the ground, his back against the fence. One child tripped and sat down heavily, jolting out an indignant wail. The man reached out a long arm. He set the small thing on its feet again as you would set a ninepin, and gave it a comforting pat. The wail died suddenly and the man slumped back. Greta laughed.

"He must like children," she said, "or they must like him. Why, he didn't even have to speak to that one."

"Sss-h," Retha warned her. "He *can't* speak, but we—we don't quite know—for sure—whether he can hear."

Whether he heard or only felt their approaching footsteps, the man turned suddenly and looked up at them between the pickets. A lean, dark, strange, and foreign face. The eyes were piercing, searching. Greta found she was standing quite still, giving this strange man a chance to look at her. Retha didn't seem to think it unusual. She was smiling at him and saying slowly, "Anthony, this is my friend Greta Addington. She's from over the mountain." Then she pulled Greta gently away. The man turned to watch until they faded into the fog.

"But, Retha, you said he couldn't *hear*, and then you *spoke* to him. And he looks almost—almost savage. And still he was minding those babies."

"I said we don't *know* whether he hears or not. Or whether he could speak if he wanted to. But he's not savage. He only looks that way when he sees a stranger. I guess it's because he's always trying to find someone—someone he knows, I mean. But, Greta, did you see his—his legs?"

"I didn't see anything but his eyes. And anyhow, he was almost hidden in that clump of monkshood. What about his legs?"

"He—he hasn't any," Retha said quietly.

"Hasn't any *legs?*" Greta could only stare in horror.

"They are gone just above his knees, so all he can do is crawl, and mind babies. But no matter how fierce he looks, *they* understand him. And he's always gentle."

"But what happened?"

Retha hesitated a moment. "We don't talk about him much. I'd like to ask Mother first if I should tell you. Let's go down to the wharf now." And Greta had to be content.

When they reached the Post Road, Retha pointed toward the shore. "See! The fog's lifting a little. You can see the end of the wharf from here and you couldn't see anything an hour ago. Come on."

Greta stood still. She couldn't explain it even to herself, but suddenly she knew how Cinderella felt when the first stroke of midnight began to sound.

"I think there isn't time to go down today, Retha," she said. "But I'd like to go next time I come. I must go home now. It'll be late when I get over the mountain."

"Your berries! You left your pail at our house," Retha reminded her.

They ran back to the house. In the doorway Mrs. Morrill stood holding the pail.

"The fog's lifting," she said quietly and held out the pail. "I put a piece of strawberry pie on top of your berries, but I don't think it'll crush them any. And come again, child. We'd like to see you often; that is, if your mother doesn't worry. You're like a visitor from another world." Then she added as an afterthought, "Coming as you do from over the mountain."

Greta thanked her and took the pail. Retha went as far as the Post Road with her. They said goodbye hurriedly. Greta left without daring to turn back and wave.

It was almost clear when she reached home, but late. Her mother greeted her with relief. Father had finished milking and sat reading the paper. Greta's conscience hurt her. She hadn't once thought of the mail and someone else had gone to the post office. She held out the pail to her mother.

"There's a surprise in it, Mother," she said. Gertrude opened the pail.

"I *am* surprised," she said. "I never dreamed you'd find so many. It's early yet for strawberries."

Greta stood very still. Then she stepped over and looked into the pail. There were the berries she had picked. *But there was nothing else in the pail!*

Suddenly she wanted to cry, but her father was looking at her over the top of his paper. He was smiling at her just with his eyes, but he looked as if he understood.

"Fog thick at Blue Cove today?" he asked.

"Heavens, child, have you been way over there?" asked her mother.

How did Father know she had been to Blue Cove? Greta no longer wanted to cry. She could look back at Father and almost smile.

"Yes, Father," she said. "It was very thick today."

"I thought so," he answered and went back to his paper.

The Clock Strikes Thirteen

by Philippa Pearce

When Tom's brother comes down with measles, Tom is sent to stay with his aunt and uncle. They live in a big old house that has been divided into several flats. Tom is cross because there is nothing for him to do and nowhere for him to play—not even a back garden, his aunt and uncle told him. Then in the middle of the night he hears the clock strike thirteen and decides to investigate.

Thirteen? Tom's mind gave a jerk: had it really struck thirteen? Even mad old clocks never struck that. He must have imagined it. Had he not been falling asleep, or already sleeping? But no, awake or dozing, he had counted up to thirteen. He was sure of it.

He was uneasy in the knowledge that this happening made some difference to him: he could feel that in his bones. The stillness had become an expectant one; the house seemed to hold its breath; the darkness pressed up to him, pressing him with a question: Come on, Tom, the clock has struck thirteen—what are you going to do about it?

"Nothing," said Tom aloud. And then, as an afterthought: "Don't be silly!"

What *could* he do, anyway? He had to stay in bed, sleeping or trying

from Tom's Midnight Garden

to sleep, for ten whole hours, as near as might be, from nine o'clock at night to seven o'clock the next morning. That was what he had promised when his uncle had reasoned with him.

Uncle Alan had been so sure of his reasoning; and yet Tom now began to feel that there had been some flaw in it . . . Uncle Alan, without discussing the idea, had taken for granted that there were twenty-four hours in a day—twice twelve hours. But suppose, instead, there were twice thirteen? Then, from nine at night to seven in the morning—with the thirteenth hour somewhere between—was more than ten hours: it was eleven. He could be in bed for ten hours, and still have an hour to spare—an hour of freedom.

But steady, steady! This was ridiculous: there simply were not thirteen hours in a half day, everyone knew that. But why had the clock said there were, then? You couldn't get round that. Yes, but everyone knew the grandfather clock struck the hours at the wrong times of day—one o'clock when it was really five, and so on. Admittedly, argued the other Tom—the one that would never let the sleepy Tom go to sleep—admittedly the clock struck the hours at the wrong time; but, all the same, they *were* hours—real hours—hours that really existed. Now the clock had struck thirteen, affirming that—for this once at least—there was an extra, thirteenth hour.

"But it just can't be true," said Tom aloud. The house, which appeared to have been following the argument, sighed impatiently. "At least, I think it isn't true; and anyway it's muddling." Meanwhile you're missing your chance, whispered the house. "I can't honorably take it," said Tom, "because I don't believe the grandfather clock was telling the truth when it struck thirteen." Oh, said the house coldly, so it's a liar, is it?

Tom sat up in bed, a little angry in his turn. "Now," he said, "I'm going to prove this, one way or the other. I'm going to see what the clock fingers say. I'm going down to the hall."

This was a real expedition. Tom put on his bedroom slippers, but decided against his dressing gown: after all, it was summer. He closed his bedroom door carefully behind him, so that it should not bang in his absence. Outside the front door of the flat he took off one of his slippers; he laid it on the floor against the doorjamb and then closed the door on to it, as on to a wedge. That would keep the door open for his return.

The lights on the first-floor landing and in the hall were turned out, for the tenants were all in bed and asleep, and Mrs. Bartholomew was asleep and dreaming. The only illumination was a sideways shaft of moonlight through the long window part way up the stairs. Tom felt his way downstairs and into the hall.

Here he was checked. He could find the grandfather clock—a tall and ancient figure of black in the lesser blackness—but he was unable to read its face. If he opened its dial-door and felt until he found the position of the clock-hands, then his sense of touch would tell him the time. He fumbled first at one side of the door, then at the other; but there seemed no catch—no way in. He remembered how the pendulum-case door had not yielded to him either, on that first day. Both must be kept locked.

Hurry! hurry! the house seemed to whisper round him. The hour is passing . . . passing . . .

Tom turned from the clock to feel for the electric-light switch. Where had it been? His fingers swept the walls in vain: nowhere.

Light—light: that was what he needed! And the only light was the moonbeam that glanced sideways through the stairway window and spent itself at once and uselessly on the wall by the window sill.

Tom studied the moonbeam, with an idea growing in his mind. From the direction in which the beam came, he saw that the moon must be shining at the back of the house. Very well, then, if he opened the door at the far end of the hall—at the back of the house, that is—he would let that moonlight in. With luck there might be enough light for him to read the clock-face.

He moved down the hall to the door at its far end. It was a door he had never seen opened—the Kitsons used the door at the front. They said that the door at the back was only a less convenient way to the street, through a backyard—a strip of paving where dustbins were kept and where the tenants of the ground-floor back flat garaged their car under a tarpaulin.

Never having had occasion to use the door, Tom had no idea how it might be secured at night. If it were locked, and the key kept else-where . . . But it was not locked, he found; only bolted. He drew the bolt and, very slowly, to make no sound, turned the doorknob.

Hurry! whispered the house; and the grandfather clock at the heart of it beat an anxious tick, tick.

Tom opened the door wide and let in the moonlight. It flooded in, as bright as daylight—the white daylight that comes before the full rising of the sun. The illumination was perfect, but Tom did not at once turn to see what it showed him of the clock-face. Instead he took a step forward on to the doorstep. He was staring, at first in surprise, then with indignation, at what he saw outside. That they should have deceived him—lied to him—like this! They had said, "It's not worth your while going out at the back, Tom." So carelessly they had described it: "A sort of backyard, very pokey, with rubbish bins. Really, there's nothing to see."

Nothing . . . Only this: a great lawn where flower beds bloomed; a towering fir tree, and thick, beetle-browed yews that humped their shapes down two sides of the lawn; on the third side, to the right, a greenhouse almost the size of a real house; from each corner of the lawn, a path that twisted away to some other depths of garden, with other trees.

Tom had stepped forward instinctively, catching his breath in surprise; now he let his breath out in a deep sigh. He would steal out here tomorrow, by daylight. They had tried to keep this from him, but they could not stop him now—not his aunt, nor his uncle, nor the back flat tenants, nor even particular Mrs. Bartholomew. He would run full tilt over the grass, leaping the flower beds: he would peer through the glittering panes of the greenhouse—perhaps open the door and go in; he would visit each alcove and archway clipped in the yew trees—he would climb the trees and make his way from one to another through thickly interlacing branches. When they came calling him, he would hide, silent and safe as a bird, among this richness of leaf and bough and tree trunk.

The scene tempted him even now: it lay so inviting and clear before him—clear-cut from the stubby leaf-pins of the nearer yew trees to the curled-back petals of the hyacinths in the crescent-shaped corner beds. Yet Tom remembered his ten hours and his honor. Regretfully he turned from the garden, back indoors to read the grandfather clock.

He recrossed the threshold, still absorbed in the thought of what he had seen outside. For that reason, perhaps, he could not at once make out how the hall had become different: his eyes informed him of some shadowy change; his bare foot was trying to tell him something . . .

The grandfather clock was still there, anyway, and must tell him the true time. It must be either twelve or one: there was no hour between. There is no thirteenth hour.

Tom never reached the clock with his inquiry, and may be excused for forgetting, on this occasion, to check its truthfulness. His attention was distracted by the opening of a door down the hall—the door of the ground-floor front flat. A maid trotted out.

Tom had seen housemaids only in pictures, but he recognized the white apron, cap and cuffs, and the black stockings. (He was not expert in fashions, but the dress seemed to him to be rather long for her.) She was carrying paper, kindling wood, and a box of matches.

He had only a second in which to observe these things. Then he realized that he ought to take cover at once; and there was no cover to take. Since he must be seen, Tom determined to be the first to speak—to explain himself.

He did not feel afraid of the maid: as she came nearer, he saw that she was only a girl. To warn her of his presence without startling her, Tom gave a cough; but she did not seem to hear it. She came on. Tom moved forward into her line of vision; she looked at him, but looked through him, too, as though he were not there. Tom's heart jumped in a way he did not understand. She was passing him.

"I say!" he protested loudly; but she paid not the slightest attention. She passed him, reached the front door of the ground-floor back flat, turned the door handle, and went in. There was no bell-ringing or unlocking of the door.

Tom was left gaping; and, meanwhile, his senses began to insist upon telling him of experiences even stranger than this encounter. His one bare foot was on cold flagstone, he knew; yet there was a contradictory softness and warmth to this flagstone. He looked down and saw that he was standing on a rug—a tiger-skin rug. There were other rugs down the hall. His eyes now took in the whole of the hall—a hall that was different. No laundry box, no milk bottles, no travel posters on the walls. The walls were decorated with a rich variety of other objects instead: a tall Gothic barometer, a fan of peacock feathers, a huge engraving of a battle (hussars and horses and shot-riddled banners) and many other pictures. There was a big dinner gong, with its wash-leathered gong-stick hanging beside it. There was a large umbrella stand holding umbrellas and walking sticks and a parasol and an air gun and what looked like the parts of a fishing rod. Along the wall projected a series of bracket-shelves, each table-high. They were of oak, except for one towards the middle of the hall, by the grandfather clock. That was of white marble, and it was piled high with glass cases of stuffed birds and animals. Enacted on its chilly surface were scenes of hot bloodshed: an owl clutched a mouse in its claws; a ferret looked up from the killing of its rabbit; in a case in the middle a red fox slunk along with a gamefowl hanging from its jaws.

In all that crowded hall, the only object that Tom recognized was the grandfather clock. He moved towards it, not to read its face, but simply to touch it—to reassure himself that this at least was as he knew it.

His hand was nearly upon it, when he heard a little breath behind him that was the maid passing back the way she had come. For some reason, she did not seem to make as much sound as before. He heard her call only faintly: "I've lit the fire in the parlor."

She was making for the door through which she had first come, and, as Tom followed her with his eyes, he received a curious impression: she reached the door, her hand was upon the knob, and then she seemed to go. That was it exactly: she went, but not through the door. She simply thinned out, and went.

Even as he stared at where she had been, Tom became aware of something going on furtively and silently about him. He looked round sharply, and caught the hall in the act of emptying itself of furniture and rugs and pictures. They were not positively going, perhaps, but rather beginning to fail to be there. The Gothic barometer, for instance, was there, before he turned to look at the red fox; when he turned back, the barometer was still there, but it had the appearance of something only sketched against the wall, and the wall was visible through it; meanwhile the fox had slunk into nothingness, and all the other creatures were going with him; and, turning back again swiftly to the barometer, Tom found that gone already.

In a matter of seconds the whole hall was

as he had seen it on his first arrival. He stood dumfounded. He was roused from his stupefaction by the chill of a draught at his back: it reminded him that the garden door was left open. Whatever else had happened, he had really opened that door; and he must shut it. He must go back to bed.

He closed the door after a long look: I shall come back, he promised silently to the trees and the lawn and the greenhouse.

Storm at Midnight

by sean o huigin

listen now
and hear the
pouring rain
listen as the
water forms in
rivulets and
gurgles round
your feet

your tail is
wet and heavy
and your mane
hangs down in
strands

listen now
listen to the
somehow silence
that is in
the air

there's still
no wind

and now
and now from
out the night
from out the
clouds a fireball
descends
a brilliant and
enormous light
that shows up
every raindrop
like a photograph
and then
the thunder
comes

the roar that
crashes and rips
up the night

listen now
the sound so
loud you cannot
even hear

the rumbling sound
as though the
earth was grinding
up
the cracking sound
of every tree in
all the world
splitting all at
once
the deep black
roar as all the
clouds mount up

like giants
rising from
the deep
and hissing as
they drop on you
in waterfalls
so strong you
cannot stand

from The Ghost Horse of the Mounties

you're in the
mud
the wind is back
and screaming
through the night

the other horses
mill and neigh
they slip like
you and struggle
to their feet

imagine now
imagine how the wind
builds up
and builds a solid
wall of rain
that hems you
in

imagine if you can
a night of light
a black night full
of roar and rain
when lightning
never stops
from ten o'clock
that summer's night
till six o'clock
the morning next
all the lightning
ever thought of
anywhere
illuminates the
land

above you see the
tops of clouds
flashing dully
with a steely gray
you know that in
between them
sharp thin bolts
of light are
flashing and
reflected on their
hills

imagine now
all around the
country's edge
a jagged line of
dancing bolts
clouds of steam
burst where
they touch the
ground
then across
sky itself a horde
of giant lightning
cracks that
make it seem
the universe
has split

imagine if you can
inside a tent
the young man huddles
scrunches up to his
companions
six men squeezed together
close as they can be

outside it seems
some monstrous beast
is pawing at the
canvas walls
its growls and
roars are pawing
at their hearts

through the canvas
water pours
each gust of wind
will slap it
through like
squeezing out a
sponge

and all the time
the light outside
grows dimmer
brighter
brilliant flashes
seem as if they'll
rip the tents

and over all
the howling
hissing
moaning
screaming
wind

The Mystery of Stonehenge

by Sheila Dalton

On the lonely, windswept Salisbury Plain in southern England stands an ancient circle of towering sarsen stone pillars. Inside are pairs of more sarsens and groupings of smaller bluestones. The sarsen pillars are four metres high, and some have a mass of over forty tonnes. On top of some of them lie huge stone lintels.

Who built this mysterious monument? When? Where did the stones come from? How did the builders raise such huge stones? And what was Stonehenge built for?

When was Stonehenge built?
Stonehenge is one of many ancient stone circles built in Europe thousands of years ago. No one knows exactly when Stonehenge was built, but the main work of the sarsen stone circle probably began around 2800 B.C., and the last part of the monument was finished around 1100 B.C. That's over 1500 years of hard work by human labor, without the use of any machines!

Who built Stonehenge?
Again, nobody knows for certain. The construction of the monument was such hard labor that at one time it was thought that slaves had done the work. Today, most archaeologists believe that the people who worked on Stonehenge did so willingly—though they're not sure why.

Where did the sarsen stones come from?
The sarsen stones were dragged to Stonehenge from quarries about thirty-two kilometres away. They were probably hauled on sleds pulled over logs, which acted as rollers. Some scientists think the stones were moved during the winter, when the sleds could slide over the snow and ice.

Where did the bluestones come from?
The bluestones, inside the sarsen stone circle, came from the Prescelly Mountains in Wales—four hundred kilometres away! Scientists think these stones (some of which have a mass of over five tonnes) may have been floated over the sea and along rivers on rafts or on dugout canoes lashed together. Overland, they were probably hauled on log sleds, as the sarsen stones were.

Modern engineers figure it would have taken 110 people working every day for 540 years to pull the bluestones over the land portion of the trip alone.

Why did the builders of Stonehenge go to so much trouble to get bluestones?
As with so many questions about Stonehenge, the answer remains a mystery. Perhaps the people believed that bluestones had magic powers. Perhaps they thought the stones held the spirits of their ancestors. Perhaps the color blue had special meaning in their religion. No one knows.

Did the builders find stones that were the right size and shape or did they cut and shape them?
Both the huge sarsen stones and the bluestones were cut and shaped—without power tools, using stone axes, stone hammers, and other tools and devices of the Stone Age.

The workers used stone axes to chip off small pieces. When they needed to make larger cuts, they scratched a line with a sharp rock where they wanted a stone to break. Then they heated the stone, probably by placing fat-soaked cat-tails along this line and setting them on fire. When the stone was hot, they splashed cold water along the line and dropped a heavy boulder onto the stone. The sudden change in temperature along the line caused the stone to crack where the workers wanted.

Shaping took months of pounding with stone hammers to square off each stone. Then the surfaces were smoothed by pushing and pulling one stone across another—for weeks.

How did builders raise the pillars and the stone lintels on top?
Although it seems incredible, workers raised these monumental stones using only stone tools and basic mechanical

devices like levers.

Archaeologists think that the builders probably positioned each pillar stone so that one end stuck out over a prepared pit. Then, levering the stone a little and bracing it, levering and bracing, levering and bracing, they gradually raised it until the end slid down into the pit.

Once the pillars were standing, the workers raised the lintel stones, probably by levering them up on two platforms of logs. A stone on one platform would be levered onto a slightly higher platform beside it. Then the workers would raise the first platform and lever the stone back onto it, and so on, back and forth on the two platforms. When the stone was finally level with the top of two pillars, the workers levered the lintel on top of them.

What did Stonehenge look like when it was finished?
When all the stones were in place, Stonehenge towered commandingly over the plain. Although the monument is incomplete today, scholars think they know what it looked like originally because of the positions of the stones.

Two banks of mounded earth about ninety-eight metres in diameter surrounded the monument. Thirty sarsen pillars, topped with a continuous circle of lintels, stand in a circle about thirty metres in diameter. Inside stood a circle of about sixty bluestones, and inside this

circle were two sets of stones arranged in two horseshoes, one inside the other. Near the centre curve of the inner horseshoe was a stone block, and east of this block was a stone marker. On the longest day of the year, the marker cast a shadow on the stone block.

How did Stonehenge get ruined?
Over hundreds of years, some of the stones gradually fell down. Others were deliberately pushed over and dragged away to make bridges and dams. In the Middle Ages, people made a ritual of toppling a stone every twenty-five years, because they thought Stonehenge had been built to worship evil gods. Later still, tourists took pieces of Stonehenge home as souvenirs. (At one time, there was even a large hammer so visitors could chip off mementos!)

Today, Stonehenge is fenced off to protect it from further ruin. Visitors must buy a ticket to get in, then walk through an underground tunnel only to the site of the monument—they can no longer enter the inner circle.

What was Stonehenge built for?
This remains the biggest mystery of all. At one time people believed that Stonehenge was a temple for worship and human sacrifices to the gods. Later, even as late as the 1970s, scientists thought that the stones were arranged to work as an astronomical clock, to predict eclipses of the sun and the moon and to mark the summer solstice, the longest day of the year.

Most scientists now think that Stonehenge was a different kind of marker, built by tribes of farmers to let other tribes know who owned the surrounding farmland. That could explain why so many generations of people were willing to work on the monument—they were establishing and protecting their right to the land, not only for themselves but for their children and for their children's children.

Still, no one really knows the secrets of the stones. Perhaps scientists will uncover secrets that give a different explanation of the mystery of Stonehenge. Or perhaps the secrets will remain hidden and the mystery of Stonehenge will never be explained.

The Beast in the Fog

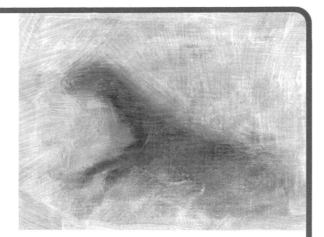

by Eleanor Cameron

What was it that stalked through the fog on the peak of San Lorenzo Mountain? Mr. Looper, the museum curator, had seen something. He called it an Elasmosaurus californicus, a survivor from the age of the dinosaurs. Tom and Jennifer had seen it too—a huge shadow, graceful and terrifying. Jennifer had her own name for it: the churnadryne.

Then a search party on the mountain heard a large creature crashing off in the fog. Convinced that it was only a stray cow, most of the searchers left. Tom and Jennifer didn't know whether to be relieved or disappointed. . . .

After a little, Jennifer and Tom and Grandmother and Mr. Looper and Willie Bead and Sam Boggins and his son, who had been standing together, were the only ones left. Everyone else had gone, including the reporters and the photographers in their cars, and Amy Bead and Agatha McWhinn, because they had to open up their shops again and wait on the trade. Even Mrs. Larkin, when they turned to look for her, had disappeared. Only her cat was there, crouched under some bushes and staring out at them with green, baleful eyes.

"Would you like to go back in the car with us, Jonathan?" asked Grandmother.

"No, my dear, I think not, thank you. I think that I shall go up on the hill."

"With that leg of yours?"

"Certainly not without it, Amelia."

"Mr. Looper," said Tom, "may I come with you?"

from The Terrible Churnadryne

213

"And I want to go too," said Jennifer. "Will you come, Grandmother?"

"Oh, child," said her grandmother, "why should I want to go? I can't climb."

"But it isn't hard. And it's so beautiful up there! You come right out on top, where you can look over the whole ocean. See, the fog's thinning, and I think the sun will be going down."

"But, why, Jennifer dear? There's no earthly use. What do you expect to see?"

"Nothing," said Jennifer. "Nothing, I guess, Grandmother."

Then why *did* she want so much to go up with Mr. Looper? She felt that she must go, that for some reason she could not explain she must not turn back now.

"Coming, Sam?" asked Willie.

"Well," said Mr. Boggins, "no, I think not, William. Mrs. Tipton's right—there's no earthly use. I guess we all agree there's no other explanation except it was Mrs. Larkin's cow. Shadows on the fog, Tom's and Jennifer's animal—everything—just an old cow. So I think the boy and I'll get along for home, Jonathan. Mrs. Boggins'll have dinner waiting. Come on, Sammy, good night, all."

"Good night, Sam," said Mr. Looper in a strange voice.

Jennifer looked up at him, but his expression did not show why his voice had sounded like that. She put her hand in his, and now the little group started up the winding path that led to the top of San Lorenzo—which was the only part of the hill, as well as the left side of it near the gorge, still covered in fog. Without a word, Grandmother came along.

I feel almost happy, Jennifer thought. . . . Yet why should she be almost happy when everyone had laughed and even Mr. Boggins had said the shadows had been nothing but Mrs. Larkin's cow and she knew now what a churnadryne really was?

Oh, but it didn't *matter* what Mrs. Larkin had said. She must remember that! Because she and Tom had seen what they had seen, and nothing could change it.

Yet—*had* it happened? She shut her eyes for an instant, and then as clearly as though hidden in secret all this time on the inside of her eyelids and waiting to be called forth, there came the image of the churnadryne. She saw it rearing up, its head back and its cream-colored neck shading down its chest and body into a beautiful dark enamelled green. She saw its wide eye staring at her from a great height, she saw the open mouth and what might have been a crest on its head. She saw again how the fog had been disturbed above its nostrils as though vapor were whirling upward. And she felt a chill go down her arms at the memory of it, as though she had seen some mythical beast it was magic to behold.

But even in that instant, while she was climbing up the path with her hand in Mr. Looper's and her head down, a crack rang out. Then there came another, and another—*crack-crack, crack!* And the sharp sounds were thrown back and forth, echoing, as though they were being volleyed against the walls of the gorge.

"What was that?" cried Grandmother.

"It sounded like gunshots," said Willie, and he stopped.

"Did any of those men who went up have a gun, Will?" asked Mr. Looper in an abrupt, stern voice.

"Not that I remember. Did they, Tom? Did you see any?"

"Nope. But, Willie, how about the sheriff? He'd have one."

"That's right, Mr. Looper. He would. And he went up with us, but I didn't see him come down."

Mr. Looper's face darkened. He stood there for a moment on the path, staring upward into the fog and over to where it still hung above the gorge. Then he turned and started climbing right across the thorn bushes toward the rim.

"Pray heaven—" Jennifer heard him mutter just as he started away. Then she understood.

"Oh, Grandmother!" She had put her hands up to her face, because she thought she was going to burst into tears; but now she took them away again and saw Tom running as hard as he could straight up the hill; and so she too took off after Mr. Looper, right through the thorn bushes the way he had gone.

She heard Grandmother calling, half-angry, half-frightened, something about the sheriff shooting again, about getting lost in the fog, and about the cliff-edge. But Jennifer could not stop.

"Mr. Looper, Mr. Looper! Wait!" She could no longer see him, nor anything but the bushes right at her side through which she forced her way, with the fog swirling in her face, above her head, everywhere around her, always closing her in as she moved. Her heart beat so hard in her chest that it hurt.

"Oh, please don't let the churnadryne be dead," she whispered. "Or wounded either, but if it's wounded, then it had better be dead. But please don't let it be either one. . . ."

Then Jennifer heard voices ahead of her, and the fog thinned and she knew that she must be near the edge of the chasm, for she heard the booming of the tide as it spent itself against the steep walls.

"Down there," she heard someone shouting, and she was certain it was the sheriff's voice. "Something big in the water . . . Couldn't be sure . . . too much fog . . . I aimed low. . . ." And then Mr. Looper's voice, angry and berating.

Now the fog cleared, just here on the side of Lorenzo, and Jennifer discovered she was right at the chasm's edge—that it was not thirty centimetres beyond her. Just above, on a little rocky promontory, were the sheriff and Mr. Looper; and the sheriff was pointing, to show Mr. Looper where he had seen the object down there in the water.

Mr. Looper's face was white.

"It may be the only one left in the world!" he was shouting back at the sheriff in a shaking voice. "Sheriff, if you've killed it, *do you understand what you've done?*"

Jennifer climbed up to them and stood gazing from one to the other. She saw that the sheriff had a revolver in his hand and that he was looking at Mr. Looper as if he thought Mr. Looper had gone mad.

"Jonathan," the sheriff said, "Jonathan, I don't *know* if I hit it. There was too much fog. But we can't have strange animals roaming around San Lorenzo scaring women and children, and things getting into the newspapers so that Redwood Cove gets a name for itself that everybody here belongs in the loony bin. If I've shot Mrs. Larkin's old cow—why, the poor thing was probably already dead, after falling all that distance."

But Mr. Looper was breathing hard.

"You're a good shot, Sheriff. I don't believe you missed it. And if you did not miss it, then you may have killed *Elasmosaurus californicus.* And it is very likely that neither I nor anyone else in this world will ever see its like again. The opportunity of a million years has possibly been lost forever."

Mr. Looper gave the sheriff one last terrible look, then turned and went on up San Lorenzo into the fog at the top and was lost to sight. The sheriff stared down at Jennifer with a kind of stunned, bewildered expression and, muttering to himself, went off down the rocky slope, so that Jennifer was left there all alone.

"Mr. Loo-ooo-per!" Jennifer called, her voice sounding thin and small and losing itself in the silence of the hill. "Mr. Loo-ooo-per!"

But there came no answer.

So she went on up, and after a little she came to where he stood—on the very summit, on the cap of stone. He was looking through veils of fog down onto the sea, not as if he were searching for something but only as if he were thinking, turning things over and over in the secrecy of his own mind.

"Maybe he's all right, Mr. Looper," said Jennifer in a quiet voice. "Please don't look that way. Maybe he's still down in his cave."

They stood there together; and, as they waited, the mist thinned to airy wisps and was gone—and there lay the vast, dark, purple sea with the glow of the sunset still in the sky tingeing the water far out. Pale yellow changed to emerald, and above that deepened to the rich blue of coming evening. How clear the air was, so that every smallest wave could be seen far away, and the dazzling crests, and the breasts of gulls riding in.

Then, just as Jennifer was looking off toward the horizon, she felt Mr. Looper's hand tighten and she heard him whisper, "Jennifer! Jennifer! Don't move—just look down."

Jennifer looked down. And there, its great body glistening from the foaming waters of the gorge, stood the churnadryne.

Its head was tilted back on its long neck as though it were testing the wind blowing in from the sea, and the color of its head—pale cream— was beautiful in the transparent light. There was a small crest along the top that diminished and was lost at the back; down the length of its neck the cream darkened to green, and then, on its chest and body, from green to deep blue. Huge flippers rested on the sand, and its great tail, thick near the top and narrowing out to the end, lay curled about it.

Like some terrible and marvellous beast out of a story told long ago, it remained motionless, so that Jennifer, scarcely daring to breathe, felt that surely this must be happening in a dream.

"Then it did not die—it did not die," whispered Mr. Looper over and over, and if Jennifer had looked up, she would have seen that there were tears in Mr. Looper's eyes. "I knew that if it weren't killed, it was here. . . ."

At last the churnadryne lifted its head—and for a single instant stared straight up into their eyes with such an intent, keen gaze that Jennifer felt the hair rise up along the backs of her arms, and at the nape of her neck.

Then, with one long lifting movement of its body, as though a wave of the sea heaved itself, it was in the water and the tide was carrying it away. An enormous comber curled in, and the churnadryne rose on the swell. Then the comber broke against it, and the churnadryne moved on.

The sea was darkening, and the sky. Now the churnadryne was swimming strongly, its head held high—just the top of its body visible above the water, and its tail looping behind.

"The last elasmosaur . . ." murmured Mr. Looper.

He will always think it was that, Jennifer said to herself, and the people of Redwood Cove will always say, "It was nothing but a cow"— but I'll know what it really was.

"It may never come back again, Jennifer," said Mr. Looper, "but you

and I know that it exists. We saw it, standing here together, looking down onto the beach, and we shall never forget it. Let them laugh—let the whole town laugh—but no one can change what has happened, can they? I'm so glad you were up here with me."

Jennifer, at the tone of his voice, tore her gaze away from the churnadryne out there in the sea. She looked up and saw for the first time Mr. Looper's expression of wonderment and joy, and knew in an instant that it did not matter *what* he called it as long as he was as happy as this.

"Jennifer—Jonathan!"

"Here we are, Grandmother. Hurry, Tom—hurry, Willie—"

There they were beside her.

"I see it!" cried Tom. "We *told* you it was real, Grandma!"

Now the ocean darkened a little more, and Jennifer could no longer be certain of what she saw. She strained her eyes to catch one final glimpse, but knew at last it was no use.

The churnadryne was gone.

Detail of *At the Crease* by Ken Danby

Hat Tricks and Home Runs

Skateboard Showdown

by Barbara Douglass

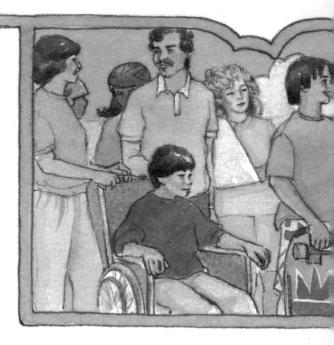

Jody's father is so eager for her to win the skateboard scramble tournament that he buys her a new top-of-the-line skateboard. Jody knows her friend, Carmen, is better than she is and deserves to win, but Carmen's board is old and has loose wheels. Jody thinks her new board will give her an unfair advantage, and she feels even worse when she discovers that Carmen has promised her little brother, who is in a wheelchair, a trip to Disneyland—the tournament prize.

By Saturday morning Jody was afraid she really was sick. Mom's eyebrows drew closer together as she placed one gentle hand on Jody's forehead.

"You don't feel feverish, honey," she said.

"It's my stomach," Jody moaned. "It always wrinkles up when I get worried, but this time it's worse. Maybe it's the flu, or—"

"James?" Mother looked at him severely.

"Nonsense," he said. "Just nerves. Jody, you'll feel fine once you have that trophy in your hands." Then he grinned confidently. "So will I. You two ready? I'll go start the car."

Mother took a deep breath and held it, as though she were trying to hold back angry words. For the first time, Jody noticed that Mom was wearing her blue sundress, not the nurse's uniform.

"You're not working today?" she asked.

"Surprise!" Mom's smile was a small one and her forehead was still

wrinkled. "I managed to trade a day off with one of the other nurses so I could be with you this morning."

Jody's stomach cramped up tighter.

Mom gave her a hug as they headed for the door. "Breathe deeply, honey, and try to relax. A few years from now you'll wonder how you ever could have worried so much over a little old skateboard contest. Honest!"

A few years from now, Jody told herself, I'll still remember this as the very worst day in my whole entire life.

At the shopping centre, Carmen was waiting in the contestants' box. She twirled the wheels on the heavy old skateboard and grinned.

"My brother came home last night and fixed it, see? Where were you Monday? I stopped by the park to tell you I had to stay home and help. My grandmother's sick and Mom's been away all week."

Without waiting for an answer, she chattered on. "Well—this is it! Are you ready? Are you excited? Are you scared? I am!" Suddenly she stopped, looking puzzled. "What's that behind your back?"

Slowly Jody held out the new skateboard. Carmen's eyes opened wide.

"It was Dad's idea, not mine," Jody explained quickly. "I was late Monday because Mom invited Andrea for lunch. When you didn't show up Tuesday or Wednesday I went to your house, but—I—"

"Never mind." Carmen spoke sharply and turned away. "I know what a dump it is. That's why I never asked you over."

"Oh, no!" Jody said. "Your house is swell. We lived in one a lot like it when I was little. Except ours was next to an auto wrecker's. It didn't smell sweet like the lumberyard. But I was really happy—"

A blast from the loudspeaker interrupted, as the announcer called for the younger contestants to line up.

Carmen studied Jody's face. "If you weren't ashamed to be seen at my place, why didn't you stay?"

"I heard you talking to your little brother—you know—about the trip to Disneyland. I just couldn't bear to show you this new board. It isn't fair, Carmen. What if your wheels come loose again?"

"Don't say that. They just can't—that's all!"

Suddenly Jody knew just what to do. She breathed a deep sigh of relief, wondering why she hadn't thought of it before.

"I've got it, Carmen! It's so simple! You'll have time to get the feel of my new board while the little kids compete. Then you can just borrow it. Whatever trick you were planning to do, it will be better on this board. Shall I show you what I've been practising? I'll bet you can do it better than I can."

Carmen shook her head thoughtfully. "I don't think I should use your new skateboard."

"If you don't, and your board gets wobbly again, Sean might win," Jody reminded her.

"You really don't care?" Carmen asked. "What about your Dad? What if I win with your board?"

"I'll explain to him," Jody said, wondering if she really would be able to. But she could see her friend weaken. "Come on," she urged. "It's the only way to make this contest fair."

Carmen grinned at last, her dark eyes sparkling. She took the slim board and ran off to practise.

For Jody, the rest of the scramble passed in a blur. She felt like one small piece of a kaleidoscope picture, tumbling about from scene to scene. She saw Dad on the sidelines, with Mom, but they weren't together. Mr. Masters stood between them. Andrea was there too, stand-

ing way in the back by herself, with her arm in a sling. Carmen's little brother sat close to the rope barrier, where he could see everything from his chair.

Jody saw Carmen sweep to the top of the ramp and spin a 540 so smoothly the skateboard was scarcely noticeable. Then, halfway down the ramp, a second 540. With the spectators already clapping, Carmen rolled effortlessly off the ramp for a third swift spin on the asphalt. Jody couldn't decide whether her friend looked more like a bird or a ballerina.

The crowd roared.

Behind her, Jody heard Sean's voice. "Well, I guess I was a little too sure of myself this time. I thought I could take it with one 540. And I thought she'd be using that clumsy old board," he said as the announcer called for number seven. "Now I sorta wish I'd practised."

Jody wasn't nervous anymore. With calm hands she pulled on the green safety pads and hooked the helmet strap under her chin. As Carmen brought back the shiny skateboard with a whispered thanks, Jody kicked off her sandals.

She borrowed Carmen's old board and four others, lined them up in the centre of the arena, pushed off, and worked up enough speed to make the jump. Even before the applause began, she could feel that it had been a good performance.

As she rolled back to the contestants' box she saw that both Mom and Dad were clapping. Carmen's little brother had his arms folded. Then it was Sean's turn.

He seemed undecided, circling several times. When he finally settled for a spinner jump, the board didn't flip quite fast enough. Sean wasn't able to complete the landing. When he fell, the crowd groaned, and then cheered when they saw he wasn't hurt. Jody was surprised to find that she felt sorry for Andrea's cousin.

But she didn't have much time to think about Sean. The judges had their heads together, adding up scores. Carmen's icy fingers squeezed Jody's hand and the loudspeaker rumbled, "Ladies and gentlemen. We have the final result for you now, of the competition for boys and girls ages ten to twelve. Will contestants number six, seven, and eight please come to the judges' stand?"

With Sean following, Jody and Carmen crossed the arena slowly and faced the judges. The announcer spoke into the microphone. "Our third-place winner today, ladies and gentlemen . . . with a total of twenty-four points . . . is . . . Sean Masters!"

One of the judges handed Sean a pink ribbon. The announcer waited for the applause to die down. Jody held her breath. I'm probably the only person, she thought, who ever entered a contest like this and ended up hoping somebody else would be the winner.

Finally the man spoke again. "In second place today . . . with a grand total of twenty-six points . . . we have . . . Jody Flynn!"

She grinned and reached for the red ribbon. This time the applause was even louder, but at last came the final announcement.

"And now, ladies and gentlemen, . . . our first-place winner . . . and skateboard champion . . . with the outstanding total of twenty-eight points out of a possible thirty"—he called out the name with a flourish—*"Carmen Mendoza!"*

No trace of jealousy remained now to spoil Jody's pleasure. She added her voice to all the others cheering for her friend. Carmen shyly accepted the gleaming trophy, the big blue ribbon, and the certificate promising a trip to Disneyland.

In seconds the three contestants were surrounded. Jody's parents came up with Mr. Masters. Andrea followed a short distance behind them. Carmen's little brother rolled his wheelchair up from the other side.

Mom reached out one arm and squeezed Jody's shoulder, drawing her close. "Your trick was fantastic, honey," she murmured.

But Jody couldn't tell, from Dad's face, what he was thinking.

"You let that girl borrow the new skateboard I bought for you," he said seriously. Mom's fingers tightened protectively on Jody's shoulder. "You realize that's probably the only thing that kept you from being the first-place winner?"

While she was still trying to think of a way to explain, Jody heard her father pull in a sharp breath. He let it out again with a sigh. "You and I don't think the same, Jody." Then, to her surprise, he grinned. His hearty voice rang out above the noisy crowd. "But I guess there's more than one way to be a Flynn. Or a champion, for that matter!" He reached for her hand and squeezed it.

"I'm proud of you, sweetheart. Really proud." Then he spoke more quietly, and there was a tremble in his voice that Jody had never heard before. "You're the best trophy a father could ever have. You know, I think I'll just put your picture in that empty spot on my shelf!"

Jody could hardly believe her ears. She had expected a scolding. Instead, Dad made her feel as though she had just won a gold medal in the Olympics. She was glad to see that all the wrinkles were gone from Mom's forehead, too. Best of all, her parents were standing side by side again, smiling at each other the way they used to, before the scramble came

between them. That made Jody's heart feel as light as her new skateboard.

Dad congratulated Carmen then, and turned to Mr. Masters.

"I'm afraid I'll have to skip the golf game this afternoon," he announced. "I have some important business with this group of champions here." He grabbed the wheelchair and began rolling Carmen's brother toward the car.

"Come on, everybody," he called back. "Let's all pile into the car. We're off to the Burger Bar for a milkshake celebration!"

"All *right!*" Jody squealed. "Let's hurry. I'll bet I'm hungry enough to eat the whole Burger Bar building—without any ketchup!"

Mom chuckled as she rushed to catch up with Dad. Sean loped after them with an eager grin. Carmen trailed along more slowly, as though she might be dream-walking. But Andrea hung back. She hadn't said one word, all this time.

Jody looked at her. Andrea's lime green shirt and shorts were smooth and clean. Her blond hair was carefully combed, and the sling supporting her arm was crisp and white.

Then Jody noticed the cast over Andrea's wrist. It was spotless too. No one had scribbled a name on it, or a joke, or a funny face.

Could a girl who looked so perfect really be shy? *There's more than one way to be a champion,* Dad said. Maybe there's more than one way to be bashful too. Jody shrugged and turned away, thinking, I don't need her when I have a friend like Carmen.

Only—she stopped suddenly—what if Mom was right about Andrea?

All at once Jody made a dash for the car. She handed her new skateboard to Mom, asked for the pen from Dad's shirt pocket, and raced back to Andrea. Half pulling, half pushing, and laughing all the way, Jody urged her into the car and plopped down beside her.

"We're going to have an autograph party!" she cried. "Every one of you start thinking of something really sharp to write on Andrea's cast. The winner goes first, Carmen," she said, handing over the pen.

The scramble to the car had tangled Andrea's hair and rumpled her clothes, but she didn't seem to notice. She didn't even tuck in her blouse. And the wide smile spreading over her face was one of the brightest that Jody had ever seen.

Weasel Grease

by Marion Renick

Jay's track team was pretty worried about the big meet with the tough team from Parsons School.

Coach Skelly admitted that the Parsons' team was tough to beat. But then he told the kids that this time they'd be using a secret weapon.

Jay stared at the little bottle Skelly showed them. Whatever was in it looked like plain water. Jay never would have taken it for a secret weapon.

Yet that is what Skelly called it. "Rub this on your arms and legs and face before you go into a race," he said. "It will make your skin so slick that you'll slip through the air like a hot spoon going through ice cream. Naturally this will help you run faster."

"Is that true?" Jay watched Skelly's face for signs of a grin.

"Science calls it 'cutting down wind resistance,'" Skelly said in a serious tone. "You'll be like an arrow—or a jet plane. You know how they are made to pass through the air easily and swiftly."

"That stuff should help on long jumps too. Let me try some!" Jay held out his hand. "We'd better rub it on Steve. He's got the yips again."

When the girls and boys took off their sweaters, Skelly poured oil into everyone's hand. "Smooth it on the front and sides of your bare arms and legs," he said. "If you haven't enough, I'll give you more."

from Take a Long Jump

"What is it?" Jill asked.

"Do other coaches have it?" Don wants to know.

"Many coaches have their own secret weapon. This is mine. It's a sly trick, I'll admit." Skelly was grinning now. "That's why I named it after a sly, rascally animal. I call it weasel grease."

"It's greasy, sure enough." Sally laughed as she rubbed it on her arms.

"Will it really help us go faster?" Steve asked.

"You just believe that it will, Steve boy," said Skelly. "Here, rub on a little more."

Nobody was discouraged now about going against a better team. The kids laughed merrily as they slapped on the weasel grease. So did Steve, who usually was licked even before he went into a contest. This time he ran down the runway on steady legs and jumped at least as far as he did in practice.

When Jay made his first jump he thought he never had gone so fast or so far. On the second round of jumps he went a little farther, outjumping everyone else. He hoped this mark would still be the winner after the other jumpers had made their third try. Next he ran in the 200-metre race and won third place against a lot of good sprinters. Then he watched the other events to see how his teammates were doing. They weren't the winners, but they were making points for second, third, or fourth places.

After a while he sat down in the grass near the officials. They were figuring scores. He heard one of them tell the others, "This is amazing. City Park is only one point behind Parsons. The score is 104 to 103. And there's only one more event to be finished. That's the long jump."

Jay wondered if his mark in that event was still leading. He hurried to the pit, where he found he had been outjumped. All the other contestants, except himself and one Parsons jumper, had taken their third jump allowed by the rules. He was glad he had one more try.

"Everything depends on you, Jaybird," Hopper said. "Skelly put me in the jump so it wouldn't be loaded with Parsons kids."

"How did you do?" Jay asked.

"Third or fourth, I think," Hopper said. "Even Steve won us a point for sixth in the 100-metre dash. If you win this, we've won the meet. Give it all you've got, Jaybird!"

Jay headed for the runway without waiting to see how far the Parsons boy was jumping. "Weasel grease, jump me farther," Jay whispered.

He didn't notice Hopper and Skelly trying to give him the good-luck sign. He stood very still, looking down the path. His mouth was dry and his legs felt like soup as he kept looking at the far end of the sand, almost seeing his heels dig in there.

Slowly he began to run. Then faster . . . faster. . . . Now the toe of his forward foot came down on the board just right. He went off with a solid, satisfying bounce, still running in the air. Farther, farther—until he began to drop. He was reaching for more distance yet when he felt the coming-to-earth bump. Sand sprayed into his face. He was glad for Skelly's hand to pull him out. He had tried very hard and he was tired.

He watched the judges stretch the tape measure, then compare figures. He heard that his jump was the longest of all. "By one centimetre," the judge said. "City Park wins the meet." Jay felt ten feet tall and ready to jump over the school building.

"That weasel grease sure is great stuff!" Over and over the kids said this on the ride home. As they were leaving the bus somebody shouted, "Hey! Now we can win the City Track and Field Meet!"

They all clapped and cheered until Skelly said, "Don't be too sure of winning. You'll be up against boys and girls from all over town. Many of them are already very good at this sport."

"But they don't have our secret weapon," said Jill.

Skelly slowly shook his head. "Don't count on that stuff. It is only baby oil. Just plain baby oil."

"But—but—I never jumped so far before." Jay was puzzled.

So were the others. They said, "But we won. The weasel grease *must* have helped."

"It showed each of you that you can do better than you thought you could." Skelly looked from one to another. "That was how it helped you."

Jay turned this over in his mind. "You mean I can *always* jump as far as I did today?"

"Any time you want to, champ. And many centimetres farther, if you keep trying," Skelly answered. "The same thing is true for every one of you kids. Never forget it."

The Pitcher

by Jeffrey Hovell

The pitcher stands like a statue under the lights
Concentrating on hitting a small, round target.

His teammates are scattered on a field,
Like pieces on a chessboard.

The job is very strange:
To fool the batter.

The crowd roars
As the pitcher steps to the mound.

He hides the ball behind his back,
Rotating it, for the correct grip.

He grits his teeth, his arms fly high.
His foot kicks out, and his arm swings back.

You see the snap of the wrist,
As the ball is released.

The ball sails through the air,
Curving to deceive the batter.

The batter swings, and misses,
As the ball snaps into the catcher's mitt.

The Base Stealer

by Robert Francis

Poised between going on and back, pulled
Both ways taut like a tightrope-walker,
Fingertips pointing the opposites,
Now bouncing tiptoe like a dropped ball
Or a kid skipping rope, come on, come on,
Running a scattering of steps sidewise,
How he teeters, skitters, tingles, teases,
Taunts them, hovers like an ecstatic bird,
He's only flirting, crowd him, crowd him,
Delicate, delicate, delicate, delicate—now!

My First Home Run

by Margaret Minter

I feel as if I'm ten feet tall,
Although in fact I'm rather small;
The reason why I feel this way?
I hit my first home run today!
And everyone was there to see,
While all my friends applauded me!
I gave that ball a mighty whack,
That sent it soaring—high and back
Behind the hands that reached *in vain;*
The only home run of the game!
My dad was pleased and very proud,
Cheering and laughing with the crowd.
But Mum was wondering what to do
With a baseball star named Mary Lou!

The Worst Team Meets the First Game

by Avi

South Orange River Middle School had a motto for its sports teams: "Everybody plays, everybody wins." It worked fine until all the guys who didn't like sports were told they had to make up a soccer team. They were all good at other things, but they sure weren't good at soccer!

On a chilly and gray September afternoon we stepped from the bus and slouched toward the Buckingham field. The leaves were just beginning to turn. Our stomachs already had. Right then and there I became opposed to capital punishment. I not only wanted to live, I firmly believed I was innocent.

We all were. Our only crime was that we didn't like sports much. Worse, we actually preferred other things. Not everything. Some things. For example, Saltz was keen on his writing, and only okay in biology. Lifsom was gung-ho about art, but his grades were generally just so-so.

So it went. Fairly normal. Or so we thought. Watching football

from S.O.R. Losers

games, rooting for teams, stuff like that, just wasn't important to us. True, Macht was a whiz at poker, and claimed that was a sport, but he didn't get much support. You'd think not being into sports was antihuman. Well, the world was about to get revenge.

And how? By the general notion that we were going to have *fun.*

Fun. It reminded me of a class trip to the S.P.C.A. Someone asked a woman there if they ever had to kill an animal. "Oh, no," she said with this ripe smile, "we just put them into a long, long sleep."

After two practices we could tell that we were heading into a long, long sleep.

When we got to the field, the Buckingham team was already lying in wait.

Mr. Lester went to speak to the other coach. Maybe to warn him. As he left, he said, "Get yourselves ready."

Get ready? Get lost is what we wanted to do.

Out in the middle of the field the referee was showing off, kicking the soccer ball up in the air with alternate feet, never once letting it touch the ground.

We watched.

"Think he's open to a bribe?" wondered Macht.

"Why not just get him for our team," Saltz said.

"Do an exchange," offered Radosh. "We'll ref. He'll play."

"Sure," said Porter, "but then we'd have to know the rules."

Porter had a point.

Then we watched the Buckingham team. They were kicking the ball about to each other as if it were on a guide wire.

"I think they know how to play," said Root, clearly upset by the possibility.

"Maybe we should ask for lessons, instead of a game," put in Dorman.

With that we all started to laugh. And couldn't stop.

Mr. Lester hurried back. When he saw us in the midst of our fit, he got worried. "Is something the matter?" he asked.

"Root here," said Hays, "had this idea that we were going to play those guys. It broke us up."

"Why, yes," said Mr. Lester, perfectly serious. "They are the opposing team."

"What are they, all-stars?" asked Eliscue.

"Oh, no," said Mr. Lester, alarmed. "It's their third-string team. Perhaps, gentlemen, you should warm up."

"When you're cold, you're cold," said Root. It was such a bad joke we stopped laughing.

"Does everybody know what position he is playing?" asked Mr. Lester.

We did, sort of. During the second practice, book in hand, he had placed us around, but I wasn't sure of the position names, except goal tender.

"Now," said Mr. Lester, "remember the important thing is to . . ." Then, so help me, he forgot what he was going to say. But Mr. Lester was, if nothing else, prepared. Right off, he went to his pocket and pulled out some papers. Notes. "Ah, yes," he said, and began to read. "It's important to concentrate. Learn to meet the ball. And, gentlemen, the most important thing of all is . . ."

We never did learn the most important thing of all. The referee blew his whistle.

The Buckingham team gathered, their blue jerseys merging into a storm cloud. Out came a thunderous cheer.

If that cheer was meant to show us that, although a third-string team, they were real and strong and feeling victorious, that we had every reason to expect defeat, it worked.

"How about us doing a cheer?" suggested Mr. Lester.

"Shazam," said Lifsom. Not only was he the only one who said anything, it didn't work. We were still us.

We sort of backed onto the field. Lifsom, who was playing up front in the middle, shook hands with the opposite Buckingham players. Maybe they decided to be nice to us. Anyway, it was our ball for starters.

As for myself, I was strolling around in the goal area trying to remember anything, which wasn't much, about the rules. How far could I go? I felt certain I could kick the ball, but on second thought, as well as third on to the seventh, I wasn't sure. Was I allowed to touch the ball with my hands, or just my elbows? Did knees count? Things like that.

In fact, I was pacing along the newly chalked goal lines, back to the field, when the whistle blew. I looked up, wondering what had gone wrong. What had gone wrong was, the game had begun.

Now the way it works, I think, or is supposed to work, is that Lifsom, being up front and middle, sort of kicks the ball back toward our side—at the moment it was Barish who was behind him—and away we would go.

But to give you a full sense of how the game went, all I can say is that somewhere, somehow, between the time the ball touched Lifsom's foot—I think it was his foot, because, as I said, I hadn't been watching—and the time it was supposed to reach Barish, Buckingham had already stolen the ball.

They didn't just steal it. They kept it. Forever. When I looked up, I saw this wall of storm-blue shirts rolling down the field, *in my direction!*

As for our guys, the ones in the red and yellow, they were doing one of four things:

Standing around.

Running the wrong way.

Backing up, furiously.

Falling down.

Or, actually, five things, because some people did a combination of two of the above, like Macht, who backed up, *and* fell down.

Anyway, you know how it is in history—battles and things—wars can truly be lost at the first shot. I understand that personally. I was at one.

Playing in front of me was Saltz, my special buddy. We not only grew up together, we lived near each other. Defended each other. Loved each other. So when he saw that advancing line of Buckingham blue attacking, attacking me, he actually did something.

First, he turned red in the face. A great red blotch. Then he started to charge at that blue line. Now, unlike me, Saltz is a big guy. With his T-shirt flapping all over the place, his arms flapping other places, his longish hair flapping in the remaining places, he *charged.*

What a sight!

For just a moment the blue line hesitated. I mean Saltz is a big guy. And the red face, the flapping, and so on . . .

The ball was squirting forward.

Saltz, I saw, was aiming right for it. My stomach, which had been travelling somewhere in the region of my throat, began to go right. I

could see that Saltz was about to send that ball a billion kilometres in the other direction.

Except . . . he missed.

Honest, he did. He charged like a mad bull, cocked his leg, or whatever you do with your leg, kicked out, missed, and kept right on going. He went, in fact, past all the Buckingham players before he realized what had happened.

And what had happened was that there was nothing between me, that ball, and Buckinghams. The ball was coming right at me. I should know—I saw it trickle past me into the net.

It was only fifteen seconds into the game. But, to tell the truth, that first few seconds was typical.

Final score:

> BUCKINGHAM: 32
> SOUTH ORANGE RIVER: 0

Or, in case you hadn't noticed, we lost our first game, badly.
We were on our way.
Down.

How Sports Came to Be

by Don L. Wulffson

Skiing

Skiing began in northern Europe and Asia long before the dawn of history. Pictures and carvings of skiers done by Stone Age people have been found in Russia and other places. Even more interesting, a perfectly preserved ski was found in a bog in Norway. After examining it, scientists concluded that the ski was close to five thousand years old!

The word *ski,* which comes from northern Europe, means "a splinter cut from a log." Pronounced "shee," it is the Scandinavian term for shoe.

According to experts, the first skis were probably made from the bones of large animals. Later came wooden skis made from slabs of pine, spruce, or ash. To make them slide better over the surface of the snow, some early skis were covered with skin from elk, reindeer, or seal. Other skis had wooden strips or runners along the bottom.

Usually the ski was strapped to the foot with leather thongs or a leather harness. A few early skis had a footrest carved into the surface of the wood.

It took a long time for skis to become standardized. In fact, in the eleventh century many persons wore a different-length ski on each foot! On the right foot they wore a short, "kicking" ski, and on the left a longer, "running" ski.

Early skiers used only one ski pole, not two. The pole, which consisted of a heavy branch, was held between the skis for steering and balance. Later,

bone points were attached to the end and a hoop to its top. Not until 1615 did skiers begin to use two poles, as we do today.

The earliest recorded skiing in North America took place in California in 1856. In that year John "Snowshoe" Thompson, a Norwegian by birth, carried the mail to miners in the high Sierras, travelling on skis much of the time. Soon the miners themselves began skiing. Eager for excitement, they took to racing down the steep mountains.

Strangely, it was an Englishman who introduced skiing to the Alpine countries of Europe. In 1888 a Colonel Napier brought skis to Switzerland, and was looked upon as a madman by the natives. The following year Napier returned with Arthur Conan Doyle, the famous creator of Sherlock Holmes. Little by little, skiing began to gain in favor with the people of the region.

The first recorded use of skis in war was in A.D. 1200. In that year King Sverre of Sweden equipped his reconnaissance troops with skis. By the sixteenth century entire armies were going into battle on skis.

By World War II (1939–1945) skiing had become an established part of modern warfare.

Surprisingly, not until the nineteenth century did people begin to think of skiing as a sport. In 1767, as part of a military exercise, Norwegian soldiers

competed by racing down steep slopes "without riding or leaning on their sticks." The first ski jump took place at Huseby Hill, near Oslo, Norway, in 1879.

Today skiing is practised throughout the world—even in such unlikely places as Morocco, Hawaii, Lebanon, and Korea. Even in places where there is no snow, people have found a way to ski—they just make their own.

Table Tennis
(Ping-pong)

Table tennis was invented in England during the nineteenth century. All the equipment used in those early days was homemade. The ball was made of string. Books put down the middle of a table made the first net. The paddle

was cut out of a piece of thick cardboard.

Balls of rubber or cork soon replaced balls made of string. Some balls were covered with a knitted web or a piece of cloth to give them more spin.

The balls we use today were originally children's toys. A man named James Gribb noticed children playing with the hollow celluloid balls. He tried them out at table tennis and discovered that they were perfectly suited to the game.

The first real ping-pong paddles looked like little drums. They had very long handles and hollow blades covered with leather.

Next, wooden paddles shaped like the ones we use today were invented. But the surface of the paddles was too slick. It did not give the player enough control.

One day a man named E. C. Goode was in a drugstore searching for a remedy for a headache. He noticed a studded rubber cash mat on the counter. The thought came to him that it would make a good surface for a ping-pong paddle. His headache forgotten, Goode bought the mat. He took it home, cut it down to the right size, and glued it to the paddle.

The new paddle gave Goode a great deal more control over the ball. It improved his game so much that he challenged the British national champion. Goode won, fifty games to three!

Badminton

The game of badminton was originally called shuttlecock. The name was changed to badminton around 1870.

At that time there lived an English duke who loved sports, especially "the game of shuttlecocks." Almost every weekend the duke invited his friends over to play the game at his home. The duke's home was a mansion—a mansion called Badminton. Little by little the game took on the name of the place where it was such a popular pastime.

The duke did not invent badminton. He only gave it its name. To understand how the sport actually began, we have to go back many centuries to the time of the ancient Babylonians.

The Babylonians were a very superstitious people. They engaged in many magic rites that they thought would reveal the future. Among these rites was one in which two people hit a ball or other object back and forth. The length of time the ball could be kept in play supposedly revealed how long the people would live.

Little by little this magic rite turned into nothing more than a game. Sometimes the game was played by just one person. Here the object was to hit the shuttlecock into the air as many times as possible without letting it drop to the ground.

In another early version of the game the object was for the players to protect a target. Both players had to stand in one place. Then they took turns hitting the shuttle at the target behind their opponent.

Originally, the shuttlecock was a round piece of cork with goose feathers stuck around its top. Early shuttles varied greatly in size, weight, and design.

At first, people used the outstretched palm as a racket. The palm was replaced by a small bat of solid wood. Eventually, a frame with strings stretched across it came into use.

Around the turn of the century the idea of using a net came into being. At the same time, boundary markers were set up and rules of the game were established.

Today, badminton is an international sport. Since 1948, annual tournaments have been held to determine the world champion. The sport is one that can be enjoyed by everyone—children and adults, carefree amateurs and highly skilled pros.

The Justine Blainey Story

Hockey ruling called 'sad day for everyone'

Toronto Star
September 26, 1985

By Heather Bird and **Lois Kalchman**

An appeal will be launched against an Ontario Supreme Court judge's decision prohibiting 12-year-old Justine Blainey from playing on a boys' hockey team, her lawyer said within hours of the ruling yesterday.

Justine's lawyer, Anna Fraser, said the decision marked "a sad day for everyone" because if discrimination is allowed on the basis of sex then it can be applied to other minorities across the country.

"That's why we've got to get it into a higher court," Fraser said.

Fraser has 30 days to file her application for leave to appeal to the Ontario Court of Appeal.

Justine, a 155-cm, 45-kg (5-foot-1, 100-pound) defenceman with the Toronto Olympics A boys' team of the Metro Toronto Hockey League, feels there isn't enough challenge for her on a girls' team.

'Very upset'

"I feel very upset, not only for myself, but for my coach, who now has to find another team player, and for all the other little girls who won't be able to play in higher levels of hockey. I'm also sorry for Abby Hoffman, who wanted for 30 years for girls to play," Justine said.

"I'm doing it for every little girl, it's not just myself," she said yesterday in both English and French at a press conference.

"The issue came up because I wanted to play. It's me, not just the adults."

She said she's still inviting the team to her birthday party and hopes to find a team she can play on this year.

Justine's mother, Caroline, said she was upset not only for Justine but for her 12-year-old son.

"I cannot accept this decision as just," she said. "I cannot accept that he's (her son) better than his sister and that the Ontario Supreme Court has said he has a sex-given right to play more and better."

Former track and field star Bruce Kidd said he felt very deeply for Justine.

"I'm also upset because this decision will sanction more sex discrimination."

Justine's coach, Danny Damario, heard the news a scant hour before the Olympics were to take to the ice at St. Michael's Arena for a game.

"I can't believe it in the 1980s, with a team the girl has proven she could play for, this would happen," Damario said.

Continued on page C3.

Continued from page C1.

Justine earned a spot as a first-string defenceman with the Olympics for their summer league schedule.

Damario refused to allow interviews with Justine's teammates because the boys were too upset.

"We've been playing rather badly. Emotionally, it's affected the kids," he said.

"Just believe me, it's very hard for me to coach this team the way they are. They don't understand what's going on."

Lawyer Jack Walker, president of the Olympics organization, called the situation "tragic."

"But on the positive side, she (Justine) took the first step. It will inevitably happen that girls will play on boys' teams."

Parents of Justine's teammates believe that since she earned her spot, she should play.

Michael Myers said his 12-year-old son Jackson is "old enough to know the difference between right and wrong and know this is wrong."

Chris Phibbs said her boy, Greg, would be disappointed if Justine can't play.

"She's a good player from what I've seen and she could certainly have a place on this team."

The battle goes on for Justine Blainey

Toronto Star
October 29, 1986

By Lois Kalchman

Justine Blainey, 13, has learned her two-year battle to play on a boys' Metropolitan Toronto Hockey League team may take another four years.

"I may not play but my daughter will," she said last night before she played her first game in the Scarborough Girls Hockey League at MacGregor Park Arena.

"I don't want to be pessimistic," said the 162-cm, 54-kg (5-foot-4, 120-pound) defenceman. "I am not giving up but the process is slow. The Ontario Hockey Association won't even let me practise with a boys' team any more."

The Ontario Supreme Court ruled that a Human Rights clause permitting sex discrimination in sports was unconstitutional. The Supreme Court of Canada refused to hear a challenge by the OHA of the lower court's ruling.

"The process (Ontario Human Rights Commission) is so excruciatingly slow and painful that if Justine waited until it was over, she would have forgotten how to play hockey," her mother Caroline said.

Her lawyer, J. Anna Fraser, said if it were to go the full route the whole thing could take until 1990.

"The Human Rights Commission hearings could go as long as 18 months or 1988," Fraser explained yesterday. "If their decision is appealed to divisional court and then the court of appeal that could be another two years. We are continuing to fight."

Meanwhile her mother sat in the stands obviously frustrated by the repeated delays.

"In this league at least she will have 36 all-star games plus skating time in house league," she said.

"Why don't they (OHA and MTHL) just leave us alone? Girls should not be limited to non-contact when our national, university, and future Olympic teams will all be contact. There is a contact league, the MTHL."

244

Girl's hockey skills atrophy during dispute, coaches say

The Globe and Mail
June 11, 1987

By Yves Lavigne

Justine Blainey, a talented hockey player respected as an equal by boys and sought after by coaches, is slowly losing her skills as she awaits the outcome of the struggle to keep her off the ice, the Ontario Human Rights Commission was told yesterday.

"She could practise every day, but unless she (plays) against her peers to develop those skills, it doesn't mean anything," coach Daniel Damario testified.

"When I saw her last, she didn't look like the player I picked (in May, 1985)," Mr. Damario said. "There's no way she can catch up for that (lost) ice time."

Testimony has indicated that the 14-year-old Grade 8 student from Toronto is too good a hockey player for girls' teams. She excels against the boys, body-checking with zeal and pinning players against the boards.

"She can throw her weight around pretty well," said David Risk, the 13-year-old captain of the Etobicoke Canucks, which had signed Justine to play defence for the 1986-87 season.

Metro Toronto Hockey League officials refused to grant Justine permission to play with the Canucks. She is alleging before the commission that the MTHL's enforcement of an Ontario Hockey Association rule that bans female players constitutes sexual discrimination.

Mr. Damario, who wanted Justine to play for his Toronto Olympics during the 1985-86 season, told the inquiry the team's general manager warned him that both coach and team could be suspended under OHA rules if Justine skated on to the ice.

Mr. Damario and Robert Brook, the coach of the Toronto East Enders, who wants Justine to play for his team in the coming season, told the inquiry skilled girls such as Justine should be allowed to play on boys' teams.

The players agree, they said.

"Their attitude was: if she could make the team, she could play on the team," Mr. Damario testified. "At that age group, if they could play, why not?"

He told the inquiry Justine is in no danger of being hurt while playing hard-checking hockey with boys. Skating skills are a great equalizer among players of different strengths, he said, and a skilled skater such as Justine could check as hard as the strongest boys on the team.

"She was always one of the ones saying, 'Let's go out there and do it.' She surprised me in regards of what she wanted to learn in hockey. She made a good student," Mr. Damario said.

Mr. Brook said he first noticed Justine's hockey talent when she tried out for another team he coached during the 1984-85 season. "She was one of the better skaters on the ice—it includes shooting, passing, balance, and basic knowledge of what she was doing."

The Globe and Mail, Toronto

Justine's win bans sex discrimination in *all* sports

Toronto Star
December 5, 1987

By **Lois Kalchman** and **Brian McAndrew**

Girls now have the right to compete for a spot on any amateur boys' sports team, the Ontario Human Rights Commission ruled yesterday.

The far-reaching ruling came in a decision granting 14-year-old Justine Blainey the right to try out for a boys' hockey team.

"It follows that . . . discrimination on the basis of sex in athletic activities is now unlawful in Ontario," ruled rights inquiry commissioner Ian Springate.

The decision goes beyond hockey and gives girls the right to compete with boys at any level in all amateur sports, said Anna Fraser, Justine's lawyer.

"You can use a special program such as the Ontario Women's Hockey Association to shelter, protect, and encourage a sport, but not as a ghetto to keep people inside," Fraser said.

"I think it will have a profound influence on all sports."

Segregation by sex remains a fact of life in many of the estimated 80 amateur sports in Ontario, including golf, football, swimming, and diving. Others, such as baseball and lacrosse, are integrated.

Justine Blainey, however, may no longer have the skills to play on a boys' hockey team after winning the 2½-year legal battle for a chance to play for an all-male club.

"It's been a long haul," said her mother, Caroline Blainey. "I'm proud of my daughter. She stuck by the struggle even though

at this point she may not be able to make a boys' team."

But the 162-cm (5-foot, 4-inch) defenceman is determined to find acceptance with a team.

"If someone says 'no' I'll just have to find another one," she told The Star last night.

Justine was 12 when she was selected to play for the Toronto Olympic peewee team, only to be benched by an Ontario Hockey Association (OHA) rule preventing her from playing because she was a girl.

Her fight took her through the Supreme Court of Canada and finally to the Ontario Human Rights Commission, which has decided prohibiting her from trying out for a team because of her sex was "unlawful and in violation of her rights."

Team loses, Justine wins

The Globe and Mail
January 18, 1988

By Alexander Bruce

Last night's 3-1 defeat for the East Enders minor bantam hockey team in Toronto was sweet victory for one of its defence-men, 15-year-old Justine Blainey.

After three years of fighting the Metro Toronto Hockey League and the Ontario Hockey Association in the courts, she finally got to play hockey the way she likes it: with the boys.

"I think she did really well out there," said Ms. Blainey's mother, Caroline. "She played well and she seemed to have fun."

In spite of her team's loss to the Aeros hockey club, Ms. Blainey managed to crack a smile for the crowd—jammed with television cameramen and photographers—as she stepped off the ice to join her team in the locker room.

"I was happy to see how well she fit in to things," said Ms. Blainey's lawyer, Anna Fraser. "Things worked out very well."

On the ice, Ms. Blainey's long absence from organized play showed only slightly. She was a little shaky on her feet and a bit unsure of her passing.

She was also smaller than some of the other players. But she kept pace, protecting her goalie well. She even managed two shots on her opponent's goal.

Her teammates, meanwhile, did not seem to care about their new defence-man's gender. They slapped her on the back when she did well and advised her when she might have done better.

It has been a long road for Ms. Blainey and her family. For three years she was excluded from competitive hockey while she fought to win permission to play boys' hockey.

She testified at the Ontario Human Rights Commission hearings that boys' hockey is more fun than girls'. She wanted to be able to bodycheck and take slapshots, actions that recently earned her suspension from the girls' league.

Last night Ms. Blainey had few opportunities to test these skills. She spent most of her time reacquainting herself with the ice and the challenges of the game.

The Globe and Mail, Toronto

The Hockey Sweater

by Roch Carrier
translated by Sheila Fischman

The winters of my childhood were long, long seasons. We lived in three places—the school, the church, and the skating rink—but our real life was on the skating rink. Real battles were won on the skating rink. Real strength appeared on the skating rink. The real leaders showed themselves on the skating rink. School was a sort of punishment. Parents always want to punish children and school is their most natural way of punishing us. However, school was also a quiet place where we could prepare for the next hockey game, lay out our next strategies. As for church, we found there the tranquillity of God: there we forgot school and dreamed about the next hockey game.

Through our daydreams it might happen that we would recite a prayer: we would ask God to help us play as well as Maurice Richard.

We all wore the same uniform as he, the red, white, and blue uniform of the Montreal Canadiens, the best hockey team in the world; we all combed our hair in the same style as Maurice Richard, and to keep it in place we used a sort of glue—a great deal of glue. We laced our skates like Maurice Richard, we taped our sticks like Maurice Richard. We cut all his pictures out of the papers. Truly, we knew everything about him.

On the ice, when the referee blew his whistle the two teams would rush at the puck; we were five Maurice Richards taking it away from five other Maurice Richards; we were ten players, all of us wearing with the same blazing enthusiasm the uniform of the Montreal Canadiens. On our backs, we all wore the famous number 9.

One day, my Montreal Canadiens sweater had become too small; then it got torn and had holes in it. My mother said: "If you wear that old sweater people are going to think we're poor!" Then she did what she did whenever we needed new clothes. She started to leaf through the catalogue the Eaton company sent us in the mail every year. My mother was proud. She didn't want to buy our clothes at the general store; the only things that were good enough for us were the latest styles from Eaton's catalogue. My mother didn't like the order forms included with the catalogue; they were written in English and she didn't understand a word of it. To order my hockey sweater, she did as she usually did; she took out her writing paper and wrote in her gentle schoolteacher's hand: "Cher Monsieur Eaton, Would you be kind enough to send me a Canadiens sweater for my son who is ten years old and a little too tall for his age and Docteur Robitaille thinks he's a little too thin? I'm sending you three dollars and please send me what's left if there's anything left. I hope your wrapping will be better than last time."

Monsieur Eaton was quick to answer my mother's letter. Two weeks later we received the sweater. That day I had one of the greatest disappointments of my life! I would even say that on that day I experienced a very great sorrow. Instead of the red, white, and blue Montreal Canadiens sweater, Monsieur Eaton had sent us a blue and white sweater with a maple leaf on the front—the sweater of the Toronto Maple Leafs.

I'd always worn the red, white, and blue Montreal Canadiens sweater; all my friends wore the red, white, and blue sweater; never had anyone in my village ever worn the Toronto sweater, never had we even seen a Toronto Maple Leafs sweater. Besides, the Toronto team was regularly trounced by the triumphant Canadiens. With tears in my eyes, I found the strength to say:

"I'll never wear that uniform."

"My boy, first you're going to try it on! If you make up your mind about things before you try, my boy, you won't go very far in this life."

My mother had pulled the blue and white Toronto Maple Leafs sweater over my shoulders and already my arms were inside the sleeves. She pulled the sweater down and carefully smoothed all the creases in the abominable maple leaf on which, right in the middle of my chest, were written the words "Toronto Maple Leafs". I wept.

"I'll never wear it."

"Why not? This sweater fits you . . . like a glove."

"Maurice Richard would never put it on his back."

"You aren't Maurice Richard. Anyway, it isn't what's on your back that counts, it's what you've got inside your head."

"You'll never put it in my head to wear a Toronto Maple Leafs sweater."

My mother sighed in despair and explained to me:

"If you don't keep this sweater that fits you perfectly I'll have to write Monsieur Eaton and explain that you don't want to wear the Toronto sweater. Monsieur Eaton's an *Anglais;* he'll be insulted because he likes the Maple Leafs. And if he's insulted do you think he'll be in a hurry to answer us? Spring will be here and you won't have played a single game, just because you didn't want to wear that perfectly nice blue sweater."

So I was obliged to wear the Maple Leafs sweater. When I arrived on the rink, all the Maurice Richards in red, white, and blue came up, one by one, to take a look. When the referee blew his whistle I went to take my usual position. The coach came and warned me I'd be better to stay on the forward line. A few minutes later the second line was called; I jumped onto the ice. The Maple Leafs sweater weighed on my shoulders like a mountain. The coach came and told me to wait; he'd need me later, on defence. By the third period I still hadn't played; one of the defencemen was hit in the nose with a stick and it was bleeding. I jumped on the ice: my moment had come! The referee blew his whistle; he gave me a penalty. He claimed I'd jumped on the ice when there were already five players. That was too much! It was unfair! It was persecution! It was because of my blue sweater! I struck my stick against the ice so hard it broke. Relieved, I bent down to pick up the debris. As I straightened up I saw the young vicar, on skates, before me.

"My child," he said, "just because you're wearing a new Toronto Maple Leafs sweater unlike the others, it doesn't mean you're going to

make the laws around here. A proper young man doesn't lose his temper. Now take off your skates and go to the church and ask God to forgive you."

Wearing my Maple Leafs sweater I went to the church, where I prayed to God; I asked him to send, as quickly as possible, moths that would eat up my Toronto Maple Leafs sweater.

Ben Johnson: The Making of a Champion

by Sharon Stewart

The story begins with a little kid whose big brother was a runner. The kid used to tag along after his brother on training runs. He got left farther and farther behind and couldn't catch up, but that didn't stop him from trying. That kid's name was Ben Johnson.

Ben was born and brought up in Falmouth, Jamaica. As his brother Edward had done before him, he ran his first races on the dusty grass of the schoolyard. From there he moved on to competitions organized by a Falmouth track group. In those days Ben's running didn't impress anyone, least of all himself. He lost most of his races—and he hated losing. Some people need to win so badly that they give up when they keep losing. Not Ben. He just got quiet and stubborn and tried harder.

In 1975, when Ben was fourteen, his family moved to Toronto, and he began racing in school track meets. His running was still nothing special. But things began to change for Ben when his brother invited him to train at a local track club. It didn't seem like much of a turning point at the time. Ben wanted to quit after two weeks. "I couldn't make it around the track once. It was too hard." No wonder it was hard—he hadn't done any real training. He lagged far behind the other runners in the club. Despite his discouragement, Ben stuck it out. Once again, he got stubborn and tried extra hard to catch up with the other runners. After six months of training, he ran 100m in 10.3 seconds, a pretty impressive feat for someone who had just begun training seriously.

With training and expert coaching, Ben's races got better and better over the next few years, and he began competing in international events. However, he still had problems to overcome. His naturally fast start made it easy for him to win short races such as the 60m dash. The trouble was that in longer races, like the 100m, Ben *tightened*, ran out of speed, in the last part of the race, and slower starters overtook and passed him to win. So in 1981, Ben added weight-lifting to his training program to help build up his strength. It worked. With greater strength came more speed and more stamina—and more wins. He took a silver medal at the Commonwealth Games in 1982 and two bronze medals at the Olympics in 1984.

At the 1984 Olympics Ben had to compete against the spectacular American sprinter, Carl Lewis, who won four gold medals. Now Carl was the one Ben had to catch up with—and beat.

Nineteen eighty-six was the year Ben Johnson really hit his stride. Early in the year he won the World Cup, and after that, eight indoor races in a row, an almost impossible feat. Then at a

Ben Johnson defeats Carl Lewis in Rome.

meet in Zurich, he defeated Carl Lewis for the first time. In 1986, he won a gold medal at the Commonwealth Games in Edinburgh, then went on to trounce Lewis at meets in San José and Moscow. Yet despite all his wins, world attention remained focussed on Lewis, who was officially listed as the world's No. 1 sprinter. Johnson was ranked No. 2—Ben was still playing catch up.

Then, in August 1987, came the World Championships in Rome. The stage was set for a showdown between Johnson and Lewis in the 100m race. Despite the fact that he hadn't beaten Johnson in two years, most people expected Lewis to win. After all, in the 100m race he would have plenty of time to catch Ben.

The two top sprinters had been assigned running lanes side by side. They did not speak to each other as they hammered their starting blocks into the track and pulled off their sweatsuits. Following the starter's orders, all the runners knelt to their blocks, then rose to set position. When the starter's pistol went off, Johnson exploded away from the blocks. It wasn't a good start—it was a *great* start! Lewis never caught up. Johnson crossed the finish line a full metre ahead. He set a new world record for the 100m—an incredible 9.83 seconds. There could no longer be any doubt about it: Ben Johnson was No. 1, the world's fastest runner. There was no one for him to catch up to anymore.

Johnson will go on to set new records, to try and beat the only runner left for him to overtake and pass—himself. Whatever races he wins in the future, whatever new records he sets, Ben Johnson plans to quit after the 1992 Summer Olympics. He wants to retire a champion, while he is still the fastest man on earth.

Ken Danby *Courage* 1987

Call Them Champions

by Sharon Stewart

An amputee skier streaks down a mountainside to claim a gold medal. A blind swimmer churns to a new record. A wheelchair racer crosses the finish line of a gruelling marathon ahead of the other competitors. Today, disabled athletes are not only playing sports, they are competing in international games. And yet, not so long ago, many people thought that *any* sport, much less international competition, was beyond the capability of people with physical disabilities.

A program of sports for physically disabled people was first developed to help rehabilitate injured veterans of the Second World War. In 1948, the first games for disabled athletes were held at Stoke Mandeville Hospital in England. The games were so successful that the organizers decided to make them an annual event. The idea of sports for the disabled soon spread to other countries, and in 1952 the Stoke Mandeville Games became the world's first international games for the disabled.

After the Stoke Mandeville Games, many countries set up local and national sports programs for the disabled, and more and more disabled people took up sports, some just for fun and others because they were interested in serious athletic competition. As more world-class competitors developed, new international games were organized to challenge them. Some, like the World

Uli Rompel, alpine skiing, blind division, followed by guide. Second place, U.S. Nationals, 1985.

◄ Linda Hamilton, track and field, amputee division. Three gold medals, Can Am Pacific Games, 1987.

Aquatic Championships and the World Winter Games for the Disabled, concentrate on just one sport or category of sport. Others, such as the World Cerebral Palsy Championships, focus on competitors with a particular disability. But some international games, like the Pan Am Games for the Disabled, offer a wide range of sports, with events for athletes with different kinds of disabilities. Probably the most famous of these games are the Olympics for the Physically Disabled, also known as the Paralympics. They are held each Olympic year, and they take place in the country that hosts the Summer Olympics, whenever that can be arranged. The Paralympics include many of the same sports as the regular Olympics, and are open to athletes with many different disabilities.

International games set a standard of achievement that inspires all disabled athletes everywhere. They also give top-level athletes the opportunity to test themselves against first-class competitors in their sports and to demonstrate their athletic abilities to the world. People involved in sports for the disabled stress that these international games are not just rehabilitation—they are a new branch of athletics. Because of this, many people now believe that the Paralympics should no longer be held separately from the regular Olympic Games. Exhibition events for physically disabled athletes at the 1988 Winter and

▲ Paul Clark (33) and Andre Viger (31), wheelchair division. Canadian Marathon Championship, 1987.

◄ Keith Lewis (24), Leslie Lam (33), and Jerry Tonello (15), wheelchair basketball. Spitfire Challenge Championship, 1987.

Summer Olympic Games—cross-country skiing at Calgary and wheelchair racing at Seoul—may help pave the way for making the Paralympics part of the regular Olympic program in the future. If that happens it will prove the point that disabled athletes have been making all along—in sport it's the ability, not the disability, that counts.

"REACH NEW HEIGHTS"

▲ Jeff Tiessen, track and field, amputee division. Silver medal, 1984 Paralympics.

◄ Cerebral palsy world record holders: Elaine Hewitt, track and swimming; Susie Chick, cycling; Laura Misciagna, wheelchair racing; Robert Mearns, track.

The Race for the Olive Crown

by Rosemary Sutcliff

Though Athens and Sparta were at war, the truce held in honor of the Olympic Games allowed Amyntas, an Athenian boy, and Leon, a Spartan, to meet and become friends at the Games. They soon realized that they would be each other's greatest rival in their event, the Double Stade footrace. When Leon cut his foot, it was almost impossible for Amyntas to keep from wondering whether the injury would affect Leon's chance of winning the race.

To keep away unworthy thoughts, Amyntas spent all his money on a special offering to Zeus, asking only to keep a clean heart and run the best race that was in him. Then, at last, it was the day of the race. . . .

"Now it's us!" someone said; and the boys were sprinting down the covered way, out into the open sun-drenched space of the Stadium.

The turf banks on either side of the broad track, and the lower slopes of the Kronon Hill that looked down upon it, were packed with a vast multitude of onlookers. Halfway down on the right-hand side, raised above the tawny grass on which everybody else sat, were the benches for the Council, looking across to the white marble seat opposite, where the Priestess of Demeter, the only woman allowed at the Games, sat as still as though she herself were carved from marble, among all the jostling, swaying, noisy throng. Men were raking over the silver sand on the track. The trumpeter stood ready.

They had taken their places now behind the long white limestone curbs of the starting line. The Umpire was calling: "Runners! Feet to the lines!"

from The Truce of the Games

Amyntas felt the scorching heat of the limestone as he braced the ball of his right foot into the shaped groove. All the panic of a while back had left him, he felt light, and clear headed, and master of himself. He had drawn the sixth place, with Leon on his left and the boy from Megara on his right. Before him the track stretched white in the sunlight, an infinity of emptiness and distance.

The starting trumpet yelped; and the line of runners sprang forward like a wave of hunting dogs slipped from the leash.

Amyntas was running smoothly and without hurry. Let the green front runners push on ahead. In this heat they would have burned themselves out before they reached the turning post. He and Leon were running neck and neck with the red-headed Macedonian. The Rhodian had gone ahead now after the front runners, the rest were still bunched. Then the Corinthian made a sprint and passed the boy from Rhodes, but fell back almost at once. The white track was reeling back underfoot, the turning post racing towards them. The bunch had thinned out, the front runners beginning to drop back already; and as they came up towards the turning post, first the boy from Macedon, and then Nikomedes catching

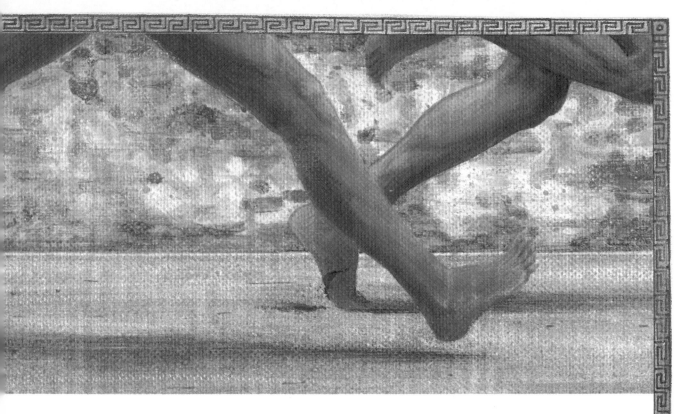

fire at last, slid into the lead, with Amyntas and Leon close behind them. Rounding the post, Amyntas skidded on the loose sand and Leon went ahead; and it was then, seeing the lean scarred back ahead of him, that Amyntas lengthened his stride, knowing that the time had come to run. They were a quarter of the way down the home lap when they passed Nikomedes; the Megaran boy had taken fire too late. They were beginning to overhaul the redhead; and Amyntas knew in his bursting heart that unless something unexpected happened, the race must be between himself and Leon. Spartan and Macedonian were going neck and neck now; the position held for a few paces, and then the redhead gradually fell behind. Amyntas was going all out, there was pain in his breast and belly and in the backs of his legs, and he did not know where his next breath was coming from; but still the thin scarred back was just ahead. The crowd were beginning to give tongue, seeing the two come through to the front; a solid roar of sound that would go on rising now until they passed the finishing post. And then suddenly Amyntas knew that something was wrong; Leon was laboring a little, beginning to lose the first keen edge of his speed. Snatching a glance downward, he saw a fleck of crimson in the sand. The cut had re-opened.

His body went on running, but for a sort of splinter of time his head seemed quite apart from the rest of him, and filled with an unmanageable swirl of thoughts and feelings. Leon might have passed the top of his speed anyway, it might be nothing to do with his foot—But the cut *had* re-opened. . . . To lose the race because of a cut foot. . . . It would be so easy not to make that final desperate effort that his whole body was crying out against. Then Leon would keep his lead. . . . And at the same time another part of himself was remembering his father standing on the quayside at Piraeus as the *Paralos* drew away—crying out that he was not running only for himself but for Athens, his City and his people. . . . A crown of wild olive would be the greatest thing that anyone could give to his friend. . . . It would be to insult Leon to let him win . . . you could not do that to your friend. . . . And then like a clean cold sword of light cutting through the swirling tangle of his thoughts, came the knowledge that greater than any of these things were the Gods. These were the Sacred Games, not some mere struggle between boys in the gymnasium. For one fleeting instant of time he remembered himself standing in the Temple before the great statue of Zeus, holding the tiny bronze bull with the silvered horns. "Let me run the best race that is in me, and think of nothing more."

He drove himself forward in one last agonizing burst of speed, he was breathing against knives, and the roar of the blood in his ears drowned the roar of the crowd. He was level with Leon—and then there was nothing ahead of him but the winning post.

The onlookers had crowded right down towards it; even above the howl of the blood in his head he heard them now, roar on solid roar of sound, shouting him on to victory. And then Hippias had caught him as he plunged past the post; and he was bending over the trainer's arm, bending over the pain in his belly, snatching at his breath and trying not to be sick. People were throwing sprigs of myrtle, he felt them flicking and falling on his head and shoulders. The sickness eased a little and his head was clearing; he began to hear friendly voices congratulating him; and Eudorus came shouldering through the crowd with a colored ribbon to tie round his head. But when he looked round for Leon, the Spartan boy had been swept away by his trainer. And a queer desolation rose in Amyntas and robbed his moment of its glory.

Afterwards in the changing room, some of the other boys came up to congratulate him. Leon did not come; but when they had cleaned off the sand and oil and sweat, and sluiced down with the little water that was allowed them, Amyntas hung about, sitting on the well curb outside while the trainer finished seeing to his friend's foot. And when Leon came out at last, he came straight across to the well, as though they had arranged to meet there. His face was as unreadable as usual.

"You will have cooled off enough by now, do you want to drink?" Amyntas said, mainly because somebody had to say something; and dipped the bronze cup that always stood on the well curb in the pail that he had drawn.

Leon took the cup from him and drank, and sat down on the well curb beside him. As Amyntas dipped the cup again and bent his head to drink in his turn, the ends of the victor's ribbon fell forward against his cheek, and he pulled it off impatiently, and dropped it beside the well.

"Why did you do that?" Leon said.

"I shall never be sure whether I won that race."

"The judges are not often mistaken, and I never heard yet of folk tying victors' ribbons on the wrong man."

Amyntas flicked a thumb at Leon's bandaged foot. "You know well enough what I mean. I'll never be sure whether I'd have come first past the post, if that hadn't opened up again."

Leon looked at him a moment in silence, then flung up his head and laughed. "Do you really think that could make any difference? It would take more than a cut foot to slow me up, Athenian!—You ran the better race, that's all."

It was said on such a harsh, bragging note that in the first moment Amyntas felt as though he had been struck in the face. Then he wondered if it was the overwhelming Spartan pride giving tongue, or simply Leon, hurt and angry and speaking the truth. Either way, he was too tired to be angry back again. And whichever it was, it seemed that Leon had shaken it off already. The noon break was over, and the trumpets were sounding for the Pentathlon.

"Up!" Leon said, when Amyntas did not move at once. "Are you going to let it be said that your own event is the only one that interests you?"

They went, quickly and together, while the trainer's eye was off them, for Leon was under orders to keep off his foot. And the people cheered them both when they appeared in the Stadium. They seldom cared much for a good loser, but Leon had come in a close second, and they had seen the blood in the sand.

The next day the heavyweight events were held; and then it was the last day of all, the Crowning Day. Ever after, Amyntas remembered that day as a quietness after great stress and turmoil. It was not, in truth, much less noisy than the days that had gone before. The roaring of the Stadium crowds was gone; but in the town of tents the crowds milled to and fro. The jugglers with knives and the eaters of fire shouted for an audience and the merchants cried their wares; and within the Sacred Enclosure where the winners received their crowns and made their sacrifices before the Temples of Zeus and Hera, there were the flutes and the songs in praise of the victors, and the deep-voiced invocations to the Gods.

But in Amyntas himself, there was the quiet. He remembered the Herald crying his name, and the light springy coolness of the wild olive crown as it was pressed down on his head; and later, the spitting light of pine torches under the plane trees, where the officials and athletes were feasting. And he remembered most, looking up out of the torchlight, and seeing, high and remote above it all, the winged tripods on the roof of the great Temple, outlined against the light of a moon two days past the full.

The boys left before the feasting was over; and in his sleeping cell Amyntas heard the poets singing in praise of some chariot team, and the applause, while he gathered his few belongings together, ready for tomorrow's early start, and stowed his olive crown among them. Already the leaves were beginning to wilt after the heat of the day. The room that had seemed so strange the first night was familiar now; part of himself; and after tonight it would not know him anymore.

Next morning in all the hustle of departure, he and Leon contrived to meet and slip off for a little on their own.

The whole valley of Olympia was a chaos of tents and booths being

taken down, merchants as well as athletes and onlookers making ready for the road. But the Sacred Enclosure itself was quiet, and the gates stood open. They went through, into the shade of the olive trees before the Temple of Zeus. A priest making the morning offering at a side altar looked at them; but they seemed to be doing no harm, and to want nothing, so he let them alone. There was a smell of frankincense in the air, and the early morning smell of last night's heavy dew on parched ground. They stood among the twisted trunks and low-hanging branches, and looked at each other and did not know what to say. Already they were remembering that there was war between Athens and Sparta, that the Truce of the Games would last them back to their own states, but no further; and the longer the silence lasted, the more they remembered.

From beyond the quiet of the Enclosure came all the sounds of the great concourse breaking up; voices calling, the stamping of impatient horses. "By this time tomorrow everyone will be gone," Amyntas said at last. "It will be just as it was before we came, for another four years."

"The Corinthians are off already."

"Catching the cool of the morning for those fine chariot horses," Amyntas said, and thought, There's so little time, why do we have to waste it like this?

"One of the charioteers had that hunting knife with the silver inlay. The one you took a fancy to. Why didn't you buy it after all?"

"I spent the money on something else." For a moment Amyntas was afraid that Leon would ask what. But the other boy only nodded and let it go.

He wished suddenly that he could give Leon something, but there was nothing among his few belongings that would make sense in the Spartan's world. It was a world so far off from his own. Too far to reach out, too far to call. Already they seemed to be drifting away from each other, drifting back to a month ago, before they had even met. He put out a hand quickly, as though to hold the other boy back for one more moment, and Leon's hand came to meet it.

"It has been good. All this month it has been good," Leon said.

"It has been good," Amyntas agreed. He wanted to say, "Until the next Games, then." But manhood and military service were only a few months away for both of them; if they did meet at another Games, there would be the faces of dead comrades, Spartan or Athenian, between them; and like enough, for one of them or both, there might be no other Games. Far more likely, if they ever saw each other again, it would be over the tops of their shields.

He had noticed before how, despite their different worlds, he and Leon sometimes thought the same thing at the same time, and answered each other as though the thought had been spoken. Leon said in his abrupt, dead-level voice, "The Gods be with you, Amyntas, and grant that we never meet again."

They put their arms round each other's necks and strained fiercely close for a moment, hard cheekbone against hard cheekbone.

"The Gods be with you, Leon."

And then Eudorus was calling, "Amyntas! Amyntas! We're all waiting!"

And Amyntas turned and ran—out through the gateway of the Sacred Enclosure, towards where the Athenian party were ready to start, and Eudorus was already coming back to look for him.

As they rode up from the Valley of Olympia and took the track towards the coast, Amyntas did not look back. The horses' legs brushed the dry dust-gray scrub beside the track, and loosed the hot aromatic scents of wild lavender and camomile and lentisk upon the air. A yellow butterfly hovered past, and watching it out of sight, it came to him suddenly, that he and Leon had exchanged gifts of a sort, after all. It was hard to give them a name, but they were real enough. And the outward and visible sign of his gift to Leon was in the little bronze bull with the silvered horns that he had left on the Offering Table before the feet of Olympian Zeus. And Leon's gift to him. . . . That had been made with the Spartan's boast that it would take more than a cut foot to slow him up. He had thought at the time that it was either the harsh Spartan pride, or the truth spoken in anger. But he understood now, quite suddenly, that it had been Leon giving up his own private and inward claim to the olive crown, so that he, Amyntas, might believe that he had rightfully won it. Amyntas knew that he would never be sure of that, never in all his life. But it made no difference to the gift.

The track had begun to run downhill, and the pale dust cloud was rising behind them. He knew that if he looked back now, there would be nothing to see.

Detail of *Kispiax Village* by Emily M. Carr

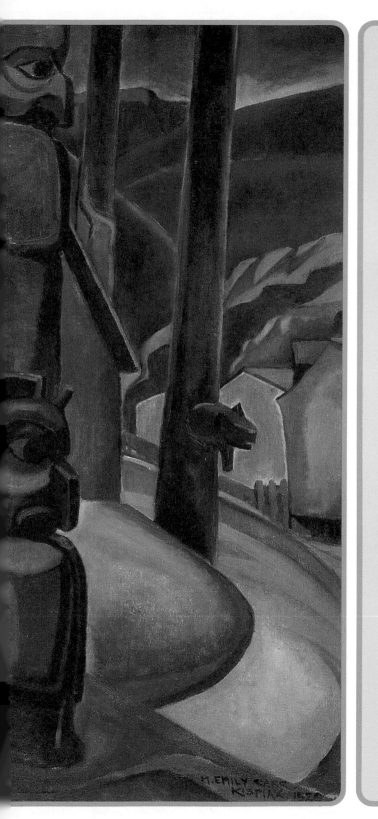

Larger than Life

Arachne

by Doris Gates

The family of Immortals dwelling on Mount Olympus was jealous of its power. Sometimes they were jealous of one another, and as in most families there were often quarrels among them. But they were united in their intolerance of any mortal who dared defy them. Such arrogance the Greeks called *hubris,* which was always punished swiftly by Nemesis, the goddess of retribution. We still use both words in our speech today. By hubris we mean not defiance of the gods but an insolent pride. Nemesis is the punishment that follows on the trail of anyone who considers himself invincible.

The story of Arachne is the story of a girl who dared defy Athena, and who suffered nemesis as a result.

Arachne was a country maiden who was famous throughout the land for her skill at weaving. No person on Earth, it was said, could weave so skilfully as she. There were some who said that not even Athena, goddess of all household arts, could weave so well as Arachne.

Among these arrogant boasters was Arachne herself, who was not at all modest about her skill. She never bothered to consider it a gift of the gods, nor was she ever humbly grateful for it. Instead, she was foolishly proud of it and even made fun of the work of girls less gifted than she. But then, one had to admit it was a wondrous sight to see her fingers moving lightly and swiftly back and forth across her loom. Her designs were intricate and beautiful, and she wove the colors of her threads with the ease and smoothness of an artist working with brush and paint. So graceful was she in all her motions that often the wood nymphs left their shadowy hiding places to watch her at work.

In time Arachne's fame and her boasting reached the ears of Athena, and the goddess decided to draw the girl into a contest that would cure her arrogant pride.

One day, when Arachne was weaving in a pleasant grove, there suddenly appeared beside her a bent old woman. She gazed for a moment at Arachne's loom and then said, "That is a pretty piece of weaving, my dear, and yet I have seen the time in my youth when I could have done as well."

At this Arachne threw up her head and said in a scornful tone, "Never did any mortal weave as I am weaving now, old woman."

"Those are rash words," said the old woman, and a strange angry light came into her gray eyes, which were exceedingly youthful for one so bent with years. "It is foolish to take too great pride in what one can do, for surely there is always someone who can do the task even better."

"Not so," cried the angry girl. "There is no one who can weave better than I."

The old woman smiled and shook her head doubtfully. "Allowing that no mortal can weave as well as you, at least among the Immortals there is one who can surpass you in the art."

Arachne left off her weaving to stare at the old woman. "And who is that, pray?"

"The goddess Athena," replied the old woman.

Arachne laughed scornfully. "Not even Athena can weave as well as I."

At these words, the wood nymphs who had come to watch Arachne began to whisper among themselves. They were frightened, for it was dangerous for any mortal to set himself above the gods in anything. Foolish Arachne!

On hearing the boastful words, the old woman's eyes again flashed angrily. But in a moment they softened, and she said, "You are young and have spoken foolishly and in haste. Surely you did not mean what you said. I will give you a chance to take back your words."

But Arachne flung up her head defiantly. "I did mean what I said, and I shall prove it."

"Prove it then," cried the old woman in a terrible voice. A cry went up from the encircling crowd, and Arachne's face turned white as a cloud bank. For the old woman had vanished, and in her place stood the shining form of the goddess Athena.

"For long," she said, "I have heard your boasting and have watched your growing vanity. Now it has led you to defy the very gods. It is time you received a lesson from which other mortals as foolish and vain as you may profit. Let the contest begin."

Another loom was set up in the pleasant grove, and Arachne and the goddess began to weave. News of the contest spread through the quiet meadow and up the mountain heights. Soon a large crowd of shepherds drew near to watch the weavers.

Athena wove upon her loom a bright tapestry that told the story of other foolish mortals who had thought themselves greater than the gods, and who had been punished for their pride. Arachne pictured on her loom the stories that told of the foolish acts of the gods.

The colors used by the two weavers were so bright they might have been plucked from the rainbow. The weaving was so perfect that the figures on each loom seemed to be alive and breathing. The watchers marvelled that such skill could be on Earth or in heaven.

At last the tapestries were finished, and the two contestants stood back to see what each had wrought upon her loom. Athena was so angered by what the girl had dared to picture in her work that she struck the tapestry with her shuttle, splitting the cloth in two. Then she struck Arachne on the forehead. Immediately there swept over the girl a deep remorse at her vanity in setting herself above the very gods. So great was her shame that she went at once and hanged herself. But when Athena beheld her lifeless body, she took pity upon the foolish Arachne.

"Live," she said, "but never must you be allowed to forget the lesson you have learned today. Though you may live, you must hang throughout all eternity—you and all who come after you and are of your flesh and blood."

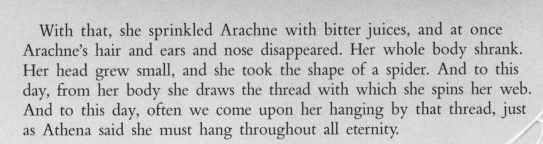

With that, she sprinkled Arachne with bitter juices, and at once Arachne's hair and ears and nose disappeared. Her whole body shrank. Her head grew small, and she took the shape of a spider. And to this day, from her body she draws the thread with which she spins her web. And to this day, often we come upon her hanging by that thread, just as Athena said she must hang throughout all eternity.

Tales of Pan

by Mordicai Gerstein

*Long, long ago, a family of
gods lived in ancient Greece. They
lived on top of Mount Olympus,
under great craggy clouds that
looked like whipped cream.*

*Zeus, the thunder god, was the king
and father of most of them. His many
children had children, and they all had uncles
and aunts and lots of cousins. They were all gods
of one thing or another. Most of the books about
them tell us how great, grand, and powerful they were.
But they could also be stupid, bad tempered, and silly, just like any other family.*

*The god Pan was one of them. He wasn't the greatest or grandest god. He didn't
want to be. He certainly wasn't the best looking. But he was the silliest, and the one
that delighted the hearts of all the others.*

The ancient Greeks sang hymns to Pan.

*"All hail to Pan," they sang. "Goat-footed, two-horned lover of noisy confusion!"
They made him offerings of wine and honey, but they also liked to joke and tell stories
about him and his relatives behind their backs.*

*Here are some of those stories about Pan and his family and the grand and silly
things they did.*

Pan Leaves Olympus

There were quarrels and occasional screaming fights, but usually Olympus was a fairly peaceful place. Pan arrived and changed it.

He climbed up and down the pillars and galloped through the throne

rooms shrieking. He threw Zeus's thunderbolts at Queen Hera. He used Uncle Apollo's harp to shoot Aunt Artemis's arrows at Uncle Ares. He laughed and made confetti out of Hermes' mail. At one day old, he was the fully grown god of noise and confusion.

"He delights my heart, but he'll drive me mad!" complained Zeus to Hermes.

"He's a menace!" shrilled Queen Hera. "And the palace looks and smells like a goat pen!"

All Pan heard from his family was "Shush!" or "Be serious!" or "Grow up!"

He tried to do as they asked. He practised sitting on his throne but it was boring. He wandered through the palace with its endless towering pillars and he felt lonely. Then he looked down at Arcadia where he'd been born. It was green and sparkling in the summer sun.

"That's where I belong!" said Pan. And with one great leap, and a howl that rocked the palace, Pan left Olympus.

All the other gods sighed a great sigh of relief. Pan landed in Arcadia, *splash!* right in the middle of a giggling stream.

"This is more like it," he said.

Pan Makes Arcadia His Home

Pan skipped and danced through the woods. Up the hills he ran to the rocky cliffs. He leapfrogged over leopards and raced mountain goats to the tops of peaks. Then he left them all behind, and leaped up mountains the goats couldn't climb. He jumped to the top of the highest, rockiest, snow-capped peak, and there Pan caught his breath and looked around. He could see all of Arcadia. There were nymphs everywhere: beautiful spirits of tree, flower, and fountain. He saw wild animals and birds of all kinds. Far below he saw hunters, shepherds, and beekeepers.

And because each god had to look after something, Pan decided to look after all of them. *"Yahooo!"* he yowled, and jumped for joy.

Then he skipped down the mountain, clapping and whistling to all the people and creatures of Arcadia.

"I am Pan!" he shouted. "I am a new god! From now on shepherds will never lose their sheep, nor sheep their shepherds. All the hives will overflow with honey, and hunters will never go hungry!"

All the people, creatures, and nymphs danced after him, clapping and cheering.

He showed them how to build proper shrines to him, and how to leave him offerings of honey, roast venison, red wine, and flowers. He watched delighted as they went off and did as he'd told them. Pan stretched and scratched his back against a tree. Then he smiled, curled up in the cool grass, and took a nap.

Pan Shouts and Invents Panic

Pan loved noise and confusion, but he also loved his afternoon naps. When Pan napped, all Arcadia, birds, beasts, and beekeepers, had to walk on tiptoe and whisper.

One afternoon while Pan was napping under a fig tree, an ant with a cold

tiptoed by. When the ant sneezed, Pan jumped up and shouted: "CAN'TYOUSEEI'MSLEEPINGKEEP THENOISEDOWN!"

It was the loudest, most surprising shout ever heard. All the sheep in Arcadia jumped straight up, their wool stuck straight out, and they ran off in every direction, while the shepherds ran in circles, and all the birds, butterflies, and bees zoomed from one end of Arcadia to the other, bumping into the rabbits, foxes, and nymphs, who got all tangled in the trees, bushes, and vines. Even Echo, way up in her craggy canyon, was so startled she was speechless.

It was a day and a half before everyone calmed down, and the ant that started it all was never seen a-gain. Pan himself was very impressed.

"What was that?" the people and creatures all asked each other.

"I call it *panic!*" said Pan, proudly. "I just invented it!"

From then on Pan used this special shout whenever someone disturbed his naps. Sometimes he used it against enemies, or to help friends or relatives in trouble. Other times he used it to scare people out of their wits, just for fun. At one time or another, everyone got a taste of "panic."

Icarus Sunset

by Richard Scrimger

Wheeling across the sky at dusk, wings outspread
Long-feathered fingers cherishing the wind,
The eagle came to them.
They watched her, high on the tower, a man and a boy
Watched the soaring minister of the air.
See, said the man, See, Icarus, how
She turns into the wind to rise,
Away to fall
Mark how she steers herself.
And the man thought, It is freedom, escape from prison
And the boy thought, It is power.
Remember, Icarus, with the wings on your back, to
Follow me, do as I do.
Yes, father.
But the boy was watching the eagle still
As she flew into the heart of the setting sun
And vanished into gold.

Long labored Daedalus, making his freedom
Carefully choosing the feathers, cunningly
Shaping the wax,
And each day the boy and he waited for the eagle
As the dusk gathered round them
And the sun fell into darkness.

Now, father? said the boy, poised on
The parapet, feathered arms wide, facing the morning.
Now, said the maker, leaping.

The wind bore them gently away,
On its back they rode as birds do
As eagles, as gods.
Follow, Icarus, cried his father
Remember, follow me.
But the boy, deaf with power, heard only
The Sun's voice, coaxing him higher.
Rise with me, Icarus, whispered the god,
I will welcome you.

Far below, Daedalus, fearful with knowledge
Strained his eyes upward, waiting for the
Hurtling blackened body that
Passed without speaking and vanished
Into the sea.

Little Badger and the Fire Spirit

by Maria Campbell

It was a long time ago when our mother, the Earth, was young. In those days, people and animals all spoke one language. There was one animal who was a very good friend of the people and he often came to visit them. His name was Gray Coyote.

Now, Gray Coyote was a gentle and considerate creature. He was also very wise. When he visited, the people all gathered around and listened to him speak. Gray Coyote had one friend who was special, a boy named Little Badger.

Gray Coyote and Little Badger spent many hours talking. You see, Little Badger was blind. Gray Coyote took him on many long walks in the forest. He taught Little Badger about the Earth he could not see, and how to smell, hear, and touch all the things around him. He taught him that everything on the earth—human, animal, insect, or plant—had a purpose. This purpose was to serve and help each other.

Little Badger's people lived in a world of plenty. Mother Earth gave them all they needed. There was never any want. However, with so much good, there had to be some bad. For Little Badger's people, the bad was the long, cold winters. On winter days, the people took refuge in their teepees, huddled together for warmth.

One cold day, as Little Badger shivered under his robe, he thought: *There must be some way for us to be warm. But how? Gray Coyote will know what to do. I will go and find him.*

And he set off to find Gray Coyote.

Outside, the wind howled in rage and blew snow around Little Badger's head. He pulled his robe tightly around himself and started for the forest.

Gray Coyote told me if I ever needed him, I was to sit under this pine tree and think very hard. He said he would hear me and come, thought Little Badger. He sat down under the tall pine and began to concentrate on Gray Coyote.

Gray Coyote was trotting through the forest when he heard a voice calling to him. He stopped and listened.

It is Little Badger, he thought. *I must hurry. He sounds very weak.*

Gray Coyote headed for the pine tree as fast as he could run. When he arrived, Little Badger was so cold his teeth rattled when he tried to talk.

"What is wrong, Little Brother?" asked Gray Coyote.

"My people are freezing to death," chattered Little Badger. "You must help us."

"How thoughtless of me," said Gray Coyote. "I have a warm coat, and I never thought of my brothers and sisters. Here, I will shield you from the cold." Gray Coyote wrapped himself around Little Badger.

"You must help us, Gray Coyote," Little Badger pleaded. "You are wise. There must be some way for us to keep warm in the winter."

Gray Coyote thought and thought. Slowly he said, "Yes, there is a way, Little Brother, but it is very dangerous."

"Tell me, Gray Coyote, before my people perish," cried Little Badger.

"There is a mountain far away from our land. Inside the mountain is fire. This fire is strange. It feeds on wood and rock and it burns forever. It would provide warmth for the people. But someone must go inside the mountain to get it."

"I will go," said Little Badger.

"Wait. I am not finished," warned Gray Coyote. "Inside the mountain lives the Fire Spirit. He has four strange creatures who stand guard for him.

"There is Mountain Goat, who can stab you with his horns, Mountain Lion, who can tear you apart with his claws, Grizzly Bear, who can kill you with one slap of his mighty paw, and Rattlesnake, whose teeth hold deadly poison. And remember, Little Brother, you are blind and will not be able to see these dangers."

"I will still go," insisted Little Badger. "Will you take me to this place?"

Gray Coyote thought for a while.

"Yes, I will take you. Go back to your people. Find among them one hundred of the fastest runners. Bring them here tomorrow when the sun comes up."

"Where are you going?" asked Little Badger as Gray Coyote turned to leave.

"I am going to call the spirits to help us," said Gray Coyote as he trotted away.

The next morning, when Little Badger met Gray Coyote by the pine tree, he had with him one hundred of the fastest runners and the wise men of the tribe. They held council, and the wise men asked the Great Spirit for strength, endurance, and courage for Little Badger, Gray Coyote, and the runners.

Then Gray Coyote spoke.

"I have talked to the spirits and they have given me guidance for our journey. They will do all in their power to help us reach the great mountain. Once we are there, Little Badger must go into the mountain alone. No power can help him until he has climbed back outside with the fire."

Now Gray Coyote said to the runners: "You must follow the direction in which I am pointing. That is where the mountain is."

He turned to the first runner. "You must run with Little Badger on your shoulders. When you have run as far as you can, the second runner will take Little Badger and do the same thing. You must wait where you are. When the last runner has gone as far as he can, I will meet him. From there, Little Badger and I will go on alone.

"I have told you of the journey there," continued Gray Coyote. "Now I will tell you of the journey back. Instead of carrying Little Badger, you will carry a stick of burning wood. You will bring it back here the same way you carried Little Badger. When you arrive here, the people of the tribe will feed the fire with small pieces of wood and keep it burning until Little Badger and I return."

The runners nodded and, picking up Little Badger, the first one started off. He ran so fast Little Badger felt he was flying through the air.

Finally, after many days, the last runner went as far as he could go. When he stopped, Gray Coyote appeared and led Little Badger to the foot of the mountain.

"Here is the mountain, Little Brother," said Gray Coyote. "From here the spirits will guide and help you to the top. Once you reach the top, you must climb down the hole and get the fire yourself. When you have the fire and have climbed out, the spirits will help you down again. I will beat this drum and sing until you return."

Little Badger took a deep breath. He was frightened, but he knew that if he failed, his people would continue to die from the cold. He listened to the beat of the drum. Suddenly, he did not feel frightened anymore and he began to climb. As he climbed, he felt the spirit of the wind steadying him, and the spirit of the rocks made the way smooth. When he reached the top, he stopped to rest. He felt a last breath of air, then it was gone and he knew he was alone. The spirits had left him.

Little Badger stood wondering how he was going to find the opening in the mountain. He began to move around slowly and to feel with his hands. A wave of warm air touched him and he knew he had found the entrance to the place of fire. He stopped and listened for a moment. When he again heard the drum Gray Coyote was beating, he carefully started down.

Suddenly, Little Badger heard a gruff voice: "WHAT ARE YOU DOING HERE? THIS PLACE IS FORBIDDEN TO YOU!"

Almost paralyzed with fear, he stayed very still. He knew he had come upon one of the guardians of the fire as it was told to him by Gray Coyote, but he did not know which one.

"I have come to see the Fire Spirit," he said, his voice shaking. "My people are cold and he is the only one who can help us."

"NO ONE CAN SEE THE FIRE SPIRIT," said the gruff voice. "YOU CANNOT PASS BY ME. IF YOU TRY, THEN I WILL KILL YOU."

Little Badger's heart pounded with fear. He had no weapons. He could not even see his enemy. As he clung to the rock ledge, he could hear Gray Coyote's drum beating. The sound comforted him, and his fear was

gone. He reached out towards the voice. When he touched the creature, it trembled, and Little Badger could feel coarse hair.

"WHY DO YOU DO THAT?" grumbled the creature. "NO ONE TOUCHES ME. MY HORNS COULD TEAR YOU APART." The words were angry, but the voice was frightened.

"Do not be afraid," said Little Badger gently. "I will not hurt you. As you can see, I have no weapons. I am blind. To know who you are, I must touch you. Ah, you are the Mountain Goat."

When Little Badger touched the Mountain Goat, he felt peace come over them. He told the creature of his mission.

The goat listened, then said, "I WILL LET YOU GO BY, BUT I CANNOT HELP YOU GO BACK. BEWARE. THERE ARE THREE MORE GUARDIANS YOU MUST PASS BEFORE YOU REACH THE FIRE SPIRIT. I WISH YOU GOOD FORTUNE, LITTLE BROTHER."

Little Badger continued climbing down inside the mountain. As he descended, he could feel the heat of the fire. When he heard a soft growl, he knew he had met the Mountain Lion.

Little Badger reached out and touched the animal. As he stroked the smooth fur, he told the Lion of his people. They could hear the drum far off in the distance and again peace settled over both of them.

Little Badger continued his slow climb down. He knew he still had to meet the Grizzly Bear and the Rattlesnake, but he was no longer afraid. If things went on as they had, he knew he would make two new friends.

It was true. When he met the Grizzly Bear and touched him, they became friends. The Bear warned him that the Rattlesnake was very dangerous.

"YOU MUST BE VERY CAREFUL, LITTLE BROTHER," he rumbled in his great voice, as the boy turned to go. "YOU MUST USE WISDOM TO GET BY RATTLER, FOR HIS MEDICINE IS VERY POWERFUL."

Little Badger continued his climb down towards the fire. Soon he met the Rattlesnake. The Snake coiled, rattled his tail, and raised his mighty head up to strike.

When Little Badger heard the sound of the rattle, he quickly said, "You must be the Snake. What a beautiful rattle you have."

Rattlesnake was so surprised that someone, especially a small boy, would dare to talk to him, and find him beautiful, that he relaxed without even realizing he had done so.

"WHY ARE YOU NOT AFRAID OF ME?" he hissed.

"I do not want to hurt you, so why should you want to hurt me?" replied Little Badger.

Rattlesnake was astonished at the little boy's words. He was thinking about what the boy had said and did not notice him leave to continue his climb.

Little Badger had almost finished his journey to meet the Fire Spirit. It was so hot, he felt his braids must be singed. He was also very tired and he stumbled. As he tried to catch his balance, a voice crackled, "NO HUMAN BEING HAS EVER SEEN THE HOME OF THE FIRE SPIRIT. WHY ARE YOU HERE?"

Little Badger knew that at last he had met the Fire Spirit.

"I cannot see your home," replied Little Badger, "for I am blind. It is very warm. If my people lived here, they would never be cold."

"COLD? COLD?" said the Fire Spirit. "WHAT IS COLD?"

As he talked, he flamed up and all the colors of the rainbow seemed to glow around him.

Little Badger could not see the flames but he felt a gust of warm air as the Spirit spoke.

"When the snows come," explained Little Badger, "my people are very cold. There is not enough warmth from the sun, so many of them die. I have come to ask you for fire to warm my people."

"TELL ME MORE," said the Fire Spirit. "I HAVE NEVER TALKED TO A HUMAN BEFORE AND THERE IS MUCH I DO NOT KNOW."

Little Badger sat down. He told the Fire Spirit about his land and his people. He told of his journey into the heart of the mountain and of the friends he had made along the way. The Fire Spirit was quiet for a long time. All that Little Badger could hear was the hiss of his flames.

Finally the Spirit spoke: "HOW LONG HAVE YOU BEEN BLIND?"

"All my life," replied Little Badger. "But I can feel and hear very well. Gray Coyote has taught me. He is like my eyes."

"GRAY COYOTE? WHO IS HE?" asked the Spirit.

"Gray Coyote is my friend," said Little Badger. He told the Fire Spirit how his friend had taught him about the world.

"He brought me to this mountain and he is waiting for me now. Listen. Can you hear him? He is beating a drum."

The Fire Spirit listened. "YES, I CAN HEAR HIM," he replied.

"The drum gave me courage and strength," said Little Badger. "It helped me make new friends."

Little Badger and the Fire Spirit sat together for a long time and listened to the faint beating of the drum.

"IT IS STRONG AND BEAUTIFUL MUSIC," said the Fire Spirit. "I WILL NEVER FORGET IT. . . . HERE, TAKE THIS BURNING STICK. IT IS THE WARMTH OF FRIENDSHIP THAT YOU BROUGHT TO THIS PLACE. IT WILL KEEP YOUR PEOPLE WARM FOREVER."

Little Badger was bursting with gratitude.

"DO NOT THANK ME FOR IT, LITTLE BROTHER. YOU SHARED YOUR WARMTH WITH ME, AND I WILL SHARE MINE WITH YOU. WHEN YOU REACH THE TOP OF THE MOUNTAIN, YOU WILL NO LONGER BE BLIND. YOU WILL SEE THE WORLD THAT YOUR FRIEND, GRAY COYOTE, HAS TAUGHT YOU

ABOUT. GO NOW, HE
WAITS FOR YOU."

Little Badger took the stick, said goodbye to the Fire Spirit, and began to climb up out of the mountain. As he climbed, he met his friends and said goodbye to them also.

When he reached the top, with the stick of fire in his hand, he saw a great light. He saw the world for the first time in his life.

He stopped for a long time and looked and looked at the world. It was so beautiful. His eyes filled with tears of happiness. He felt the Spirit of the wind touch his hair gently and whisper, "Listen, Little Brother."

From far below, at the foot of the mountain, came the beating of the drum. As Little Badger listened, he heard two drums, then three.

How can there be three drums? he wondered. He listened again. Now there were four, five, then six drums. Soon the air was filled with the sound of many drums, all of different sizes, making different and beautiful sounds.

Suddenly Little Badger smiled. He knew. Gray Coyote's magic drum was his heartbeat. The other drums were the beating hearts of all living things.

Little Badger laughed as he climbed down the mountain. Around him was the sound of the drums, the pulse of the world, the music of the universe.

Savitri and Satyavan

by Madhur Jaffrey

nce upon a time there lived a King and Queen who, after many years of being childless, gave birth to a daughter.

She was the most beautiful baby the parents could have hoped for, and they named her Savitri.

When Savitri grew up and it was time for her to marry, her father said to her, "Dearest child, we hate to part with you. You have given us the greatest joy that humans can ever know. But it is time for you to start a family of your own. Is there any man you wish to marry?"

"No, father," replied Savitri, "I have not yet met a man I would care to spend my life with."

"Perhaps we should send for pictures of all the nobles in the country. You might come upon a face you like," said the King and he sent his court painter to bring back portraits of all the nobles and rulers in the country.

Savitri examined the portraits, one after the other, and shook her head. The men in the portraits all looked so very ordinary, even though they were all emperors, kings, and princes.

The King then said to his daughter, "It might be best if you went to all the big cities of the world to find a husband for yourself. I will provide you with the proper escort of men, elephants, camels, and horses. Good luck. I hope you can find a man to love."

Savitri set out with a large procession of men, elephants, camels, and horses. In her effort to visit all the cities of the world, she had to cross many oceans and deserts. She did this fearlessly. But she never found a man she could love.

When she returned home, her father said to her, "You have looked in all the big cities of the world and have found no man that you wish to marry. Perhaps you should now search through all the forests of the world."

Savitri set out again with a large procession of men, elephants, camels, and horses, and began searching through all the forests of the world. She did this fearlessly.

She had looked through the last forest and was just about to return home when she came upon a young man who was cutting wood.

"What is your name?" she asked.

"Satyavan, Your Highness," he replied.

"Please do not address me as 'Your Highness'," she said, "my name is Savitri. What do you do for a living?"

"I do nothing much," the young man replied. "I have very old, blind parents. I live with them in a small, thatched cottage at the edge of the forest. Every morning I go out to cut wood and gather food. In the evening I make a fire for my parents, cook their dinner, and feed them. That is all I do."

Savitri returned to her father's palace and said, "Dearest mother and father. I have finally found a man to love and marry. His name is Satyavan and he lives in a cottage by a forest not too far from here."

"But will you be able to live a simple life in a simple cottage?" asked her father. "This young man obviously has no money."

"That makes no difference at all to me," Savitri said. "He is capable, honest, good, and caring. That is what I respect and love him for."

The King sent a message to the blind couple's cottage saying that Princess Savitri wished to marry their son, Satyavan. When Satyavan arrived home that evening with his heavy load of wood his parents said, "There are messengers here from the King. Princess Savitri wishes to marry you."

"I love the young lady in question," replied Satyavan, "but it will be impossible to marry her. She has money, jewels, elephants, camels, and servants. What can *I* offer her?"

Tears rolled down the faces of his blind parents. "Son," cried the mother, "we never told you this, but long ago, before you were born, your father too was a ruler with a kingdom of his own. His wicked brother blinded us and stole our birthright. You should have been born a prince and heir to the kingdom, quite worthy of the beautiful Savitri. We have fallen on hard times, but if you two love each other, why should you not marry? Who knows what the future has in store for anybody?"

So a message was sent back to the King saying that Satyavan had agreed to the match.

On the day of the wedding, the King and Queen held a huge reception. Everyone of any importance was invited.

That is how it happened that the wisest Sage in the kingdom appeared at the scene.

Just before the wedding ceremony, the Sage took the King aside and whispered, "It is my duty to warn you. The young man your daughter is to marry is decent and of good character, but his stars are crossed. He will die very shortly. This marriage would be a tragic mistake."

The King felt ill when he heard this. He called his daughter and told her what the Sage had said, adding, "Perhaps it is best to call the marriage off."

"No, father," Savitri said solemnly, "I will marry Satyavan, whatever our future may hold."

Savitri was no fool, however. She had heard that the Sage knew of heavenly remedies for earthly problems.

"Oh dearest Sage," Savitri said to him, "surely there is a way I can prevent my husband from dying. You, in your great wisdom, must offer me some hope. There must be something I can do?"

The Sage thought deeply. "You can extend your husband's life by fasting. Eat nothing but fruit, roots, and leaves for a year, and Satyavan will live for those twelve months. After that he *must* die."

With a sense of doom hanging over the bride's family, the wedding did take place. The groom and his parents were told nothing of what the future held for them.

Savitri began to lead a simple life with her husband and parents-in-law. Early each morning, Satyavan set out for the forest to cut wood and to forage for food. When he was gone, Savitri made the beds, swept the house, and shepherded her in-laws around wherever they wished to go. She also prayed and fasted.

One day Savitri's mother-in-law said to her, "Child, we know how rich a family you come from. Since we have lost our kingdom, we can offer you no fineries, but Satyavan does collect enough food for all of us. We have noticed that you eat just fruit, roots, and leaves and never touch any grain. That is not a healthy diet. We are beginning to worry about you."

"Oh, please do not worry about me," begged Savitri. "I love to eat fruit."

The twelve months were almost over. On the very last day, Savitri got up with her husband and announced that she would accompany him into the forest.

"Child, what will you do in the forest? The work is hard and there are all kinds of dangerous animals," said her mother-in-law.

"Do stay home," said Satyavan, "the forest is not a comfortable place."

"I have travelled through all the forests of the world. I was not uncomfortable and I was not frightened. Let me go with you today."

Satyavan had no answer for his wife. He loved her a lot and trusted her instincts. "Come along then, we'd better start quickly. The sun is almost up."

So they set out towards the heart of the forest.

Once there, Satyavan climbed a tree and began to saw off its dried-up branches.

It was a scorchingly hot day in May. The trees had shed the last withered yellowing leaves. Savitri looked for a cool spot to sit down and just could not find any. Her heart was beating like a two-sided drum. Any moment now the year would end.

"Ahhh . . ." came a cry from Satyavan.

Savitri ran towards him, "Are you all right?"

"I have a piercing headache."

"Come down from the tree. It's the heat. I will run and find some shade." Savitri found a banyan tree and helped Satyavan towards it. Many of the banyan tree's branches had gone deep into the earth and come up again to form a deliciously cool grove. The leaves rustled gently to fan the couple.

"Put your head in my lap," Savitri said to Satyavan, "and rest."

Satyavan put his head down, gave a low moan, and died.

Savitri looked up. There, in the distance coming towards her, was

Yamraj, the King of the Underworld. He was riding a male water buffalo, and Savitri knew that he was coming to claim Satyavan's soul. She turned to the banyan tree and implored, "Banyan tree, banyan tree, look after my husband. Shield him and keep him cool. I will return one day to claim him."

Yamraj took Satyavan's soul and started to ride away. Savitri followed on foot. She followed for miles and miles. Yamraj finally turned around and said, "Why are you following me, woman?"

"You are taking my husband's soul away. Why don't you take me as well? I cannot live without him."

"Go back, go back to your home and do not bother me," Yamraj said. But Savitri kept following.

Yamraj turned around again. "Stop following me, woman," he cried. Savitri paid no heed to him.

"Well, woman," said Yamraj, "I can see that you are quite determined.

I will grant you just one wish. As long as you do not ask for your husband's soul."

"May my in-laws have their sight back?" asked Savitri.

"All right, all right," said Yamraj, "now go home."

After several more miles Yamraj glanced back. There was Savitri, still following.

"You really are quite persistant," Yamraj said. "I'll grant you one other wish. Just remember, do not ask for your husband's soul."

"Could my father-in-law get back the kingdom he lost?" Savitri asked.

"Yes, yes," said Yamraj, "now go, go."

Several miles later, Yamraj looked back again.

Savitri was still following.

"I do not understand you. I've granted you two wishes and yet you keep following me. This is the last wish I am offering you. Remember, you can ask for anything but your husband's soul."

"May I be the mother of many sons?" Savitri asked.

"Yes, yes," Yamraj said. "Now *go*. Go back home."

Several miles later Yamraj looked back only to see Savitri still there. "Why are you still following me?" Yamraj asked. "I have already granted you your wish of many sons."

"How will I have many sons?" Savitri asked. "You are carrying away the soul of the only husband I have. I will never marry again. You have granted me a false wish. It can *never* come true."

"I have had enough," Yamraj said. "I am quite exhausted. Here, take back your husband's soul."

Savitri rushed back to the banyan tree so her husband's body and soul could be joined again.

"O banyan tree," she said, "thank you for looking after my husband. In the years to come, may all married women come to you and offer thanks and prayers."

Satyavan opened his eyes and said, "My headache has gone."

"Yes," said Savitri, "thanks to the kind banyan tree that offered us its shade. Let us go home now where a surprise awaits you. I will not tell you what it is."

Satyavan put his arm around his wife's shoulders and they began to walk slowly back home.

Strong Man Who Holds Up the World

by Joan Skogan

 ges ago, when many of the Tsimshian people lived in Metlakatla Passage, the chief of one of the villages had four sons. The three older boys were lively, but the youngest one seemed lazy and slow and the others often teased him.

The time came for the men of the village to prepare for the sea-lion hunt. Far across the northern seas lay the rocky island where the sea lions gathered. The waves roared and crashed over the island. A man had to be able to leap to the rocks and overcome the huge beasts, or be killed himself.

The three older brothers were training for the hunt. Every morning they swam in the ocean to accustom their bodies to the cold. When they returned, their father, the chief, lashed their backs with berry branches to harden the boys to pain. They drank a brew from the devil's club plant, and wrenched the branches from spruce trees to develop their strength. While they tested themselves, their younger brother lay in the warm ashes beside the fire. His brothers scorned and insulted him, saying, "We would starve if we depended on you to hunt for us." But the boy slept on by the fire.

Unknown to the others, while they slept at night, the youngest boy swam alone in the cold, dark waters of the Pass. His body slipped easily through the waves as he swam out farther than the others had ever been, and each night went a little farther yet. He lashed his own back with branches, and sipped the devil's club tea before he slept by the fire. His brothers teased, "You are covered with ashes. Don't you ever bathe?" but he said nothing to them.

One night when he was swimming, a loon came towards him as if to speak. "What do you have to tell me, supernatural one?" said the boy.

The loon answered, "I have strength to give you, Brother. Take hold of my feet and we will dive together." The boy held onto the loon, and they dove to the bottom of the sea where a cave appeared. The loon instructed the boy, "Enter the cave and bathe in the spring you will find there. When you return to your village, you, too, must practise breaking the branches of the spruce trees. Say nothing of this to anyone."

The youngest brother did these things, and his strength grew until he could bend the spruce tree to the ground. All in the village were bitter against him now, yet he said nothing of his secret practices.

On the morning of the sea-lion hunt, the older brothers took their harpoons with cedar lines and stepped into the canoes. The youngest brother rose from his place by the fire and walked to the beach. "I will go with you," he said, but his uncles and the older men angrily refused to take him, saying, "You should have prepared yourself. A lazy, dirty fool like you will only be in the way."

His youngest uncle took pity on him. "You can come with me—surely you can help in some small ways. Perhaps you will learn something." The hunters paddled their canoes, lifting and falling on the long swells, until they heard the roaring of the sea lions on the high, barren rock.

One of the uncles stood in the bow of the first canoe and made ready to leap as it climbed the wave crest, but another wave caught them and crushed the canoe on the rocks. The men fell into the sea and were lost. The other hunters hung back. Then the youngest brother stood, balancing himself in the rolling canoe, calling, "I shall jump to the rock." Though the others believed he, too, would drown, they could not stop him. He leaped and clung to the rock, then ran to attack the largest sea lion. He thrust the animal over and broke its back. He killed several more sea lions before the rest escaped, then he slung the carcasses into the canoes plunging in the wild seas around the island. Every house in the village was rich with meat. For a time there was no more talk about the laziest boy in Metlakatla.

The youngest brother was growing to manhood, but he continued in his sleepy ways. People forgot that he had proved himself strong and brave. Winter turned to spring, and the men of Metlakatla began to prepare for the competitions of strength between the northern villages. The young man still slept in the ashes. Everyone said to him, "You are filthy—why can't you be like the others?" Only his youngest uncle said, "Leave him alone. Do not forget he shamed you all once."

As before, the youngest brother swam alone at night, often meeting the loon, who advised him to practise uprooting spruce trees to strengthen himself. This the young man did, until he could tear the largest trees from the earth and cast them into the ocean.

Those from distant villages gathered together with the people of Metlakatla for the tribal contests. A large pile of stones was collected for the first contest. For days the men took turns throwing. A man from the Nass River threw farther than the others, and his people were excited and taunted the Metlakatla people. When the young man who slept by the fire offered to take part, his own people yelled, "Filthy One, you have not trained at all! Do not bring any more shame upon us!"

But the youngest brother smiled, saying, "These stones you have used are fit only for children." He chose a huge boulder from the beach and threw it far past the stone of the Nass River man. His people danced and cheered, but the young man only wandered back to his fire.

He joined the contests again for the wrestling matches. A huge man, almost a giant, from Kitamaat Village, defeated the other competitors, and the Kitamaat people laughed and jeered, "Where is the Filthy One? He was lucky before. Let us see what he can do." When he whom they called "Filthy One" came to meet the Kitamaat champion, he seemed in danger of being killed by the giant. The Kitamaat man rushed forward, but the youngest brother grasped him and threw his body into the air, overcoming him completely. All the people murmured among themselves, for they realized now that this young man was no ordinary person.

The final contest was the uprooting of trees, the test of complete strength. Many men tried, but only one succeeded in pulling out a fair-sized tree. The young man smiled and said, "We should not play with

saplings." He wrenched from the ground the biggest spruce tree on the hill and threw it over the cliff. The people from all the villages stood in silence. This man was a supernatural being.

The young man's strength became known in all parts of the north; even the animals heard about him. One by one they came to test themselves against his strength: the cougar, the wolf, even Medeek, the great grizzly bear. The man from Metlakatla conquered them all.

The forest itself tested him. The trees crowded onto the beach, but he uprooted them and thrust them back. He pushed away the mountains when they tried to smother the village. He was the strongest man in the world, though he still slept by the fire much of the time.

One night, when all in the village slept, a strange canoe landed on the beach in front of Metlakatla. The men in the canoe said to one another, "This is the place. This is where he lives." The steersman jumped ashore and went directly to where the strong man was sleeping.

Gently, he shook him awake, "Come, my dear, your grandfather has need of you. You are ready for your great task." Without a word, the young man followed the stranger to the canoe. The steersman said, "Let us be on our way," and the canoe became a blackfish, skimming the waves with the travellers on his back.

Far from land, they sighted a rock. Here the blackfish stopped, and they stepped from the canoe. The strangers took the form of loons, and the one who had been steersman said, "We have brought you here because your grandfather, He Who Holds Up the World, has grown weary. He has waited for your training to be completed. Now you are ready. Come." He took the young man along a path leading into the rock. Loons and ducks guarded the trail. The man from Metlakatla entered an opening in the ground and descended a long ladder.

When he reached the bottom of the ladder, he saw a very old man with a huge hemlock pole braced against his shoulder. The aged one said, "I have waited long for you, but I had to be certain you would have the strength to do this work. Now, I will instruct you. The ducks and loons will be your messengers. They will bring your food. The blue bill duck will oil your joints, so you will never become stiff. Remember, you must stay still. If you move at all, you will cause an earthquake. Should you collapse, the world will be destroyed. Now I am going to rest." Slowly, the old one rose, and the young man took his place.

Next morning, when the people of the village did not see their strong young man beside the fire, they searched for him and were greatly concerned. The youngest uncle said, "Surely he has been called away to some task fit for his great strength." The Tsimshian never saw the young man again, yet the earth of Metlakatla was steady beneath their feet, and today the ducks still dive deep into the sea.

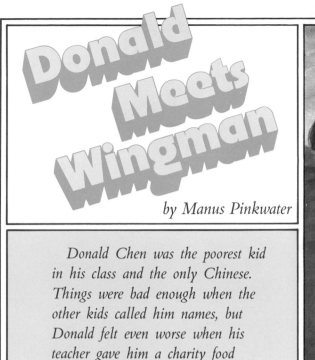

Donald Meets Wingman

by Manus Pinkwater

Donald Chen was the poorest kid in his class and the only Chinese. Things were bad enough when the other kids called him names, but Donald felt even worse when his teacher gave him a charity food basket for Thanksgiving. So he stopped going to school. . . .

Donald had a schoolbag. Every morning he would fill it with comic books. Then he would start out for school, but he would turn right a block before the school and head for the river. It was only a few blocks, across Broadway, across Fort Washington Avenue, then down a little street to a footbridge across the Henry Hudson Parkway.

When Donald Chen, Chen Chi-Wing, crossed that footbridge, he entered a little park. There were trees there; the river flowed past, with the wild jungles of New Jersey on the other side. Stretching over everything, so big that he couldn't see the whole thing at once, was the George Washington Bridge.

He knew how to climb the bridge. No other kid he knew was able to do it. The only hard part, really, was scrambling up the bottom part, which was like a wall. Once he got to the big steel beams, it was easy to go from one to the other. With his schoolbag hanging from his belt, he climbed. The steel beams, which looked like spider webs from the lit-

from Wingman

tle park below the bridge, were big enough to walk on. They slanted up, meeting other beams—roads leading to roads.

He worked his way up to the place where the bridge curves out over the river. He could hear the cars and trucks rumbling over his head. The river flowed slowly beneath him, and boats passed underneath. Pigeons fluttered and sea gulls glided beneath and about him, but he didn't pay much attention. He just checked these things when he arrived in the morning to make sure everything was still the same. Then he would open his schoolbag.

Donald read comic books all day. He read *Skywolf, Captain Marvel, Spy Smasher,* and *Plastic Man.* He read *Batman, Airboy, The Spirit,* and *Superman.* They were real people. They were strong. Everybody respected them. Crooks were afraid of them.

The steel beams of the bridge were made in the shape of a letter H. There was room for Donald to sit inside the H, and when he lay on his stomach, nobody could see him. As he read the comics, the rumbling of the cars on the bridge sounded farther away, and after a while it would fade out, and Donald would read his comics in silence.

In the afternoon, Donald would leave the bridge. It always made him sad to realize that school would be letting out, and it was time to go home. As he crossed the little footbridge over the highway, his feet felt heavy, as though he were tired. When he got home, his father would give him a bowl of vegetable soup, and Donald would do some work in the laundry. His father never caught on that Donald was not going to school.

Donald went to the bridge for a long time. It was getting to be real winter. It snowed a couple of times, but Donald never minded the cold. He put a few comic books under him, and was very comfortable.

When Donald met Wingman, he met him on the bridge. Donald looked up from the Aquaman story he was reading, and there was someone standing over him, legs apart, balancing on the edges of the beam. He had steel armor that covered his body, his arms and legs were bare, and he carried a long sword. On his head he wore a strange pointed helmet, and over his shoulders a cape made of gray feathers. It looked like a pair of wings. He seemed to shine all over. He was Chinese.

Donald held his breath. The shining figure looked stern and friendly at once. Suddenly, with a rush of feathers, the figure jumped off the beam. Donald felt his heart thump once, hard. He realized all at once that it was very high up and dangerous on the bridge; he had never thought about it before. At the same moment, he looked down over the side. The man in armor was gone. Donald knew he could not have fallen all that way at once. He looked up and saw something like a big gray bird disappear, flying into the sun.

Donald thought about what he had seen. It seemed that the winged man had just lighted on his particular beam by accident, as pigeons sometimes did, not knowing Donald was there. And just as the pigeons did, he had flown away when Donald had looked at him. Donald decided to be careful not to look at him if he came back. That way, maybe he would stay.

Donald was too excited to read anymore. Usually he could read comics anytime. He even read comics the two times his family had been kicked out of their apartment. He read comics the day his mother went to the hospital. But Wingman's appearance excited him. He had never seen anything like him outside a comic book. Now he was impatient with the stories, and the colors looked dull.

Donald stopped reading and looked out over the river. The sky was blue and clear. A tugboat in the distance made puffs of white smoke. Sea gulls soared and dived, calling to one another. Donald noticed that his nose was running. He thought he might bring his jacket the next day.

Donald didn't see Wingman again that day. He thought about him. He remembered every tiny moment. Sometimes he remembered so clearly that he could almost see him. Almost, but not quite. At night he dreamed Wingman's appearance again and again.

The next day Donald climbed to his beam and opened his schoolbag. *Police Comics Number 58: Plastic Man Meets the Green Terror;* but he didn't really read. He just turned the pages and waited for Wingman. He went through comic after comic, waiting. Then he got involved in a Captain Marvel story. Mr. Mind, a tiny worm in a general's uniform, was the head of a gang called "Mr. Mind's Monster Society of Evil," and Captain Marvel was trying to stop them from stealing two magical black pearls. As Donald read, the bridge noises faded away and things became silent.

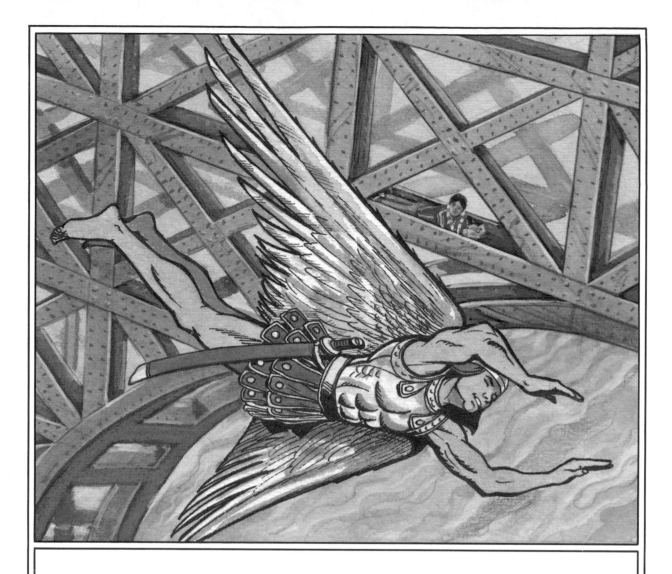

In the middle of a fight between Captain Marvel and Captain Nazi, Donald realized that Wingman was there. Donald remembered not to look at him. He saw Wingman's feet balanced on the edges of the beam, and went back to his comic book, pretending to read, turning the pages slowly.

Donald's heart was pounding. As he turned the pages of comic after comic, he would glance up and see the feet. He wanted to look at Wingman, but he was afraid of startling him. Then Wingman sat down. There was a rustle of feathers, and Donald knew that Wingman was sitting across the beam from him, his feet dangling toward the river. Donald looked up slowly. He took in every detail, the sword, the armor, the cape of gray feathers, Wingman's face.

Wingman looked at Donald, smiled, and pushed himself off the beam. Donald looked down and saw Wingman falling, wrapped in his cape. He held his breath. Then the cape unfolded into two gray wings, and Wingman skimmed just above the river, like a sea gull. Then he soared up in a great loop backward, over the bridge. Donald turned and saw him coming from the other side, right toward Donald's beam. As he approached, Wingman gathered his cape around him and hurtled right past Donald like a bullet. Then he spread his cape, and tilted his wings from side to side as though he were waving as he flew away, disappearing among the tall buildings of Manhattan.

Donald felt very happy. He felt as though he were flying too. He didn't read any more comics that day. He sat on the bridge and remembered how Wingman looked flying over the river.

Donald put some sandwiches in his schoolbag in the morning. He went to the bridge and waited for Wingman. Once again he turned the pages of a comic book, not paying attention. Once again he got caught up in a story, this time about Plastic Man, caught by the police for a crime he did not commit. The bridge became silent as Donald read.

When Donald looked up, Wingman was there, sitting across the beam as he had the day before. He was looking out over the river, not noticing Donald. Donald sat for a long time looking at Wingman. Neither of them moved. Wingman appeared to be watching something too far away for Donald to see. Hours passed. Donald was content to study Wingman's cape, sword, and armor. The bridge was silent. Wingman was more interesting than any comic. Wingman never moved. Even the river seemed to be standing still.

Then Donald felt a start, as though he had just come awake, although he hadn't been sleeping. The bridge began to roar with traffic, the river began to move. Donald reached into his schoolbag and took out two sandwiches, salami and peanut butter combination. He put one on the beam next to Wingman and waited to see what would happen. Wingman didn't move. He was still watching something far away. Donald held his own sandwich in his hand and waited.

Still looking into the distance, Wingman reached for the sandwich beside him. He held it in his hand and gave a strange cry. Donald jumped; his hair stood up. Wingman gave the call again, a sad sound that came from high up in his nose. It made Donald's skin tingle.

Wingman's eyes lifted. Donald looked out over the river and saw a big bird flying toward them fast. Very fast. As Donald looked, it got bigger and bigger; then it was right before them. It was as big as Donald himself. Its feathers were gray like those in Wingman's cape. Its beak was black and hooked and sharp. An eagle! It landed between Donald and Wingman. Wingman unwrapped his sandwich and gave half to the bird. Then he took a bite from the other half, and looked at Donald. Donald gave half his sandwich to the bird too. It swallowed it in one gulp after shaking it in its beak. Donald and Wingman smiled at each other and ate their sandwiches.

For the rest of the afternoon, Donald and Wingman sat on the beam in the sunshine. The eagle practised tightrope-walking up and down the edge of the beam between them, sometimes spreading its wings to keep its balance. When it was time to go home, Donald smiled goodbye to Wingman and climbed down the bridge. When he reached the bottom, he looked up. He could just see Wingman sitting on the beam. The eagle was flying in circles, under and over the bridge and making piercing cries again and again.

When Donald got home, his uncle Li-Noon was there. He was cooking. Whenever Uncle Noon came they had a feast. He had brought roast pork and lo mein noodles from Chinatown, and big oranges and dry sweet cakes. He also brought a little bottle of whiskey, and he and Donald's father each had a drink out of little glasses. Donald's father ironed in the laundry and Uncle Noon cut up vegetables in the kitchen, and they shouted to each other from room to room, talking Chinese too fast for the children to understand.

At supper Uncle Noon gave presents to the children. Wing's sister got crayons, his little brother got a puzzle made of bent nails, and Donald got lucky money in a red envelope, and a comic book. It was one he had, but he could trade it.

Before he went to bed, Donald tried to draw a picture of Wingman and the eagle. He used his sister's new crayons. He put it in his schoolbag to show Wingman the next day.

Geeder and Zeely

by Virginia Hamilton

Elizabeth just loves to imagine things. She starts the summer by giving herself a new name, Geeder. Then she meets tall, beautiful Zeely Tayber and she just knows there is something special about her. One day Geeder comes across a picture of a Watutsi princess in a magazine—and she looks just like Zeely. Naturally Geeder can't resist telling people that Zeely is really a queen. Then Zeely asks to meet Geeder, and tells her a Watutsi tale.

Geeder sat quite still, with the photograph of the Watutsi woman on her lap. She had held her hand pressed against it when Zeely first began her tale. Now, she smoothed her fingers over the photograph. "Oh, Miss Zeely," Geeder said, "I thought you were special even before I found the picture." It was as if she spoke to herself and not to Zeely.

Zeely stared at Geeder. "I asked you to come here because I wanted to tell you the tale my mother told," she said. "It means everything but you don't seem to care about it."

"Well, it really is a nice story," said Geeder. "I mean, I like it so much, with all that snow and that man and the girl." She clutched the photograph with both hands and then thrust it away to the ground. "But it's only a story. I came here today because . . . because *you* wanted me to! You wanted me to come to *be* with you, Miss Zeely!"

Zeely's eyes widened suddenly. Her long fingers covered her mouth in surprise. "Ahhh, now I see!" she said. "I did not realize that was why you came."

from Zeely

307

"You are the most different person I've ever met," Geeder said.

Zeely laughed softly. She drew her long legs up under her chin and folded her arms around them. In this way, she rocked slowly from side to side. Her eyes closed and there was a smile upon her lips.

Geeder watched her. All the time that Zeely had told her tale, she had sat stiff and tall in her long robe. Her shoulders had stood out sharply; her face had been all angles. Now, her features seemed to soften and flow into the deep shadows the trees made. Her hands and forearms were hidden in the long grass around her legs. Geeder looked at Zeely's black, black hair, dark as night, and it became a part of the darkening leaves above her head.

Geeder said, "It's you that comes down the roadway late at night, isn't it, Miss Zeely?" She spoke into Zeely's ear.

Zeely nodded her head but did not open her eyes. "I come to look after my pigs," she said.

"And you carry a feed pail," said Geeder. "The moon going down slants onto it and it looks like it floats in the air. The moon is behind your back and so you don't have a face. It looks just like you don't have a head or any arms and you glide right above the ground."

"So," Zeely said, "you have seen me? I have seen you."

"You go by the house just before dawn," Geeder said. "You come early in the morning, anyhow. Why must you come so way late at night?"

"And why must you sleep there in the grass," Zeely asked, "so way late at night?"

"I like the stars," Geeder said, "and the moonshine."

"I like the night," said Zeely. She opened her eyes and stretched out her legs. Her shoulders drooped forward and her head fell back, slightly, as she studied the trees.

"Where I came from," Zeely said, "Canada, there was a lake.

"Oh, it was not a large lake," she said. "You could swim it, going slowly, in about fifteen minutes. I have done that. I have swum it when there was no moon or stars to light my way. Do you know what it is like to swim at night?"

"No," Geeder said, "I don't swim well, yet."

Zeely smiled, her eyes still in the trees. "It is like no other where," she said. "It is being in something that is all movement, that you cannot see, and it ceases to be wet. You must be very calm or you will not find your way out of it."

"Is that why you like the night?" asked Geeder.

"You see," Zeely said, looking at Geeder now, "the children wouldn't often swim in that lake, even in the daytime. A tiny old woman lived beside it. She wore a big bow in her hair that was very dirty. On top of the bow she wore a man's straw hat. She walked, bent forward, with a big cane for support. Often, she cackled to herself and pointed her cane at things. The children were afraid of her but I was not. Sometimes, I'd be swimming in the lake in the daytime, and she'd come upon me. 'Zeely Tayber,' she would call, 'I see you!' And I would call back to her, 'And I see *you!*' Then, she would call again. 'One of these times,

I'll catch you!' she would say, and she would cackle and point her cane at me.

"Oh, no," Zeely said, "I was not afraid of her like the others were. I thought of her as a friend, almost. Then . . ."

"Then, what?" Geeder said.

Zeely looked away from Geeder. Her eyes turned inward upon themselves as Geeder had seen them do before.

"One night," Zeely said, "I had finished swimming and was pulling on my clothes when I heard footsteps on the path. I heard a cackle and I knew who it was. All at once, fear took hold of me. I had not ever thought of that little woman walking around at night, you see. At that moment, I was terrified. Quickly, I gathered my clothes and stood between a bush and tree, well hidden, I thought. And there she came along the path."

"Oh," said Geeder, softly. Her eyes were wide.

"She did nothing for a moment," Zeely said. "She stood there beside the lake looking at the dark water. Then, she looked around. She went up to a stone lying there beside her and touched it with her cane. It moved. It was a turtle and it scurried into the water."

"No!" said Geeder.

"Oh, yes," Zeely said. "And there was a fallen branch, twisted upon itself there, right next to the path. Vines grew over it. She poked one vine with her cane. It rippled. It was a snake and it slithered off into a bush near where I stood."

"No!" said Geeder.

"I couldn't believe my eyes," Zeely said, "I was so amazed by what I had seen."

"You must have been just scared to death!" Geeder said. She leaned against Zeely now, looking up at her, and Zeely leaned against Geeder. Neither realized how close they had become, sitting there under the great trees.

"I was scared," Zeely said. "The woman kept cackling. Her back was turned to me. But I must have choked out loud on my fear, for suddenly she was silent. She spun around and stood there, facing the darkness where I was hidden.

" 'Zeely Tayber,' she said, 'I see you!' And I remember, I began to cry.

" 'Zeely Tayber,' she said again. She raised her cane right at me, and she was coming toward me. I could see her bow moving in the air. Suddenly, she had me by the arms. She was cackling again—I thought she would never stop.

"At last, she spoke," Zeely said. " 'Zeely Tayber,' she said, 'you have made a poor soul happy. You are the night and I have caught you!' "

"Oh!" said Geeder. "What a thing to happen!"

"Yes," said Zeely.

"What did you do?" asked Geeder.

"Do?" Zeely said. "I did nothing. Soon, the woman let me loose and went on her way, laughing and singing to herself. I was stunned by what she had said to me and I stood there in the darkness for many minutes. All at once in my mind everything was as clear as day. I liked the dark. I walked and swam in the dark and because of that, I was the *night!*

"Finally," Zeely said, "I told my mother about what had happened. My mother said that I simply had not known darkness well enough to tell the difference between a stone and a turtle and a vine and a snake. She said the snake and turtle had been there all the time. She said that since the woman was not quite right in her head, she had decided that I was the night because my skin was so dark."

"Did you believe what your mother said?" asked Geeder.

"I came to believe it," Zeely said. "I believe it now. But I was sorry my mother had said what she did. It meant I was only myself, that I was Zeely and no more."

Geeder sighed and looked down at her hands. "Things . . . are what they are, I guess," she said, quietly.

"Yes," said Zeely. "No pretty robe was able to make me more than what I was and no little woman could make me the night."

"But you *are* different," Geeder said. "You are the most different person I've ever talked to."

"Am I?" Zeely said, her voice kind. "And you want to be different, too?"

Geeder was suddenly shy. She took hold of her beads and ran her fingers quickly over them. "I'd like to be just like you, I guess, Miss Zeely," she said.

Zeely smiled. "To be so tall that wherever you went, people stared and questioned? You'd like to be able to call a hog to you and have it follow you as though it were a puppy?" She laughed. The sound of it was harsh. "Hogs see me as just another animal—did you know that? Their scent is my scent, that is all there is to it. As for being so tall, I would like once in a while not to have people notice me or wonder about my height. No," Zeely added, "I don't think you'd enjoy being like me or being different the way I am."

"I guess not, then," Geeder said. "I mean, I don't know." She stopped in confusion. She would never have imagined that Zeely didn't like being tall. "I want to be . . . to be . . ." She paused.

"Whoever it is you are when you're not being Geeder," Zeely said, finishing for her. "The person you are when you're not making up stories. Not Geeder and not even me, but yourself—is that what you want, Elizabeth?" Zeely looked deeply at Geeder, as if the image of her were fading away. "I stopped making up tales a long time ago," she said, "and now I am myself."

Geeder was so startled she could not say anything. And the way Zeely called her Elizabeth, just as though they were the same age, caused a pleasant, quiet feeling to grow within her. What she had promised herself at the beginning of the summer crossed Geeder's mind. *I won't be silly. I won't play silly games with silly girls.*

But I *was* silly, she thought. I made up myself as Geeder and I made up Zeely to be a queen.

She let go of her bright necklaces and smoothed her hands over her hair.

"Myself . . ." she whispered. "Yes, I guess so."

Zeely Tayber ruffled the creases from her long robe and then stood up to leave. She was tall and beautiful there, before Geeder. Her expression was soft.

"I want to thank you, Geeder," she said, "for helping me with the sow last Saturday. I don't know how much you know about hogs, but they are miserable creatures. My father is tired of them and so am I. I take care of them as much as I can, to see they are treated well. It is hard work and I don't have much time for friends."

She touched Geeder lightly on the hair. Her long fingers fluttered there a moment, as lithe as the wings of a butterfly, before they were gone. Zeely knew before Geeder did that Geeder was close to tears.

"You have a most fine way of dreaming," Zeely said. "Hold on to that. But remember the turtle, remember the snake. I always have."

Geeder didn't see Zeely leave the clearing. The colors of bush and tree swam in her eyes and Zeely melted away within them.

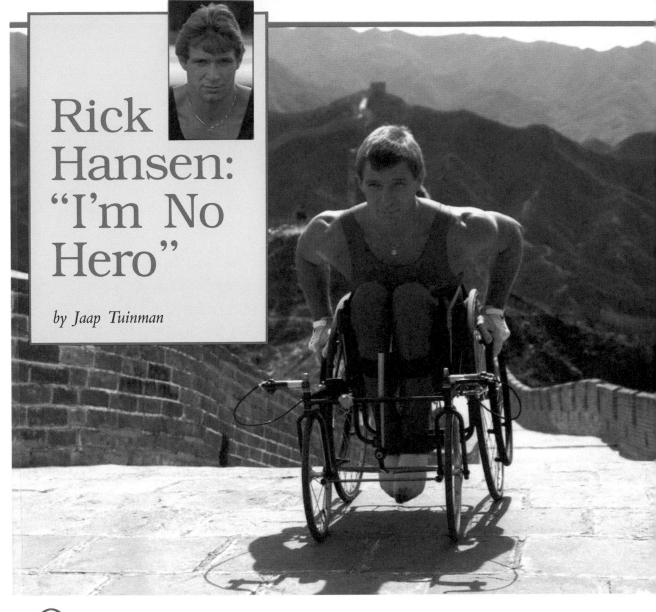

Rick Hansen: "I'm No Hero"

by Jaap Tuinman

On April 12, 1986, Rick Hansen pushes his wheelchair up the steep inclines of the Great Wall of China. The effort is enormous, but he persists. The Great Wall has been a personal symbol on his journey: if he can climb the Great Wall, which has withstood all attacks from invading forces, then he will know that there is no wall too big to overcome. He reaches the top and rests. He has come a long way.

The long journey to the top of the Great Wall begins thirteen years earlier, in the summer of 1973, in the Cariboo country of British Columbia. Rick Hansen and his friend Don Adler are sitting in the back of a pickup truck, hitchhiking home from a fishing trip after their own truck gets stuck. On a stretch of rough washboard road, the driver loses control, and the truck flips over. Both boys are thrown free. Don escapes uninjured, but Rick lands on a metal toolbox and breaks his back. In a few seconds a healthy, athletic, confident kid of fifteen becomes a paraplegic—permanently paralyzed from the waist down.

Within weeks Rick begins his struggle to regain independence. Only seven months after the accident, he leaves the rehabilitation centre and drives himself home in a car equipped with hand controls. But his struggle is far from over. His journey has just begun, and he has to battle pain and fear and loneliness and frustration every bit of the way.

First he goes back to high school to get his diploma. Then he attends the University of British Columbia and graduates with a B.A. degree in physical education—the first disabled person ever to do so. At school and after graduation he participates in wheelchair sports. He plays wheelchair basketball with a Vancouver team, where he becomes friends with teammate Terry Fox. He trains for racing events and within a few years becomes a world-class wheelchair marathon champion, winning nineteen international marathon events. In 1983, he shares Canada's athlete-of-the-year award with hockey star Wayne Gretzky.

But athletic championships and awards are not the stuff of Rick Hansen's real dream, the dream he has been cherishing for years—an around-the-world wheelchair tour to raise money for spinal-injury research and to focus world attention on the problems of disabled people. He begins planning seriously to make his dream a reality.

On March 21, 1985, Rick Hansen, with his support team, sets off from Oakridge Shopping Centre in Vancouver. He gives the first turn of his wheels on a round-the-world journey of 40 073 km, a distance equal to the Earth's circumference.

Right from the beginning the trip is tough, tougher even than Rick Hansen has anticipated. On only the second day out he is grappling with injuries, 64 km/h headwinds, pouring rain, and zero-degree temperatures. Somehow, he keeps going. He pushes his chair thousands of kilometres—up gruelling mountain climbs, along endlessly lonely open stretches. He suffers from muscle injuries, tendonitis, and flu. For weeks, undetected fumes from the engine of the motorhome in which he rests and sleeps sap his energy. Thieves rob him, four times, making off with a video-camera, irreplaceable tapes of part of the tour, and thousands of dollars' worth of special clothing and equipment. But worse than the pain and the sickness and the robberies is the indifference of the people. So many don't seem to understand why he is making the journey; they don't care about or share his dream.

Still, Hansen keeps pushing—his wheelchair, the people with him, and above all, himself. He has wheeled his chair down the west coast of the United States and across the south, through countries in Europe and the Middle East, on to Australia and New Zealand. And now, a year after the first turn of the wheels in Vancouver, he sits on top of the Great Wall of China. Yes, he has come a long way, but he still has a long way to go. He gives a turn to the wheels and starts rolling again.

From the Wall, Hansen's route leads on to Shanghai, then to South Korea and Japan. After that he flies to Miami and travels up the east coast of the United States. On August 24, 1986, he leaves Bar Harbor, Maine, and flies to Newfoundland. Now he begins his journey west across Canada, from the easternmost point at Cape Spear back to Vancouver.

So far Rick Hansen's tour has only been a partial success: much publicity, little money. To achieve his goal of $10 million for spinal research, Canadians will have to come through in a big way. And they do, beyond Hansen's most optimistic hopes. The road from Newfoundland to Vancouver is every bit as tough as any he has travelled abroad, but every turn of the wheels is made easier by the cheers and the generosity of Canadians all along the route. People of all ages and all walks of life, businesses and governments, moved by the courage and determination of the Man in Motion, want to share his dream.

The journey across Canada takes nine months—so many stops along the route to greet crowds of contributors, so many TV appearances and banquets to speak for spinal research and for paraplegics. One stop is at a monument near Thunder Bay, where his friend Terry Fox had to end his Marathon of Hope.

On March 20, 1987, two years less a day from the first turn of his wheels in Vancouver, Rick Hansen crosses the border into British Columbia, his home province. Hundreds of people are waiting for him, including many friends and relatives, and his mother and father. At this point only 3200 km of his tour remain, but they include three crossings of awesome mountain ranges. On this part of the tour, as elsewhere, Rick meets with people who have overcome disabilities or are working hard to do so. The press publicizes these meetings,

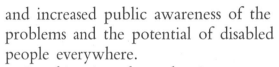

and everywhere he goes, Hansen is greeted with enthusiastic support. In Williams Lake, where he grew up, virtually the entire town is present at a rally in his honor. "I'm just trying to do all I can," he tells the crowd. "I'm no hero."

Finally, on May 22, 1987, Rick Hansen comes home to Vancouver and wheels into the shopping centre he started from 26 months before. In those months he has rolled more than 40 000 km, visited 34 countries around the world, and achieved both his goals: he has raised $20 million for spinal research

and increased public awareness of the problems and the potential of disabled people everywhere.

On this triumphant day in Vancouver, Rick Hansen hears many words of welcome, but the ones he treasures above all are those of an eighteen-year-old girl who was badly injured in a car accident two years earlier. She walks with difficulty, but unassisted, to the microphone. "One year ago," she says, "I was in a wheelchair. You showed me how to reach for the stars. You gave me that encouragement to do the best I can. I thank you for letting me share a part of your dream."

To her, and to the people everywhere who supported him, Rick Hansen says, "Thank you, all of you, for sharing mine."

Detail of *Northern Lights* by Paterson Ewen

Worlds to Discover

New Dimensions in Inventions

My Uncle Dan

by *Ted Hughes*

My Uncle Dan's an inventor. You may think that's very fine.
You may wish he were your uncle instead of being mine—
If he wanted he could make a watch that bounces when it drops,
He could make a helicopter out of string and bottle tops
Or any really useful thing you can't get in the shops.
      But Uncle Dan has other ideas:
      The bottomless glass for ginger beers,
      The toothless saw that's safe for the tree,
      A special word for a spelling bee
      (Like Lionocerangoutangadder),
      Or the roll-uppable rubber ladder,
      The mystery pie that bites when it's bit—
      My Uncle Dan invented it.

My Uncle Dan sits in his den inventing night and day.
His eyes peer from his hair and beard like mice from a load of hay.
And does he make the shoes that will go for walks without
    your feet?
A shrinker to shrink instantly the elephants you meet?
A carver that just from the air carves steaks cooked and ready
    to eat?
      No, no, he has other intentions—
      Only perfectly useless inventions:
      Glassless windows (they never break),
      A medicine to cure the earthquake,
      The unspillable screwed-down cup,
      The stairs that go neither down nor up
      The door you simply paint on a wall—
      Uncle Dan invented them all.

Michael Built a Bicycle

by Jack Prelutsky

Michael built a bicycle
unsuitable for speed,
it's crammed with more accessories
than anyone could need,
there's an AM-FM radio,
a deck to play cassettes,
a refrigerator-freezer,
and a pair of TV sets.

There are shelves for shirts and
  sweaters,
there are hangers for his jeans,
a drawer for socks and underwear,
a rack for magazines,
there's a fishtank and a birdcage
perched upon the handlebars,
a bookcase, and a telescope
to watch the moon and stars.

There's a telephone, a blender,
and a stove to cook his meals,
there's a sink to do the dishes
somehow fastened to the wheels,
there's a portable piano,
and a set of model trains,
an automatic bumbershoot
that opens when it rains.

There's a desk for typing letters
on his fabulous machine,
a stall for taking showers,
and a broom to keep things clean,
but you'll never see him ride it,
for it isn't quite complete,
Michael left no room for pedals,
and there isn't any seat.

321

How Inventions Happen

by Valerie Wyatt

Inventions happen in many ways—almost as many ways as there are inventors. But here are five ways that have brought success to many people.

Wait for Inspiration

Many inventions come about because their inventors have a flash of inspiration, or "eureka moment." The word "eureka" comes from something that happened a long time ago in ancient Greece. The Greek mathematician Archimedes was stepping into his bath one day when, thanks to a flash of inspiration, he got the answer to a problem that had been bothering him. Archimedes was so excited by his idea that he jumped out of the bath and ran naked into the streets, yelling "Heureka! Heureka!" We've dropped the *H* but the meaning is still the same: "I have found it!" The eureka moment is responsible for many inventions, including Post-it™ Notes.

The story of Post-it Notes began in the 3M Corporation during the 1960s. The corporation was trying to find a superpowerful new glue, and Spence Silver was working on the project. Silver was a chemist with a playful streak. He sometimes changed chemical "recipes" he was working on, adding a bit more of this and a bit less of that, just to see what would happen. One day, while fiddling with a recipe, he ended up with the glue that wouldn't. Silver's glue looked like a real failure. It would stick two things together, but then you could pull them apart again. The problem was that people didn't want temporary glue; they wanted long-lasting glue.

No one at the company was particularly impressed with the stuff—except its inventor. He was convinced that it had a use. However, the glue had a few problems. For instance, it had no memory. When he put the glue on a piece of paper, stuck it to a desk, and lifted it off again, the glue might stay on the paper or it might "forget" and stick to the desk instead. It didn't "remember" where it had been.

Silver worked on the glue for almost ten years. During that time, he managed to improve its memory, but the only way he could think of to use it didn't catch on. It was a bulletin board coated with the glue. Although the board was useful—you could stick papers to it and then remove them later—few were sold. People preferred the old-style bulletin board with tacks to hold things on.

The sometimes-it-sticks-sometimes-it-doesn't glue caught the attention of one of Silver's co-workers, Arthur Fry. It stuck in the back of his mind. One Sunday in 1974, while singing in a church choir, he kept losing his place in the songbook because his bookmarks fell out. Fry had a flash of inspiration:

what if Silver's glue were stuck onto paper to make removable bookmarks? Fry didn't shout out "Eureka!" the way Archimedes had done (and he was fully dressed at the time), but his eureka moment led to the invention of Post-it Notes. Soon these small blank notes with Silver's glue along one edge were being churned out by the millions.

Post-it Notes are used in homes, schools, and offices around the world. You can write on them and stick them anywhere—on another piece of paper, on phones and fridges, even on people. Post-it Notes might have been invented without Arthur Fry's eureka moment. But sometimes a flash of inspiration is needed to work out problems. No one knows where these flashes come from. One theory, though, is that part of your mind is working away on a problem even when you're doing ordinary every-day things. Then suddenly two ideas will come together and—*eureka!*—you've got it!

Work Together

People sometimes think of inventors as hermit-like loners in lab coats. But many things have been invented by groups of inventors working together. Teamwork allows inventors to put their heads together and brainstorm to find solutions to problems. As the old saying goes, "Two heads are better than one."

That expression certainly proved true in the case of two Americans, Leopold Godowsky and Leopold Mannes. They invented color film in 1935 after more than fifteen years of working together.

The two inventors first got to know each other in high school. Both were the sons of musicians, and both wanted to be musicians. As a hobby they tinkered with photography. Since the world was in color, it seemed natural to them to find a way to capture it on film in color. They began their experiments while they were still in school.

A lot of other inventors were working on the same idea. At first people thought you would need three layers of film to produce a color picture. One layer would be yellow, another red, and the third blue. Only when you put the three together, one on top of the other, would you be able to see all the colors of the rainbow. The two Leopolds tried this too, but the pictures that resulted were blurry. They thought there must be a better solution. They decided to use separate layers of chemicals on one piece of film instead of several layers of film.

The two Leopolds began experimenting. Their research so impressed the Kodak Camera Company that they were hired on and given laboratory space.

The two musicians were not what you might think of as typical inventors. For example, to time the various parts of their experiments, they sang songs. As musicians they knew how long each bit of song lasted, and it was more fun to sing than to use a clock. While onlookers (and onlisteners) at Kodak scratched their heads, Godowsky and Mannes sang and brainstormed their way to the first color film in 1935.

Today most inventions come not from solitary inventors but from large corporations and universities where teamwork is common. Some companies even make sure that every team knows what every other team is doing. That way, if a problem arises, there are lots of people who can put their minds to it. After all, if two heads are better than one, hundreds must be better still.

Borrow from the Past

Most inventions are not the work of a single individual or even a single team. They're the result of tens, sometimes hundreds of people's work over tens, hundreds, or even thousands of years. Each inventor adds a new idea and builds on what has gone before. Borrowing from the past is how people learned to build modern airplanes.

Today we think of the Wright brothers as the pioneers of flight. But long before the Wrights' famous first flight on December 17, 1903, the real pioneers of flight were strapping themselves into sets of wings and throwing themselves off towers and cliffs.

One of the earliest, an Arab named Abu'l-Qasim 'Abbas bin Firnas (or 'Abbas for short), was a bit of a mad inventor. He loved music and invented a metronome to help him keep time. He built a machine that was said to produce thunder and lightning in his living room. And he conducted a number of experiments on flight. One day in 875, 'Abbas glued vulture feathers all over his body, climbed a high tower, and jumped off. One onlooker claimed that 'Abbas flew quite a distance. Probably most of the distance was straight down. The flight ended in a crash. Some observers blamed the absence of a tail for his downfall.

Other fliers followed. In about the year 1000 an Iranian "flew" to his death, and a monk in England broke both his legs after a nasty landing. In most cases these early "fliers" weren't aware of each other's accomplishments. They got their inspiration from the

birds. But by the mid-1800s, would-be fliers were keenly aware of who was up in the air and how others were doing it.

Some inventors believed that balloons were the way to go. One flier who thought that the future of flight lay not with balloons but with heavier-than-air craft was Otto Lilienthal. He built gliders that look a bit like today's hang-gliders and made thousands of test flights in the 1890s. The longest of these flights covered 229 metres—six times longer than Orville Wright's first powered flight ten years later. Lilienthal was the first to realize that flying machines had to have controls to keep them flying properly. Unfortunately, like so many other early fliers, he died in a crash while testing his theories.

When the Wright brothers heard of Lilienthal's death and his experimental gliders, they began to read everything they could about human flight. They borrowed ideas from earlier inventors, added some new ideas of their own, and built the first successful powered plane, aptly named the *Flyer.* As news of the *Flyer's* historic flight on December 17, 1903, was reported in newspapers, other airplane inventors started to work. Learning from experience and continually making design improvements, aircraft inventors (today called aeronautical engineers) have gone from ungainly planes made of fabric, wood, and wire to supersonic jets, short-takeoff-and-landing planes, and other modern-day marvels of flight.

Be Observant and Curious

Lots of inventions happen simply because people notice something unusual and start thinking about it. For example, during World War II an American named Percy Spencer made magnetrons used in radar systems to detect planes and ships by beaming out microwaves and noting the reflections bounced back.

Spencer noticed that you could warm your hands by holding them close to the magnetrons. They gave off about as much heat as a large light bulb. But it wasn't until he found a melted candy in his pocket that he started to think about cooking food with microwaves. At first the microwaves weren't strong and constant enough to do much more than melt things, but by the end of the war that problem had been solved.

Spencer and his co-workers began to experiment. First they held a bag of popcorn in front of a microwave beam. The popcorn jumped around inside the bag. Then they hung a pork chop on a string in front of the microwaves. It cooked! Spencer believed it was time to put on a demonstration for his company's board of directors. He wanted to convince them that it was possible to cook with microwaves and that the company should start manufacturing microwave ovens.

When the day of the demonstration

arrived, the board members assembled around the magnetron. Spencer placed an egg on a stand where the microwaves would be concentrated and told the operator to turn on the microwaves. Anyone who has cooked an egg in a microwave oven knows that you must pierce the shell or the egg will explode. Spencer had probably already discovered this, but he couldn't resist using an unpierced egg. When the microwaves began—*kablam!*—the egg exploded all over the assembled board members. This unforgettable demonstration of the cooking power of microwaves won the board members' approval. The High Frequency Dielectric Heating Apparatus (today called a microwave oven) was patented in 1953. By the 1960s household models were popping up in homes everywhere.

Thanks to Percy Spencer's keen sense of observation and curiosity you can warm up a cup of cocoa in seconds and cook dinner in minutes. Many other inventions also owe their existence mainly to observation and curiosity. For instance, Velcro™ might never have been invented if a Swiss engineer named Georges de Mestral hadn't noticed that burrs and seeds stuck to his socks after he had been out in the woods. Using a magnifying glass, de Mestral found out how these plant hitchhikers did it. They had tiny barbs that hooked into the soft sock fabric.

De Mestral wondered if he could make a fabric fastener using the same idea. He came up with a fastener made of two strips of cloth: one strip had hundreds of tiny hooks, and the other had hundreds of tiny loops. When the two came together the hooks grabbed the loops so securely that you had to *rrrrrip!* the pieces apart. De Mestral patented his invention in 1957. Since then Velcro has been used on everything from sneakers and snowsuits to spacesuits and artificial hearts.

Work Hard

Few inventions happen overnight. Even something as simple as Velcro took eight years to invent. Inventors experiment, make changes, and experiment again—often for years. But sometimes, no matter how hard an inventor works, his or her invention doesn't. Something is missing, and that "something" is luck.

No one put more hard work into an invention than Charles Goodyear. But without luck, all his hard work would have been useless. As a young man growing up in New England in the early 1800s, Goodyear was fascinated by the strange new substance called rubber, made from the sap of certain tropical plants. He was amazed at how you could stretch a piece of rubber and then watch it snap back to its original size.

At first a lot of other people shared Goodyear's enthusiasm. They bought the new boots and raincoats that were being waterproofed with rubber. But rubber had problems: it became sticky in hot weather and cracked in cold. Soon people were putting their rubberized clothing in the back of the closet and leaving it there.

Charles Goodyear never lost his enthusiasm for rubber. He was determined to find a way to solve the temperature problems so that rubber could be used year-round. The main problem seemed to be not the rubber itself but the turpentine that was mixed with the rubber to soften it. Goodyear began experimenting with other softeners.

Goodyear mixed in everything he could think of—chemicals, ink, some say even soup. When a new batch of rubber was ready, he would roll it out, often with his wife's rolling pin, and wait to see what would happen. In winter, he nailed blobs of rubber to the side of the house to see if they would crack. As failure followed failure, Goodyear became poorer and poorer. At times he had to sell his children's schoolbooks to raise money. Sometimes he even did his experiments while in jail for failing to pay his debts.

Nothing seemed to work. But then he mixed in some nitric acid and the problems seemed to be solved. Goodyear patented the "acid gas" technique and sold a huge order of the "new" rubber mailbags to the U.S. government. It wasn't until the mailbags were returned sticky and limp that Goodyear realized he had failed again.

One day not long after the mailbags were returned, Goodyear accidentally dropped a blob of rubber mixed with sulfur and white lead on a hot stove. He didn't notice it until the next day. When he picked it up, he could hardly believe his eyes; the rubber felt like leather. It was soft and flexible and not sticky at all.

The accident pointed Goodyear in the right direction. It showed him that heat and chemicals were both necessary to make rubber flexible year-round. In 1844 he patented his process, later called "vulcanization" after Vulcan, the Roman god of fire.

Accidents have played a part in other inventions too. In 1878 a Procter and Gamble worker took a lunch break and forgot to turn off a machine that stirred soap. When he got back, the soap mixture was full of air bubbles and so light that it floated rather than sinking under water. Customers loved the new floating soap called Ivory, and the company was swamped with orders. Now that's what you'd call a happy accident.

The Secret Lake

by Janet Foster

We always knew there was a lake hidden somewhere in the woods far to the south of our cabin, but we had never seen it. It was so small that it had never been given a proper name and its tiny heart shape appeared on only a few of the larger county maps. Maybe that's why the local people seldom showed much interest in it. "Too small for fishing," some of them said. Our neighbor told us he'd seen the lake once, but that was a long time ago, and he couldn't even remember how he had come across it while he was logging in the dense bush. "Country changes a lot," he admitted, stroking his chin thoughtfully. "Don't reckon it would be easy to find now." I wasn't discouraged. I knew that somewhere, lost in the deep, dark woods at the very back of our land, there was a secret lake waiting to be found.

On a cold, clear day in late autumn, just as the maple leaves were beginning to turn crimson and frost tickled our fingers and noses, we bundled up and set off with a compass to find the little lake.

The first part was easy. Passing through the old gate below the cabin, we picked up Rabbit Trail, which wound through the tall stands of cedar and skirted the woods at the edge of the Centre Field. It had been

from The Wilds of Whip-poor-will Farm

an old cattle trail once and now we called it Rabbit Trail because the snowshoe rabbits liked to use it too.

Once past the Centre Field, we followed the Birch and Maple Wood trails through the forest and then we turned and hiked up along the High Ridge Trail. A red squirrel scolded us from the top of a tall spruce tree and little bands of black-capped chickadees flitted among the branches searching for tiny seeds. I brushed past a low juniper bush and startled a ruffed grouse that was roosting underneath. As the frightened bird rose into the air, its wingbeats made such an explosion of noise that for a second or two my heart stopped.

After we left High Ridge the woods became much deeper and darker. The trails had ended. Now we were on our own, and it was time to consult the compass. We struck out in a southeasterly direction, having taken a rough bearing while back at the cabin of where we thought the lake should be. As long as we continued in more or less a straight line, we would come to the secret lake, or so we hoped. But it was tough going. Our route led through thickets of prickly ash bushes that scratched our cheeks and tore at our clothing, past cedar swamps so thick we could hardly find our way through. We scrambled over giant rocks and boulders left by an ancient glacier and hopped across fast-flowing streams. We hiked through pine groves that were as still and silent as cathedrals, past maple trees so big I couldn't reach my arms around their trunks. And we saw birch trees so white and gleaming they must have been freshly scrubbed that very morning.

On and on we went, always checking our direction against the compass and wondering if we were ever going to reach the secret lake.

Then, from a small clearing on top of a low hill where we paused to catch our breath, I saw something sparkling through the trees ahead. We were there!

Racing each other through the last dense cedar swamp, we pushed aside the heavy branches and burst out onto the grassy banks of the little lake. It was as smooth as glass and ringed with golden tamarack trees. The water was clear and very deep. A small school of sunfish lazily swam by close to shore, their brightly colored scales flashing in the sunlight. They stayed and watched us for a moment or two and then, with a flick of their tails and feathery fins, cruised slowly on. A painted tur-

tle struggled up through the thick carpet of underwater vegetation and hung motionless on the surface until my sudden movement sent it diving for the bottom again. One or two late-season dragonflies skimmed low over the water, and on shore, a huge green bullfrog solemnly surveyed the lake with glassy, gold-rimmed eyes.

The lake was very quiet. Only the sound of a woodpecker drumming on a dead tree somewhere back in the woods broke the silence. Fumbling in my pack for the binoculars, I scanned the far side of the lake. Something close to shore was rippling the reflections. I carefully focussed the binoculars on a small, dark head that was moving through the still water, leaving a familiar V of spreading ripples. Trailing behind was a long, freshly cut, leafy poplar branch. A beaver was busy laying in his winter store!

As we watched, the beaver swam to the centre of the lake and then veered across toward a narrow point of land on our left. Just as it reached the shore, there was a loud splash and both beaver and branch disappeared under the water. I examined the point carefully with the binoculars and saw a huge mound of sticks at the edge of the shore. "It's the beaver's house," I whispered to John, handing him the binoculars.

Quietly we began to make our way around the bay. The shoreline was well flooded and there were deep channels cut in the bank where poplar branches had been dragged into the lake. Not far from the lodge we looked down into the clear water and saw the beaver's food supply, a great pile of twigs and branches poked carefully into the side of the bank. In winter, when the lake froze over, the beaver would be able to swim underwater from the lodge to the food store without having to come up through the ice.

As we reached the beaver lodge, there was a sudden rippling of the water and a beaver appeared. This was not the same one I had seen through the binoculars. It was much smaller and I decided it had to be the female. She floated on the surface just a short distance from us, then, leaving scarcely a ripple, dived. A few moments later, she surfaced near the middle of the lake and swam off toward the far shore. Climbing out onto the bank, she shook the beads of water from her matted fur and waddled off into the bushes. I had an idea she was going for more poplar branches. We were lucky to see the beaver at all for normally they work only at night. But perhaps they were working overtime to get their winter food supply in before freeze-up.

The beaver lodge was a giant mound of sticks and branches all woven together and held with mud. It sat at the edge of the lake and the beavers' hidden entrance was a long channel that led in from the lake and disappeared between two tree roots under the bank. The tunnel would lead right up into the middle of the house so that the beaver could come and go from the lodge without ever being seen.

I wanted to take an even closer look—the male beaver was still inside—but John quickly motioned me away and pointed out into the lake. The female was coming back. There was no place to hide so we just crouched down on the bank and waited.

She swam steadily toward us, holding her nose well above water and trailing a leafy poplar branch even longer than the one her mate had brought back. Suddenly she stopped swimming. Letting go of the branch, she turned her wet head from side to side, sniffing the air. I tried to sink even lower into the grass, but it was no good. A sudden breeze had come up and it was carrying our scent straight toward her. The beaver dived, and this time, as she rolled forward, the top of her flat broad tail hit the water with a resounding *whack!* that echoed clear across the lake. It was the beaver's warning signal to her mate.

We waited a long time, but the beaver did not surface again. "C'mon," John finally said as the sun sank lower and lower in the sky. "She's probably back inside the house by now. We'd better find our way back before dark."

And that's how the secret lake officially came to be known as Beaver House Lake! We went back again and again, finding easier routes every time and tying strands of brightly colored wool on the trees to mark the trail. Just before Christmas, we snowshoed in and crossed the frozen lake to the lodge, now buried beneath a mound of fresh snow. A long line of fox tracks circled the lake and ran right over the top of the beaver house. But there was no reason to fear for the beaver. They were safely down inside the lodge and their underwater food supply was within easy swimming distance. We would not see them again until the ice melted in spring.

Biruté Galdikas and the Red Apes

by Margery Facklam

Biruté Galdikas was fascinated by orangutans, the least known and most mysterious of all the great apes. She was especially curious about them because they live alone, not in groups or families, like other apes. Biruté and her husband, Rod Brindamour, travelled deep in the rain forest of Indonesia to study how orangutans live in the wild. They got more orangutans than they were prepared for. The Indonesian Forestry Service brought them orphaned babies that had been illegally captured and sold as pets, and so had never learned to live in the wild. Biruté and Rod took the baby orangs into their camp, a bark-walled thatch-roofed hut, and tried to prepare them to live in the rain forest.

Sugito was the first little orphan to become one of Biruté's babies. He was one year old and had been kept in a small crate before the authorities found him. When he climbed into Biruté's arms the first time, he decided she was his mother. If he had been raised in the forest, he would have been carried everywhere for at least a year and a half. He never let go of Biruté, not even when she went into the river for a bath or when she went to bed. When she tried to change her clothes with the little orang hugging her, he fought and howled as she shifted him from one side to the other.

It wasn't long before there was a houseful of babies. It was impossible to keep the animals outside the fragile hut. They even had one orang who poked her head right up through the thatch roof to see if it was still raining. And the animals took everything. At night, if Biruté and Rod did not give them something to wrap up in or settle into for a substitute nest, they would bang around all night until they found something—clothes, blankets, anything.

The little orangs loved to put things in their mouths—flashlight batteries, toothpaste, brushes. Biruté said that there was nothing without orang tooth-marks on it. They tasted everything and ripped apart books, clothes, even an umbrella. Sugito loved to wait until Biruté wasn't looking and then spit a mouthful of chewed rice into her tea.

"I was sometimes convinced that they were using their high ape intelligence to maximum capacity just thinking up ways to drive us crazy. Cempaka would dump bowls of salt in my tea. Sobiarso would eat flashlight bulbs, and both she and Rio would suck all our fountain pens dry. I would find old socks in my morning coffee. It was a continual battle of wits, and they won!"

Biruté watched the wild orang mothers for clues to raising her orphans. She learned that "Help yourself" is the rule in the wild, too. Because the young orangs do not have to learn to play with other orangs or get along in a group, they do not need social rules. The babies may have temper tantrums when they want something the mother is eating, but the mother just waits until the baby is through screaming, paying little attention to the fuss. She does not hand the baby food. The baby takes it from her mouth and learns the taste of foods it can eat. Biruté and

Rod collected two hundred different foods the orangs eat, including fruits, berries, leaves, bark, insects, and eggs. Biruté has never yet seen an orangutan eat meat. One of her orphans took a dead mouse away from a cat and examined it closely, but he threw it away with a look of disgust on his expressive face.

Gradually, the orphans learned to fend for themselves. When their ape-proof house, complete with screens, was finally ready, Biruté and Rod moved in, leaving the other camp to the orangs. The apes had a great time tearing it apart, but they had to sleep in the forest as a result. Rod and Biruté often took the orangs by the hand and walked them through the paths into the trees. Rod spent hours one day showing a little orang how to bend branches to make a nest, but the orang just stared at him blankly.

Although Biruté felt a little sad when the orphans were finally ready to live in the forest, she also felt like a proud parent whose child has graduated from school.

Rod and Biruté continued their study of wild orangs even while they worked with the halfway house. They went out every day, walking the paths, listening. Sometimes the only clue to the whereabouts of an orang was the sound of twigs breaking or the sound of fruit pits dropping to the ground. Once in a while they would hear the crashing of branches as the orangs broke off limbs, some as big as logs, and sent them hurtling down as a warning.

Throatpouch was the first male orang who allowed Biruté and Rod near. They had been following him constantly for two weeks, and they had known him for about two months when they realized that he had accepted them. Throatpouch was in a tree, and Rod and Biruté were sitting below, resting, when suddenly the big male came down the trunk of the tree and looked at them.

Biruté said, "I thought, well, it's all over. It's finished. We're going to be attacked." But he just totally ignored them, turned his back on them and began eating the termites that he had dug up with his claws.

Biruté began to learn the pattern of the orangs' day. She charted their pathways, learned what territories were inhabited by whom, and began to see some relationships. She was no longer surprised to see the big orangs walking on the ground; they are so heavy that ground travel is easier. The big males often make simple nests on the ground, especially for their afternoon rest. They go into the fifteen- and twenty-metre-high betel palms and ironwoods mainly to eat and sleep.

Orangutan hands are specially adapted for swinging on branches. The fingers are long and can hook securely around a limb. The thumb is short and stubby and stays out of the way when the ape swings. The young orangs and lighter females swing from limb to limb, but when a tree is far away, they swing the branch they are on and use it like a pendulum to leap to the next tree.

Biruté found that the females travel about ten kilometres a day in their home range, but it is not a private territory. They often met other females travelling with their young, or adolescent females feeding together for a while. She saw young orangs play together for short periods and sometimes even groom each other, but they were all short contacts, and when the animals were sexually mature they no longer played together.

Biruté says her most vivid memory is of the time she came face to face with a large adult male on the ground. It was a scorching-hot day. She was walking along a path when she saw a huge orangutan ambling along, head down, paying no attention to anything. Suddenly he stopped in his tracks, less than four metres from her. For many seconds they stared at each other. Biruté described the scene: "I guess he was evaluating the bizarre sight in front of him—a pale-faced primatologist with large black sunglasses, clutching an enormous bag full of dirty laundry."

There was nowhere to go. The narrow path was fenced in by tall ferns that almost closed in overhead like a tunnel. "But strangely, I felt no fear," Biruté said. "I simply marvelled at how magnificent he looked with his coat blazing orange in the full sunlight."

Then he whirled away abruptly and padded back down the trail.

Although she had been surprised to meet an orang on the path, she was no longer surprised to see a big male on the ground after having known Nick.

Nick was a male they had followed

from dawn to dusk for sixty-four days. They were determined never to let him out of their sight. When he built his nest for the night, they rested or returned to camp if it was not too far, and they were at the nest site by dawn when Nick awoke.

On the forty-fifth day of following Nick, they saw him looking for termites, and they had a moment that Biruté said she hardly dared hope for. Nick broke off a piece of wood, which they thought he might use as a tool, as the chimps did. But he only examined it closely, looking for termites, before he threw it down.

Biruté and Rod sat down on the end of the log where Nick was feeding. Suddenly, Nick stopped eating and swung around to look at the intruders. He stood upright and moved toward them until he was only a couple of metres away. Biruté and Rod did not move. They kept their heads down, their eyes away from Nick's. Direct eye contact is a sure sign of aggression among the apes. They waited. Slowly, Nick dropped to a crouch again. Still they waited. After what seemed like forever, Nick moved back to his end of the log and began to poke around again for termites. He was truly habituated. Rod and Biruté were part of his daily life.

Years later, Nick showed them another difference between orangs and the other apes. One day they watched as he waded out into the shallow lake near the camp and munched on reeds growing near the shore. Biruté says it took four years to see this because Nick was not secure enough with them to leave the safe tropical rain forest for the more open area of the lake.

Chimps and gorillas avoid the water whenever they can. They step across streams. But the orangs' habitat has so many waterways that they have adapted to it, although they do not swim. Like the other apes, they do not like the rain: but unlike the chimps and gorillas, who sit in misery in the rain, the orangs do something about it. They build platforms over their nests and often sleep, dry and comfortable, through the long afternoon rains. If they don't have time to build a roof, they hold large leaves like umbrellas over themselves.

Biruté has come to understand the three distinct units of orangutan society—the mothers and infants, the adolescents, and the solitary males. The old males are often seen with bent or broken toes and fingers. Biruté and Rod watched fights between adult males, which probably accounted for some of the deformities of the animals. But they have also seen these animals fall from the trees, and certainly they have broken bones from that.

The orangutans are intelligent animals.

Those in the halfway house used household tools all the time. One day a female watched Biruté make pancakes. Then she grabbed a glass, a handful of flour, a handful of sugar, and some eggs, put them all together, and beat them with a spoon. The orangs often used sticks to poke at things, and little Sugito would bring Biruté a cherished bottle of coke and an opener. She knew exactly what the opener did.

Biruté thought that perhaps the abundance of food, along with not having to share it with a community, explained why the orangutans never learned to make or use primitive tools. But that was only a few years into the study. After five and a half years, Biruté saw an orangutan break off a dead branch and use it as a backscratcher. "Certainly, this was not a very dramatic instance of tool use," she told a group when she was lecturing in the United States, "but it was, nonetheless, tool use."

Biruté and Rod learned a lot about the life of the red apes, and how their habitat in the Asian rain forests has been responsible for adaptations different from those of their African relatives. But they know that there is more that they have yet to learn.

"A five-and-a-half-year study such as ours represents only a good beginning when one is dealing with long-lived complex primates such as orangutans," Biruté explains. Orangs have lived to the age of fifty-seven years in captivity.

But Biruté and Rod studied orangutans long enough to begin to see the relationships between generations of these animals. They watched an older female orang they know to be the grandmother of one of the youngsters, and they learned much from these animals. They did not witness the aggression and cannibalism seen in the gorillas and chimps, except with a once-captive orang they did not consider normal. So there is much more study ahead, and many more questions to answer. Like other animal watchers, they agree that the more they find out, the more questions they learn to ask.

The "wild person of the forest" is not so much a mystery as he once was.

Blue Lotus Beads

by Jane Adams

When Nadine Jennings was fourteen, the doctor decided that she should spend a winter out of Canada, after a severe attack of pneumonia. Her parents were in Egypt; Professor Jennings was excavating in the ancient ruined city of Bubastes, near the town of Zagazig in the Delta. Nadine was happy to go there, instead of spending another lonely year at boarding school.

Her parents lived in a house built on the edge of a canal that had been old in the time of the Pharaohs, and the garden was full of fruit trees and flowers. Nadine's father bought a pony for her, and she often went riding with him to the ruins where his men were excavating the tombs. They would take their lunch and stay all day, and here it was that Nadine's strange adventure began, one clear day in late February.

She lay in the sandy grass at the foot of a broken pillar that had once supported an altar to Bast, the great cat-headed goddess. She had almost fallen asleep, when a light touch on her shoulder roused her.

Looking up, she saw a dark-eyed girl of her own age dressed in a fine linen gown that fell from her throat to her ankles in delicate pleats. Her long black hair was crowned with a wreath of blue lotus flowers. She smiled at Nadine out of sad eyes, pointed to the broken temple well beside her, and vanished.

Nadine stumbled to her feet and ran in search of her father.

"Oh, Dad," she gasped. "Dad, where is she?"

He looked at her anxiously, felt her forehead and pulse to see if the sun had "touched" her, as the Egyptians say. Nadine assured him she was well, and breathlessly poured out her story.

"Just a dream," her father concluded. "You must have fallen asleep."

But one of his foremen standing by looked curiously from Nadine to her father and back again. "She has seen the 'Little Sitt'," he said quietly, "the 'Little Lady'."

"What do you mean?"

The man explained that many children who had come to the old well had seen this vision of a girl in white, who sighed but never spoke. It was a ghost, and legend claimed that someday she would find whoever she was seeking, and then would come no more.

"What utter nonsense!"

"Was it a ghost, Dad?"

"Tush, what a story! There's no such thing as a ghost."

But even as Professor Jennings spoke, someone laughed high above their heads, and a stone was thrown from the ruins nearby, then another and another, as if some angry child was pelting them. He called out sharply in Arabic, but not one of the workmen dared venture up the ruined wall from where the laughter came. In the sudden silence each felt a chill.

Nadine was glad to mount her pony again; to gallop home through the sunset, leaving the creeping shadows of the ruins behind. She rushed into the house to tell her mother the story. Although Mrs. Jennings laughed, she did not entirely disbelieve.

Some weeks later, when Nadine was alone, she slipped away to the ruined temple, far from the tombs where the workmen were digging. She sat there quietly. She knew there had been a good deal of talk about the "ghost of the ruins" lately. Several things had gone wrong at the excavations. A workman who jeered had fallen sick. Queer, eerie singing had been heard by a night watchman.

But Nadine wasn't afraid of the pretty, sad-eyed girl of long ago. She waited patiently, while the sun sank lower, throwing dusty fingers of light across the temple court.

Soon a shadow stole towards her. She saw the same wistful figure.

"Who are you?"

"I am Tachot, daughter of Phra, the great physician of the divine Pharaohs. For thousands of years I have waited here for you, Sen-Senb, the seller of flowers in the temple, to give you back your blue lotus beads."

"I'm not Sen-Senb. I'm Nadine Jennings, and I've never had any blue lotus beads in my life."

"*Once* you were Sen-Senb, the temple slave of Bast, the cat-headed one. And in those days, beyond the shadows, I did you a wrong for which I have been waiting to atone all these years. Listen and I will show you that which you have forgotten."

A cloud drifted over Nadine's eyes. When she opened them, the ruins had vanished, and in their place stood a huge dark temple. Arches soared up into the remote dimness of the roof, and the narrow windows showed a star-strewn sky. The floor beneath her feet was of painted stone. All around her, in the dark, gleamed the mysterious angry eyes of the temple cats, who in their hundreds haunted the shrine of their guardian goddess.

Nadine slept with many other girls on a mat on the floor. Her hair was short and created a thick fringe across her forehead. Her gown of gray homespun linen was narrow and fell straight from her chin to her bare feet.

Dawn came and she rose, shivering in the chilly morning. She put away her mat and trooped to the baths, where old slave women waited to pour water over her from red porous jars. Afterwards she was scented and oiled, garlanded in flowers, and dressed in white linen.

Nadine and the other flower sellers were soon busy in the inner court sorting the roses, lilies, jasmine, marigolds, and oleanders that the country women had brought in. They arranged them into stiff bouquets which they piled into flat baskets for sale. As she passed through the temple court with her basket on her head, slaves were washing the floors and the altars, heaping fresh fruits and flowers before the shrine.

Nadine, as in a dream, saw that other girl, that other self, pass by singing lightly with her companions to the temple court inside the great bronze gates. There they waited patiently in the dust for rich and generous worshippers.

Many people passed by: poor women with their babies, men in skull caps, beautiful ladies in litters borne by slaves, with women beside them carrying huge painted fans to keep the flies away. Court officers dashed up in chariots that shone like gold.

Suddenly, from between the painted curtains of a wooden litter, she saw the face of Tachot, the ghost child of the ruins, smiling down on her as she bent to look at a bouquet. Tachot waved to a slave to accept the flowers, then flung a roll of copper coins at the flower seller's feet. She beckoned to one of her women to bring her silver slippers so she could descend from her litter. As Nadine bent to pick up the coins, a necklace of blue lotus beads fell outside the loosely fitting neck of her dress. Tachot saw it, and stared at it as if it had enchanted her.

"Where did you get that necklace, slave?"

"Lady, it has been mine all my life. There is no means of unfastening the catch from my neck."

"How many years have you been here, slave?"

"The gods alone know, lady! They tell me since babyhood. I remember no other mother than the great goddess whose slave I am."

"I will buy the necklace from you. I will give you a piece of gold for it."

"My lady is kind to notice such an unworthy person as myself, yet I cannot part with my necklace. My mother hung it round my neck. When my years of service are done and the goddess is appeased, it is by this token she will know me."

Tachot shrugged her shoulders and her slaves pushed the flower girl aside as she passed into the temple. But Sen-Senb knew that it was not over yet. She felt a cloud on her heart at the displeasure of the spoiled young beauty and knew the incident would bring trouble.

That night, sleeping among her companions, a light touch on her shoulder awakened her, and a slave beckoned her to follow. She was led into the inner part of the temple, close to the altar of sacrifice and the great temple well. She saw the High Priest of Bast and a veiled figure that she recognized as that of Tachot, daughter of Phra the physician.

"Sen-Senb, the great Lady Tachot does you the honor to require of you the paltry blue beads that are around your neck."

Sen-Senb, the temple slave, fell on her face before him. Yet timid as she was by nature, broken by the hard life and the strict discipline of the temple service, something courageous rose in her. It helped her to lift her head and gave her the strength to defy the demands of the High Priest.

"They are mine, my father. They have never been taken from my neck. May the great goddess forgive me, but I cannot give them up!"

"The goddess demands them from you."

Sen-Senb held firm against their threats and Tachot's offered gold.

Then the great priest made a sign to a tall slave beside him, who immediately wrenched the necklace from Sen-Senb's throat in one swift movement, then presented it to the eagerly waiting Tachot. The lady took it and read the engraving on the scarab with which it was linked together, and smiled as she placed a bag of gold at the feet of the goddess.

A shrill cry from Sen-Senb was stifled by the huge hand of the slave. But all had turned to look at her as she screamed, so no one except herself saw Tachot drop the beads into the fathomless recesses of the temple well.

Darkness engulfed the dream and when Nadine woke, it was to the broken altar, the singing wind, the creeping flowers and grasses of the ruined temple court. Beside her sat the wistful figure. And not a metre away lay the temple well of her strange dream. The outstretched hand of Tachot pointed down the well.

"There the beads still lie, Sen-Senb, caught in a cranny of the well. You know the story, and now you shall hear its meaning. You were my half sister, stolen from your father in revenge for a slight he paid to the goddess Bast, and made her slave. Your mother died of grief. Years later your father married a widow who already had one child. Myself.

"I was made the heiress. I was rich, petted, adored. Yet your father never loved me, and I knew if he found *you* my position would be small in his household.

"Those blue lotus beads were our only link with your family. When I read the inscription I knew you were truly your father's daughter. And I flung them into the well so you could never prove your birth.

"I died without ever telling anyone except the priest, who—for much gold—kept my secret.

"You were married to a poor date seller and spent your life wandering the desert. And in your turn, you died. Now, Sen-Senb, the beads again are yours. I shall sleep in peace at last . . ."

The voice sank away into the silence, and Nadine roused herself with a start. There was no one present and all she could hear was the wind.

She scrambled to her feet and her call brought her father and some of his men hurrying to the spot. She poured out her story. Although he laughed at it, her father sent one of the men down the well just to prove there was nothing there: that it was only a dream.

Down . . . down . . . down. Nadine peered over and saw a lantern flickering far below. Suddenly her seeker gave a signal and eager hands hauled him up. When he climbed out and stood blinking in the sunshine, Nadine saw in his hands a broken necklace of blue lotus beads.

In the falling dusk she watched her father turning the beads over in his hands. The natives glanced fearfully over their shoulders, as if expecting to see Tachot. A long shuddering sigh, like a rising wind, rose and fell. Then the silence of the evening descended.

The Painted Caves of Altamira

by Joy Hollamby-Lane

"Papa, papa. Mira, toros pintados! Look at the pictures of bulls, daddy!" shouted Maria.

"Where?" asked her father.

"Here, above my head!" Maria replied.

Hurrying to her side, Maria's father looked up. For days he had been digging up bones and stone tools in this cave, but not once had he glanced at the ceiling. It was covered with pictures! Not bulls, but bison—standing, grazing, and running. He had never seen anything like it before.

It had all started eleven years earlier.

A farmer hunting for foxes lost his dog on the hillside. He whistled and called the dog by name, but it didn't return. Finally he went back to the outcrop of rocks where he'd last seen the dog. Now, very faintly, he could hear the animal whining and barking. The sounds were coming from a hole amongst the rocks; apparently the dog had followed a fox into the hole and now couldn't get out. The farmer knelt down and started clearing the rocks, enlarging the hole.

"Hold on, you silly dog. I'll have you out in a minute," he called to the frightened animal.

Finally the hole was big enough for the farmer to get his head and shoulders through. Reaching down, he pulled the dog out by the scruff of its neck. But now the farmer was curious. The dog's barking had been ringing as though he'd been in a cavern. Caves were not uncommon in this area of northern Spain, but none had been reported on Altamira before.

Ensuring that the entrance was safe and no rocks would fall on him, the farmer lowered himself through the hole. He had no light with him and the sunshine coming through the hole gave little illumination, but there was enough light to show the farmer that he really was in a cave. Not far from the entrance was a pile of rocks that had fallen from the ceiling. There

wasn't enough space for the farmer to squeeze past the rocks, so he picked up a stone and threw it over the pile. He heard it land and roll and by the sound he knew that the cave was fairly large.

Back on the hillside the farmer whistled to his dog, then hurried to his village of Santillana del Mar to tell of his discovery. But no one seemed very interested. After all, what is one more cave? Just another place to lose a straying sheep or cow that had broken through the stone wall of its pasture.

It wasn't until seven years later that an employee on the nearby estate of a nobleman, Don Marcelino Santiago Tomás Sanz de Sautuola, heard about the cave and told his employer. He knew the Señor was interested in the modern sciences, especially geology and prehistory.

Don Marcelino immediately took two of his workmen and rode the two and a half kilometres to Altamira. They enlarged the entrance to the cave and went inside, but, like the farmer, were stopped by the rock fall. With shovels they started to clear the rocks, but while he was digging Don Marcelino noticed animal bones—all split in half lengthwise—and amongst them stones fashioned like the stone tools he'd seen in museums.

The nobleman realized he must have found the cave dwelling of prehistoric men. Gathering several of the bones and stone tools, he went to visit an old friend at the university in Madrid. Don Juan Vilanova y Piera confirmed the nobleman's belief that the cave had been a prehistoric dwelling.

"These bones were split by men to get at the marrow in the centre," Don Vilanova said.

"And what about the stones?" asked Don Marcelino.

"They are tools," replied the professor. "Tools of the Paleolithic Age, of stone-age men."

"What steps would you suggest I follow to excavate the cave?" asked the nobleman.

"You've never been to a prehistory dig, have you?" asked Don Vilanova.

"No, unfortunately I haven't," replied Don Marcelino.

"Then I'd suggest you spend some time at one before you dig any further," his friend replied.

For the next four years, Don Marcelino visited other prehistoric sites, museums, and exhibitions. At the Second Universal Exhibition, at Paris in 1878, he examined the scrapers, arrowheads, knives, and borers of flint found in the cave shelters of the Perigord. Finally, in the spring of 1879, he returned to the cave of Altamira.

With his workmen Don Marcelino reopened the original entrance to the cave and removed the rock pile that had fallen from the roof. Then he started to dig, slowly and carefully. Almost at once he found bones and teeth of bison, stag, and horse, and the shells of oysters and other mollusks that must have come from the nearby seashore.

Amongst the bones and shells were flint tools and knives, bone awls and needles. Some of the shells had deposits of black and dark red pigments stuck to them and there were lumps of the same pigments scattered amongst the bones.

Don Marcelino worked his way right to the end of the big, main cavern. Here he found the skeleton of a cave bear. These creatures were almost twice the size of grizzly bears and much more ferocious. Stone-age men sometimes fought fierce battles with them for possession of a cave.

When the nobleman had satisfied himself that this was as far as the cave went, he returned to a passage that led to the left at the entrance to the main room. This passage was narrow, and in places barely a metre high. Don Marcelino had to stoop and crawl along it. At the end he found another room, smaller than the main cavern, and rectangular in shape. Here he prepared to dig again.

Each night, when he went home, he took with him the bones, shells, and tools found during the day. Then, after dinner, he would show them to his twelve-year-old daughter, Maria, who was keenly interested in her father's hobby. He sometimes found it hard to answer some of her questions because at that time not very much was known about our cave-dwelling ancestors.

One morning, as Don Marcelino was about to leave for the cave, Maria came running out of the house.

"Take me with you, please, daddy," she said.

"Oh, no, Maria," her father replied. "It's cold and dark in the cave and you'd soon get bored."

"No, I won't. Honestly, daddy. I want to see the cave for myself. Please, daddy?"

"Well, go and ask your mother what she thinks."

Away went Maria, and Don Marcelino sent one of his men to get her horse; he knew he wasn't going to get away without her that day.

But her father had been right; it wasn't long before Maria got tired of squatting to watch her father dig slowly and carefully, sifting every shovelful, examining every bone and stone he found. Finally, she got up and wandered away by herself. It was then that Don Marcelino heard his daughter shout, *"Papa, papa. Mira, toros pintados!"*

Father and daughter held up their torches and examined the ceiling. Here was a whole horde of beasts, some of them species which the Señor did not recognize, although he was an ardent naturalist and hunter. But so excellent were the paintings that he realized the artist had lived amongst these animals and was familiar with every muscle and movement of them. Don Marcelino noticed that the painter had used the natural contours and bosses of the stone to give a three-dimensional effect; when the lights were moved, the animals seemed to move too.

With his torch Don Marcelino went carefully over the ceiling and walls of the whole cavern. Near the entrance to the passage was an outstanding collection of about twenty animals, all apparently life-size and painted in several shades to give the animals a more lifelike appearance. Amongst them were three animals which seemed out of place: a gray boar, a wild horse, and a doe. The colors were as fresh as if they had been applied within the last few days, yet the paintings had been created some 10 000 years earlier; stalactites obliterated parts of them.

Again the nobleman went to Madrid. Maria had wanted to go with him, but he felt the 650-kilometre journey by horse-and-coach would be too tiring for her. But he promised that when he returned with Don Vilanova, she should lead the professor to the pictures.

In Madrid Don Vilanova was surprised at his friend's excitement and secretly felt the nobleman was exaggerating; but some pictures carved on bone had been found in France just the year before. The professor agreed to accompany his friend back to Altamira.

Led by Maria, they explored the whole cave. Behind the group of bison were earlier charcoal sketches of the animals. On the other side of the chamber were two lifelike horses and, between them, the imprint of three hands. Two of the hands had been traced, and the third had been made by pressing a hand covered with paint against the rock. As these were all left-hand prints, the artist must have been right-handed. Many of the paintings were in three colors. This explained the shells with dried pigment; they had been the artist's paint pots.

The excitement of the friends grew with each new discovery. In the main cavern the roof had been too high for the artist to reach, but wherever there was a level space on the walls, there was a picture. Sometimes the artist had had to stand on a stalagmite or rock protrusion to reach a flat surface to paint. In another place, where once the wall must have been as soft as wet cement, a bison head had been sketched with a finger and was surrounded by parallel grooves also made by fingers. In some places the animals had been etched with a sharp instrument, while others had been outlined with charcoal.

Cave painting, Lascaux, France.   Cave painting, Altamira, Spain.   Indian petroglyphs, Utah.

Maria was the first child to discover Paleolithic cave art, but she was not the last. Three brothers in France, the sons of Count Begouen, were on an expedition with their teacher when they discovered clay bisons in dark passages of the caves at Tuc d'Audoubert, and the neighboring Trois Frères (Three Brothers) cave where a "horned god" looks down on hundreds of splendid engravings. And on September 10, 1940, a group of boys at Montegnac, also in France, slipped through a narrow shaft in the rocks and found themselves in a cavern that is now called the Hall of Great Bulls; these are the incredible frescoes of Lascaux.

Such prehistoric art has been found all over the world. There are several painted caves in South Africa, some of them found in the 1970s. In Canada, Indian paintings on rocks and cliffs can be seen at Agawa on Lake Superior, and petroglyphs (rock carvings) on Vancouver Island.

Why did stone-age men paint lifelike animals in caves? No one knows for sure, but there are several theories. Some experts think the pictures were painted to ensure good fortune in the hunt; others believe it was a form of worship. I like to think that some of them were done just because the artist liked to paint! Perhaps the bison at Altamira were created by a young man who wanted to show the women and children how the hunters had found such a group of animals on a particular hunt. Perhaps, like professors teaching anatomy to future doctors today, teachers used the paintings to inform future hunters about the animals they would pursue.

Whatever the reason, people—maybe you—will continue to find cave and rock paintings for a long time to come.

On the Way to Canada

by Margaret J. Anderson

Elspeth MacDonald's parents planned to leave Scotland to start a new life in Canada, where they had relatives. Before the family could leave Glasgow, both parents died. Elspeth knew that the authorities would separate her and her brother, Robbie, so she decided to run away. She had the steamship tickets and a little money, and she knew that her uncle lived in a place called Manitoba.

The children travelled by train to Liverpool, and joined the throng of people waiting to board the ship bound for Canada. To keep Robbie quiet, Elspeth invented a hide-and-seek game about Shadow Bairns who had to hide so they wouldn't catch them.

Elspeth could feel the surge of movement when the first passengers were allowed on the ship somewhere far ahead. She was surrounded by tall men in heavy coats, smelling of wet wool and tobacco. The suitcase was hard to manage, and she worried about getting separated from Robbie. He was having his own troubles, being continually shoved aside and buffeted by suitcases and hampers.

from The Journey of the Shadow Bairns

As they were pushed nearer the ship, Elspeth tried to plan what she would say to the ticket collector. It should be easy to convince him that she and Rob had been separated from their parents in this crush, but how was she to find out where they should go on the boat? Was she supposed to have tickets for rooms or beds? She looked up at the side of the ship, rising above the dock like a great white wall. Was it like a train inside, with lots of seats?

Her worries were interrupted by a small but urgent request from Robbie.

"Robbie, you've got to wait!" said Elspeth, desperately looking at the mob of people hemming them in.

"I can't wait," said Robbie tearfully.

"It won't be long now," Elspeth lied, knowing that it could well be hours before they were on the boat.

"I can't wait!" said Robbie again, and promptly wet his blue serge trousers. Right then, Elspeth decided that running away had been a mistake.

There were more problems than she could cope with. When she got on the boat she'd tell the ticket collector that they were by themselves. Let *him* worry about Rob's wet trousers. With that decision made, it was easier to wait her turn to board the *Lake Manitoba*.

They were squashed tighter now, so tight that Elspeth could not even look down at her own feet, but she eventually felt the edge of the gangplank and shuffled forward and up. The travelling bag caught on a ridge of board nailed crosswise on the ramp. She felt the pressure of the crowd behind her as she struggled to free it. The handle was slipping from her grasp, but she managed to jerk the bag up. "Hang on to me, Robbie!" she shouted, but her words were lost, muffled by the crush of bodies around her.

At last they were on the deck. Elspeth looked wildly around for Robbie, only to find that he was right beside her, flushed and tousled, but much less worried and frightened than she was. There was no sign of any official looking at tickets, so Elspeth and Robbie joined the crowd pouring down the stairway. When they saw some other children, they instinctively followed them, and found that all families with children were lodged together in the middle hold.

Elspeth felt vaguely disappointed that the boat wasn't more like the train. There the seats had been covered in soft red velvet and the little lamp fixtures had been gold. Here everything was of raw wood and bare boards, as if it were still being built. The hold was partitioned off by upright posts. Boards nailed to these formed crude bunks, sometimes two deep, sometimes three. Instead of mattresses there was loose straw, and the floor was covered with sawdust.

The hold was a huge room, dimly lit by paraffin lamps. As more and more people crowded in, it seemed smaller and became unbearably hot and noisy. People were claiming bunks, spreading their belongings around, shouting at their children. Tentatively, Elspeth set their bundles on a bottom bunk, but a woman immediately told her to move along because that bunk was taken.

In the far corner, Elspeth spotted a narrow opening between the bunks on the end wall and those on the side. Wriggling into it, she found that the ends of the two sets of bunks and the side of the ship formed a space like a tiny room. Pulling Robbie in beside her, she whispered,

"This is where the Shadow Bairns are going to live."

Robbie liked their corner. Right away he began to build Pig-Bear a castle out of the sawdust on the floor. Elspeth filched some straw from neighboring bunks, just in case they had to sleep there on the floor. She hoped that once everyone was settled she would be able to claim a left-over bunk without causing any fuss, but the way people were still pouring in there weren't going to be any bunks left. Already arguments and even fights were breaking out. People were being forced to give up some of the bunks they had claimed and put two or three children in one bed.

Elspeth spread their blankets and sorted out their clothes. She helped Robbie change his trousers, laying aside the wet ones until she could find out where to wash them. Getting on the boat now seemed so easy that she was ready to cope again. She wouldn't tell anyone they were alone—not yet. After all, she had even thought of bringing along a bar of yellow laundry soap.

The bunks on either side were occupied now, but no one paid any attention to them. One woman hung blankets over the end of her bunks, which made their corner very dark.

"Pig-Bear can't see," Robbie complained. "And I'm too hot. I want a drink of water."

"I'll get you a drink soon," Elspeth promised, wondering what they were going to do about meals. She was beginning to realize there was a lot she didn't know. "We'll go back up and take a look around, but you're to stay right beside me."

"Like a Shadow Bairn," Robbie said, nodding solemnly.

They crawled out of their corner and made their way through the crowded hold. The first flight of stairs was more like a ladder than a staircase. They had to push their way between people who were still on their way down. Two more flights brought them to the deck.

It was a relief to be outside. A thin drizzle of rain was falling, but the day seemed bright in contrast to the gloom below. They stood in a sheltered place between a lifeboat and the rail, absorbed in the bustling activity all around them. Passengers still hurried up the gangplanks, cranes swung precarious loads of luggage from the dock to the hold, and a mob of gulls was fighting over a basket of bread that had burst open

on the dock. The smell of the sea, the wet salt wind, and the cries of the birds reminded Elspeth of their faraway home in the Highlands. For a moment, even she who had so little to leave behind suffered a pang of homesickness, but that was forgotten when a straggling band assembled on the dock played "God be with you till we meet again."

"They're singing to us!" Robbie said, jumping up and down with excitement and clapping his hands.

The pulse of the engines and the shudder of the boat drowned out the last quavering notes. A cheer went up from those staying on the shore, answered by a louder cheer from the deck. When the ship pulled away and the people on the dock were just a dark blur, all waving white handkerchiefs, Robbie was still waving back. He thought that everyone was saying goodbye to him.

Elspeth watched the receding shore. *They* couldn't get Robbie now. She put her arm protectively around his shoulders, pulling him closer to her. If only Mama and Papa could be here too. She tried to shake off the black feeling of loneliness that slipped over her when she thought of her parents. She turned to Robbie. "We've done it, Robbie! We ran away and no one stopped us!" But somewhere in her mind came the answering thought—no one really cared. Abruptly, Elspeth turned her back on England and pulled Robbie over to the stairs.

At the bottom of the first flight they passed a dining room where a steward was setting out a tub of ship biscuits and another of hard-boiled eggs. As soon as his back was turned, Elspeth dashed forward and shoved four eggs into her pockets. She took a biscuit for each of them.

"Was it all right to take them?" Robbie asked nervously when Elspeth divided the spoils back in the hold. "Won't they be angry?"

"It's our supper. It's meant for us," Elspeth reassured him. "It's just better to eat it here by ourselves. I'll take our mugs and fetch tea, but you wait here."

The ship biscuit was about fifteen centimetres across and three centimetres thick, so it kept Robbie quiet for a long time. For both of them an egg was a rare treat, and they'd never had two each before.

By evening, Rob and Elspeth knew their way around the ship. They heard plenty of angry complaints about the crowded holds and makeshift washrooms, but they thought nothing of it because they had shared a toilet with five other families back in Glasgow.

Robbie didn't want to sleep, with all the excitement and noise. On one side of them a baby was crying. On the other, a man and his wife were arguing.

"I'll lie down here right beside you," Elspeth said, tucking a blanket around Robbie. "Look, here's Pig-Bear!"

The quarrelling voices became still, and they could hear the mother singing softly to her crying baby. Tears filled Elspeth's eyes as she recognized the sweet, sad music of "Bonny Doon," a song that Mama used to sing. "Ye mind me of departed joys, departed never to return." Elspeth began to cry.

Robbie reached up and touched Elspeth's wet cheek. "Don't cry, Elspeth!" he said softly. *"They'll* never find us here. *They* won't know where to look."

She snuggled closer to him. Was it easier or harder for Robbie, not being burdened with so many memories? she wondered. As time went by, he would forget Mama and Papa. But at least he still had her, and she had him. Comforted by this thought, she finally drifted off to sleep to the soothing sound of hymns.

For the first time since Mama had died, Robbie slept through the night. They were awakened by the sounds of the families around them beginning their second day at sea. Elspeth went to wash a few clothes in a scant bucket of water one of the stewards had provided, leaving Robbie behind. When she returned to the hold she was surprised to find that he was not alone. Two freckle-faced girls stared up at Elspeth. They both had fine, light-red hair, almost orange, twisted into tight braids. They looked about eight or nine years old. Elspeth was sure she had seen them before.

"They're Rachel and Rebecca," Robbie said eagerly. "They want to be Shadow Bairns."

"Shadow Bairns are quiet," Elspeth said sternly. "How do they know about Shadow Bairns if *you* were quiet?"

"Pig-Bear went out and that one—Rachel—found him. I had to go out and get him. Shadow Bairns stick together."

Elspeth looked at the girls and wondered how Robbie knew which one was Rachel. They looked exactly alike. Then she remembered where she had seen them before. At Carlisle Station, with their father and mother and brother, saying goodbye to the old ladies.

"Please, will you let us be Shadow Bairns?" Rebecca asked.

"Let them," Robbie pleaded.

Elspeth looked at his eager face. It might help to have friends on the boat, even though they were younger than she was. And playing with them would keep Robbie amused. "All right," she said.

"I knew she'd let us! I knew she would!" Rachel said to Robbie.

"But first you have to show that you know *how* to be Shadow Bairns. You have to creep through the hold and up to the deck and hide behind the lifeboat near the top of the stairs without your brother seeing you."

"How do you know about our brother?" Rebecca asked.

"Elspeth knows everything," Robbie answered proudly. "I'll show you the lifeboat."

Elspeth watched them go, looking forward to a few minutes to herself. Robbie and the twins merged with the shadows, passing through the hold with exaggerated caution, but no one paid any attention to them. It was easy to be a Shadow Bairn! Easy to go unnoticed, even in a place where there wasn't enough room for everyone. Elspeth suddenly found that she didn't want to be alone after all. Taking the clothes she had just washed, she followed the children to the deck, giving them time to reach the lifeboat first.

They had pulled a piece of loose canvas around them to shut out the wind, and were sitting together, snug in its shelter.

"We did it! We did it!" shouted one of the twins.

"Shadow Bairns are quiet," Elspeth reminded her.

"Tell us more about Shadow Bairns."

Elspeth sat down beside them and told them about this place called Manitoba where the Shadow Bairns were going. She could see the place clearly just from the sound of its name. It was a small town, with steep mountains behind, close to a huge lake, like the picture Miss Johnstone had shown them. The houses were white, crowded close together, and had steep red roofs and doors of different colors.

"What color is Uncle Donald's door?" Robbie asked.

"Blue," Elspeth answered. "Blue like the water in the lake. And all around the lake are beaches of silver sand."

The story was interrupted by an angry shout. "So that's where you brats are hiding! I should throw you overboard, because that's where Papa and Mama think you are by now, and I'm getting the blame for it! You come back down to your bunk and stay there!"

"We can't, Matthew! We're Shadow Bairns," said Rachel.

"We weren't to tell," shouted Rebecca.

The boy grabbed the twins and pulled them toward the stairs, both of them yelling loudly.

"Maybe their brother wants to be a Shadow Bairn too," Robbie suggested when they were gone.

Elspeth shook her head. He was too old to pretend things like that. Besides, he hadn't even noticed her and Robbie.

"I'm hungry," Robbie said.

"Maybe there are still some eggs and biscuits," Elspeth answered hopefully. "Let's go down to the dining room."

The stewards were bringing in pots of stew and mashed potatoes. Elspeth and Robbie hesitated in the doorway, drawn by the warm smell of the food, but afraid to go into the crowded dining room.

"Have your ma and pa lost their appetites already?" a friendly steward asked. "Come on in and help yourselves."

They filled their bowls and sat close together at one of the big tables, eating quickly and feeling like uninvited guests at a party. The benches were nailed to the floor, and the tables had raised edges that made it difficult for Robbie to reach his food. They soon understood the reason for the raised edges when bowls and mugs slid across the table as the ship rolled.

"Hold on to your dish, Rob," Elspeth warned. Too late. Robbie's plate had shot across the table.

"One bowl of this muck is enough for me!" said the man opposite, pushing it back.

Robbie laughed, and they both began to feel more at ease.

After dinner they went down to the hold. The mother was singing to her baby, and someone was snoring loudly on the other side. Their dark corner now seemed familiar and welcoming. A feeling of well-being settled over Elspeth. She and Robbie were together, part of this huge family of people, all going to Canada.

The New Land

by William Kurelek and Margaret S. Engelhart

In the early nineteenth century, large numbers of European immigrants began arriving in Canada. Most came because they were poor and hoped to make better lives for themselves here. The painter William Kurelek was the son of such an immigrant, and these paintings of his show some of what pioneering farmers experienced in the new land.

Arriving in the New World: Full of hope, a pioneering couple build their first shelter in the wilderness.

from They Sought a New World

Taken from *Jewish Life in Canada* ©1976 William Kurelek and Abraham J. Arnold, published by Hurtig Publishers.

◄ Arriving on the Prairies: When they saw the vast emptiness, did they wonder if they should have come?

Children's Work: Boys or girls were given the job of bringing cows home and doing the actual milking. ▼

Taken from *They Sought a New World* ©1985 Estate of the late William Kurelek, published by Tundra Books.

At the Mercy of Nature: A single spark could destroy a field and wipe away hope for a harvest.

In Sickness and in Health: When the mother fell ill, this father ploughed with his baby strapped to his back.

Taken from *They Sought a New World* © 1985 Estate of the late William Kurelek, published by Tundra Books.

▲ A Farm Wedding: The preparations could take months and the festivities could go on for several days. Relatives travelled great distances to attend as it was a rare chance for a family reunion.

Taken from *They Sought a New World* © 1985 Estate of the late William Kurelek, published by Tundra Books.

▲ Looking Back: For a fortunate few, success came beyond anything they ever dreamed possible. Looking Ahead: Others would continue to hope for a better life for their children and grandchildren.

If I Forget Thee, O Earth

by Arthur C. Clarke

When Marvin was ten years old, his father took him through the long, echoing corridors that led up through Administration and Power, until at last they came to the uppermost levels of all and were among the swiftly growing vegetation of the Farmlands. Marvin liked it here: it was fun watching the great, slender plants creeping with almost visible eagerness toward the sunlight as it filtered down through the plastic domes to meet them. The smell of life was everywhere, awakening inexpressible longings in his heart: no longer was he breathing the dry, cool air of the residential levels, purged of all smells but the faint tang of ozone. He wished he could stay here for a little while, but Father would not let him. They went onward until they had reached the entrance to the Observatory, which he had never visited: but they did not stop, and Marvin knew with a sense of rising excitement that there could be only one goal left. For the first time in his life, he was going Outside.

There were a dozen of the surface vehicles, with their wide balloon tires and pressurized cabins, in the great servicing chamber. His father must have been expected, for they were led at once to the little scout car waiting by the huge circular door of the airlock. Tense with expectancy, Marvin settled himself down in the cramped cabin while his father started the motor and checked the controls. The inner door of the lock slid open and then closed behind them: he heard the roar of the great air pumps fade slowly away as the pressure dropped to zero. Then the "Vacuum" sign flashed on, the outer door parted, and before Marvin lay the land which he had never yet entered.

He had seen it in photographs, of course: he had watched it imaged on television screens a hundred times. But now it was lying all around him, burning beneath the fierce sun that crawled so slowly across the jet-black sky. He stared into the west, away from the blinding splendor of the sun—and there were the stars, as he had been told but had never quite believed. He gazed at them for a long time, marvelling that anything could be so bright and yet so tiny. They were intense unscintillating points, and suddenly he remembered a rhyme he had once read in one of his father's books:

> Twinkle, twinkle, little star,
> How I wonder what you are.

Well, *he* knew what the stars were. Whoever asked that question must have been very stupid. And what did they mean by "twinkle"? You could see at a glance that all the stars shone with the same steady, unwavering light. He abandoned the puzzle and turned his attention to the landscape around him.

They were racing across a level plain at almost a hundred miles an hour, the great balloon tires sending up little spurts of dust behind them. There was no sign of the Colony: in the few minutes while he had been gazing at the stars, its domes and radio towers had fallen below the horizon. Yet there were other indications of man's presence, for about a mile ahead Marvin could see the curiously shaped structures clustering round the head of a mine. Now and then a puff of vapor would emerge from a squat smokestack and would instantly disperse.

They were past the mine in a moment: Father was driving with a reckless and exhilarating skill as if—it was a strange thought to come into a child's mind—he were trying to escape from something. In a few minutes they had reached the edge of the plateau on which the Colony had been built. The ground fell sharply away beneath them in a dizzying slope whose lower stretches were lost in shadow. Ahead, as far as the eye could reach, was a jumbled wasteland of craters, mountain ranges, and ravines. The crests of the mountains, catching the low sun, burned like islands of fire in a sea of darkness: and above them the stars still shone as steadfastly as ever.

There could be no way forward—yet there was. Marvin clenched his fists as the car edged over the slope and started the long descent. Then he saw the barely visible track leading down the mountainside, and relaxed a little. Other men, it seemed, had gone this way before.

Night fell with a shocking abruptness as they crossed the shadow line and the sun dropped below the crest of the plateau. The twin search-lights sprang into life, casting blue-white bands on the rocks ahead, so that there was scarcely need to check their speed. For hours they drove through valleys and past the foot of mountains whose peaks seemed to comb the stars, and sometimes they emerged for a moment into the sun-light as they climbed over higher ground.

And now on the right was a wrinkled, dusty plain, and on the left, its ramparts and terraces rising mile after mile into the sky, was a wall of mountains that marched into the distance until its peaks sank from sight below the rim of the world. There was no sign that men had ever explored this land, but once they passed the skeleton of a crashed rocket, and beside it a stone cairn surmounted by a metal cross.

It seemed to Marvin that the mountains stretched on forever: but at last, many hours later, the range ended in a towering, precipitous head-land that rose steeply from a cluster of little hills. They drove down into a shallow valley that curved in a great arc toward the far side of the mountains: and as they did so, Marvin slowly realized that something very strange was happening in the land ahead.

The sun was now low behind the hills on the right: the valley before them should be in total darkness. Yet it was awash with a cold white radiance that came spilling over the crags beneath which they were driv-ing. Then, suddenly, they were out in the open plain, and the source of the light lay before them in all its glory.

It was very quiet in the little cabin now that the motors had stopped. The only sound was the faint whisper of the oxygen feed and an occasional metallic crepitation as the outer walls of the vehicle radi-ated away their heat. For no warmth at all came from the great silver crescent that floated low above the far horizon and flooded all this land with pearly light. It was so brilliant that minutes passed before Marvin could accept its challenge and look steadfastly into its glare, but at last he could discern the outlines of continents, the hazy border of the at-mosphere, and the white islands of cloud. And even at this distance, he could see the glitter of sunlight on the polar ice.

It was beautiful, and it called to his heart across the abyss of space. There in that shining crescent were all the wonders that he had never known—the hues of sunset skies, the moaning of the sea on pebbled shores, the patter of falling rain, the unhurried benison of snow. These and a thousand others should have been his rightful heritage, but he knew them only from the books and ancient records, and the thought filled him with the anguish of exile.

Why could they not return? It seemed so peaceful beneath those lines of marching cloud. Then Marvin, his eyes no longer blinded by the glare, saw that the portion of the disk that should have been in darkness was gleaming faintly with an evil phosphorescence: and he remembered. He was looking upon the funeral pyre of a world—upon the radioactive aftermath of Armageddon. Across a quarter of a million miles of space, the glow of dying atoms was still visible, a perennial reminder of the ruinous past. It would be centuries yet before that deadly glow died from the rocks and life could return again to fill that silent, empty world.

And now Father began to speak, telling Marvin the story which until this moment had meant no more to him than the fairy tales he had once been told. There were many things he could not understand: it was impossible for him to picture the glowing, multicolored pattern of life on the planet he had never seen. Nor could he comprehend the forces that had destroyed it in the end, leaving the Colony, preserved by its isolation, as the sole survivor. Yet he could share the agony of those final days, when the Colony had learned at last that never again would the supply ships come flaming down through the stars with gifts from home. One by one the radio stations had ceased to call: on the shadowed globe the lights of the cities had dimmed and died, and they were alone at last, as no men had ever been alone before, carrying in their hands the future of the race.

Then had followed the years of despair, and the long-drawn battle for survival in this fierce and hostile world. That battle had been won, though barely: this little oasis of life was safe against the worst that Nature could do. But unless there was a goal, a future toward which it could work, the Colony would lose the will to live, and neither machines nor skill nor science could save it then.

So, at last, Marvin understood the purpose of this pilgrimage. He would never walk beside the rivers of that lost and legendary world, or listen to the thunder raging above its softly rounded hills. Yet one day—how far ahead?—his children's children would return to claim their heritage. The winds and the rains would scour the poisons from the burning lands and carry them to the sea, and in the depths of the sea they would waste their venom until they could harm no living things. Then the great ships that were still waiting here on the silent, dusty plains could lift once more into space, along the road that led to home.

That was the dream: and one day, Marvin knew with a sudden flash of insight, he would pass it on to his own son, here at this same spot with the mountains behind him and the silver light from the sky streaming into his face.

He did not look back as they began the homeward journey. He could not bear to see the cold glory of the crescent Earth fade from the rocks around him, as he went to rejoin his people in their long exile.

Detail of *And the Spirit Will Guide* by Linda Beth Sanderson

Tom and Alice and Anne, with an e!

373

Who's Who in Children's Books

by Sharon Stewart

Alice has learned a *lot* of rules and lessons, but when she pops down a rabbit hole into Wonderland, she finds that most of them no longer apply. Despite this, nothing fazes Alice, from conversing with a disappearing cat to playing croquet with hedgehogs for balls and flamingoes for mallets!

Alice in Wonderland by Lewis Carroll

Bruno Walton and **Boots O'Neal** are the black sheep of their boarding school, MacDonald Hall, because they come up with crazy ideas, like putting Fizz-All in a rival team's swimming pool and investing school funds in the stock market. They are aided in their hilarious schemes by the inmates of Miss Scrimmage's Finishing School for Young Ladies.

Go Jump in the Pool by Gordon Korman

Caddie Woodlawn is a red-headed tomboy who lives in pioneer times. Caddie is better at ploughing than at cooking, and she would rather mend clocks than sew. Her curiosity and boldness always get her into scrapes, but her courage and quick thinking get her out again.

Caddie Woodlawn by Carol Ryrie Brink

Dorothy just can't seem to help having adventures. First a cyclone whirls her off to the land of Oz and drops her house on a wicked witch, killing her. Then she meets three valiant companions, and together they find the Emerald City, dissolve a witch, and unmask the Wizard of Oz. No matter how exciting her adventures are, though, Dorothy wants to get back home to Kansas.

The Wizard of Oz by L. Frank Baum

Ellen Grae Derryberry is a matutinophile who likes boiled peanuts by the pound, fishing, and Grover, her friend. What she doesn't care for are soap and water and starched petticoats. Ellen Grae's specialty is telling tall stories to anyone and everyone.

Ellen Grae by Vera and Bill Cleaver

Figgy Gryshevich would like to go on playing Monopoly on his friend Ada's porch for the rest of his life. But when you have a grandfather like the Goat Man, life isn't that easy. Even a lucky rabbit's foot can't protect Figgy from his troubles, but his loyalty and concern for his grandfather win him friends who care and help.

After the Goat Man by Betsy Byars

Ged goes to the magic Isle of Roke to learn the arts of wizardry. Though he is gifted, Ged is loud, proud, and full of temper. In a duel of magic with a rival, he accidentally lets a deadly shadow-beast loose upon the world. Ged must then set forth on a quest to save both himself and all the lands of Earthsea from its evil power.

Wizard of Earthsea by Ursula LeGuin

Heidi lives high on a mountainside in Switzerland. Free-spirited and lively, she wins the heart of her crusty old grandfather, befriends a surly goatherd, and persuades an invalid girl to walk again. Heidi's joy and optimism change the lives of everybody about her.

Heidi by Johanna Spyri

Ilse Burnley loves using fancy words, especially when she gets angry. In one quarrel she calls her friend Emily a "proud, stuck-up, conceited, top-lofty biped"! But Ilse is warm-hearted and true, and though she may call Emily a serpent and a crocodile one minute, she's quite likely to hug her the next.

Emily of New Moon by L.M. Montgomery.

Julilly, who is just twelve years old, is sold to do heavy labor on a plantation in the deep South. She discovers she is strong enough to survive and to help and protect her friend, Liza, too. Julilly's courage and determination keep them both going on the long road to freedom in Canada.

Underground to Canada by Barbara Smucker

Kungo, an Inuit boy, is away from home when raiders kill his parents and kidnap his sister. Kungo sets off to find Ittok, a legendary archer, because he hopes that he, too, can become a great archer and avenge his family. But when Kungo's moment of vengence comes at last, he finds that Ittok has taught him not just archery but wisdom and kindness too.

The White Archer by James Houston

Lewis Barnavelt has always thought of himself as cowardly and not very good at anything. Yet when he becomes involved

in mysterious events in his uncle's house, Lewis discovers that there is more to him than he had suspected. In the end his insight and special kind of courage defeat the schemes of an evil wizard.

The House with a Clock in Its Walls by John Bellairs

Mowgli, the wolf boy, knows little of the ways of human beings. He is loyal to his pack leader, Akela, and loving toward his friends, Baloo the Bear and Bagheera the Black Panther. To his enemy, Shere Khan the Tiger, Mowgli is unforgiving, and he carries out his vow of revenge. Such is the Law of the Jungle.

The Jungle Book by Rudyard Kipling

Nicholas Knock is a venturesome boy whose mind has funny edges. He goes for walks in the universe and comes home late, and he loves a silver honkabeest. When it disappears, he goes on hunting it, for he has found he can't do without it.

Nicholas Knock and Other People by Dennis Lee

Olwen Pendennis is the hereditary keeper of an interstellar beacon on the distant planet of Isis. Her life is carefree and joyous, until settlers arrive from Earth. Through the pain she suffers when they reject her because she looks different from them, Olwen comes to understand that her struggle to hold onto her pride and self-respect is part of the price of growing up.

The Keeper of the Isis Light by Monica Hughes

Pippi Longstocking is the strongest girl in the world, and she lives by herself in the Villa Villekulla. She has Mr. Nilsson, a monkey, for company, and she keeps a horse on the porch. She doesn't have any grown-ups around to tell her what to do, so poor Pippi just does exactly what she pleases every single day!

Pippi Longstocking by Astrid Lindgren

Queenie Peavy has never been more than a stone's throw away from trouble. She has said "I don't care" so many times that she almost believes it. But Queenie does care. Her father is in jail, and she idealizes and defends him. When it is almost too late, she at last learns to be honest with herself and to face things as they really are.

Queenie Peavy by Robert Burch

Robin Squires yearns to travel to the New World. When he does go there with his uncle, his curiosity and kind heart get him into trouble. It takes every bit of his

courage to endure the hardships, enslavement, and deadly danger that await him on mysterious Oak Island.

The Hand of Robin Squires by Joan Clark

Storm Boy loves the beach and the ocean of his home in South Australia, and he can't bear to be indoors, no matter what the weather. He is a friend to all living things, yet it is his friendship with a great white pelican that teaches him the most about caring and loving and saying goodbye.

Storm Boy by Colin Thiele

Tom Sawyer is a terrible trial to his poor Aunt Polly, who is trying to bring him up to be respectable. Tom steals jam and runs away to be a pirate chief. He's fond of dead cats, and his best friend is the disreputable Huckleberry Finn. Tom is usually in trouble, but somehow he always gets out of it unscathed.

The Adventures of Tom Sawyer by Mark Twain

Valerie has always been jealous of her sister and brother, right up to the minute they all blunder into an alien space trap. But when she wakes up alone on the planet of the popeyes, all Valerie can think about is finding Susan and John. It takes all her wits and nerve to find a way for all of them to escape from the outlaw planet.

Space Trap by Monica Hughes

Will Stanton discovers on his eleventh birthday that he is one of the Old Ones, immortals who keep the world from domination by the forces of evil. Both terrified and thrilled by the new powers he is developing, Will feels most of all the awesome responsibility, because it is midwinter . . . and the Dark is rising.

The Dark Is Rising by Susan Cooper

Yunggamurra is a river-spirit, dark and silver as moonlit water. Laughing and playful, she sings cold-hearted songs of enchantment. It is the magic of Wirrun of the People that transforms Yunggamurra and teaches her to be a human being.

The Dark Bright Water by Patricia Wrightson

Zan Hagen loves to compete, and nothing means more to her than being on the school baseball team. Sidelined by an injury, Zan becomes bored and desperate. Then her friend, Rinehart, introduces her to running, and Zan discovers the greatest challenge of all—competing against herself.

Zanboomer by R.R. Knudson

The Roundup

by Morley Callaghan

When Luke's father died, he went to live with his aunt and uncle. He was lonely, and his only companion was Dan, an old half-blind collie. Luke's Uncle Henry thought Dan was useless and ought to be done away with. But Mr. Kemp, who lived on the next farm, told Luke that Dan was still a fine dog and would be finer still with some careful brushing and grooming. It seemed to Luke that at least one person understood how he felt about Dan.

"I was out for a walk and Dan turned in here," Luke began solemnly. "I thought I'd come in, Mr. Kemp."

"Why, you wouldn't be much of a neighbor if you didn't come in, Luke. Why, you certainly did a good job on Dan. He looks about ten pounds thinner, a fine, sleek dog."

"He looks younger, don't you think, Mr. Kemp?"

"Years younger, Luke."

"Uncle Henry didn't think so."

"Maybe your uncle didn't really look at him."

"Oh, he looked at him, all right."

"But not as if he had never seen him before."

"Yeah. That's right, and that's important, eh, Mr. Kemp?"

"It certainly is important, Luke. Come on, let's get those cows."

"Well, what do we do, Mr. Kemp?" Luke asked enthusiastically.

"I'll tell you what I do, Luke," Mr. Kemp said amiably as they passed the stable and headed for the open pasture land stretching out from the back of the house. "I just get behind the last cow in the field and say, 'Co boss,' and throw a little pebble at her heels and she lurches along like a drunken sailor, and soon they all start moving. There are only about twelve of them. But an energetic lad like you with a smart dog might round them up like a cowboy riding the range. See what I mean?"

Turning to the left, they cut by the corner of the Kemp woodlot and ahead was the pasture land stretching out, rolling a little, in the rising mist. From there you could see the grazing cows, fat brown-and-white Jersey cows. "I'll tell you what," Mr. Kemp said, when they came to a smooth flat stone. "I'm a lazy man. I could sit here and smoke a pipe and watch you and Dan handle the job, Luke. You might have the making of a great cowboy. How do I know? Don't be afraid of making a little noise and if you want to you can ride herd on them. Let's see how you can handle this, son."

With a happy grin on his face he sat down and fumbled in his pocket for his pipe. What pleased Luke was that he could see that Mr. Kemp enjoyed being there with him and would also enjoy watching him round up the cows. In the little silence between them their eyes met, and Luke had the strange feeling that Mr. Kemp knew all that he, Luke, would like to do, and that these things were right and good because they had been done many times before; the contemplation of these things seemed to give Mr. Kemp a simple pleasure in being alive in the world. Of course, Luke didn't express it to himself in this way. But he had a sudden friendly awareness that everything, simply everything, the time of the evening, the cows in the field, the sun going down, himself there with the dog, was all as it should be. Grinning, he said, "I think I can get them heading this way, Mr. Kemp."

"Take it easy, son. Once they pass this stone they're on their way, and Joe, my hired man, will get them in the sheds."

"Come on, Dan," Luke called, and they both began to trot across the pasture. Before they had gone fifty paces he felt himself imbued with a strange excitement, stimulating his imagination and giving a fantastic glow to the whole scene. The mist from the lush pasture land rose around him like the low thin smoke from campfires; hovering over the ground it swirled like smoke settling after artillery fire. The cows became a great herd that had to be rounded up quickly and driven along the pass in the direct fire of the rustlers who were there in the campfire smoke. His regular trot became a gallop. As Dan galloped with him and he called softly, "Will we ride 'em, Dan! Give the word, Dan. Of course, there's only you and me." He addressed Dan as the leader, as if he recognized that Dan, from then on in their play and in his dreams, was to be the one who was older and possessed of an ancient, instinctive wisdom.

When they were far across the field beyond the last lazy brown cow, Luke suddenly swerved as if reining in his mount, a mount that only he could ride, and Dan swerved too. Luke didn't deign to pick up a stone or stick and hurl it at the lazy cow grazing there peacefully. He yelled, "Just as you say, Dan. Hi, hi, to the hills. To the hills. Sure, we'll ride 'em, Dan," and he rushed at the cows. Dan, now barking fiercely, darted at the legs of the startled cow, which jerked up its head, backed away, lashing its flanks with its tail, and trotted heavily away from the boy and the dog.

Forgetting about his lame leg the collie swerved around crazily with Luke, hurling himself at the rear hoofs and cutting in recklessly under the belly. Each time Luke yelled, "Hi, hi, hi," the old dog barked with fierce excitement. But the mist was rising, the mist like a terrible barrage smoke from the hidden gunfire, coming closer. While Dan circled and barked and drove the herd together, Luke was left alone to face the rustlers. Panting, he dropped to his knees as if the horse, perfectly trained, was kneeling beside him; he took aim; he heard the roar of his gun. But that little twinge in his shoulder—a hot stab—yes—he had been hit, the shoulder suddenly became painful. He let his left arm fall heavily at his side. But he couldn't abandon the position, not when Dan counted on him; not when Dan, riding as he never rode before and firing in the air, had three of the herd trotting along in the beginning of the stampede. "Good old Dan, he can do the job alone if they don't wing him," Luke whispered to his horse. "Come on, boy, on your feet." Mounting, he rode after Dan, ducking low on the saddle.

"Hi, hi, Dan," he yelled. And Dan trotted back to him, panting and blowing and limping badly now. "I'm sorry, Dan. Maybe I let you down. But they got me in the shoulder. Oh, Dan, they got you in the leg." Dan's good eye only danced and shone with pleasure. From one of the cows came a long "Moo-oo," and then an answering "Moo-oo," from across the field.

"They're all in motion now, Dan. It's just as you figured it. Soon we'll be out of danger. I'll try and hold out, Dan. Soon the whole great herd will be in motion. And woe betide those rustlers if they try to stop them. They'll be trampled underfoot, pounded to a pulp. Don't worry about me, Dan, I'm taking it easy."

As they rode off again across the field, he was with concern that Dan, limping badly, wasn't swerving and barking. Though tiring, he wanted to go on. With his good eye he said he wanted to go on. So Luke, too, began to limp badly. "Oh, oh," he moaned. "They got me in the leg, too, Dan. I'm afraid I'm holding you back."

His moan was so real that Dan, wheeling, looked up with the same intelligent and sympathetic concern that Luke had offered to him; the dog tried to jump up and put his paws on Luke's chest; the tongue came out, reaching for Luke's hands. "I can hold out if you can, Dan," Luke cried. And they whirled on after the cows.

Driven by the shouting, circling, and barking, the twelve cows now in a group moved slowly in the direction of the corner of the woodlot and the lane leading to the sheds. No longer could they be startled into trotting, they loafed along, mooing and swinging their heads at the barking dog. But they were like a real herd with their lashing tails, their big surprised eyes, and their snorting nostrils. And to Luke their animal smell was like a strange intoxicating odor, belonging to his dream in which he rode along, lean and tired on his saddle now, chatting with his boss, Dan, for the herd was filing past the outpost, where Mr. Kemp waited.

"Well, Luke," Mr. Kemp called, "that was a great show."

"Eh? Was it?" Luke answered with an embarrassed smile, for in his mind he was still far away from Mr. Kemp; but now, coming closer to him in his thoughts, and then suddenly very close to him, he smiled shyly.

"Where's Dan?" he asked awkwardly. "Hey, Dan, come here. Here we are back with Mr. Kemp." He seemed to be apologizing to Dan for restoring him to the reality of the pasture land, and Mr. Kemp, and the sawmill, and making him an old dog again. But Dan was now willing to be quiet. He flopped down at Luke's feet. "Was it all right the way we did it, Mr. Kemp?" Luke asked.

"It was never done better, Luke."

"Well, that's fine."

"Yes, Luke, it was done with dash and distinction and splendid imagination."

"Dan's a little lame. I hope his leg won't get worse, Mr. Kemp. I hope it doesn't stiffen up. I don't think he's such a very old dog, do you, Mr. Kemp?"

"Oh, Dan's good for a few years yet, Luke."

"If you owned him you wouldn't want to get rid of him, would you, Mr. Kemp?"

"Me? Well, not if he meant much to me, Luke. A man never deliberately gets rid of anything he loves, Luke, does he? But the trouble is, a dog often has more loyalty than a man and sometimes he can't count on his owner's loyalty. Come on, sit down and rest awhile, Luke."

As Luke sat down Mr. Kemp said rhetorically, "Let's sit upon the ground awhile and tell sad stories of the death of kings. That's a quotation from *Richard the Second*, son, a play. In our case, it's the death of dogs we're talking about."

He began to tell a story about a dog he had owned when he was a boy, a dog that had grown up with him. He talked in a slow, drawling tone. It was getting a little cooler and the night breeze that follows the sinking sun was rustling through the leaves of the trees. Luke, sitting beside the eloquent old man, had his face raised to him, his eyes wondering.

"And this dog, a little Boston bull, was pretty old," Mr. Kemp went on. "I don't know how old, maybe twelve years. It was going along the road with me one day, trotting on ahead, and suddenly it seemed to stiffen and roll over. Well, it was a heart attack. Now here's the funny thing, son. That dog knew it was finished. Yet it kept trying to twist its body around in a pathetic convulsive movement so it could turn its head to me and look at me, look right into my eyes. It wanted to make this last gesture of affectionate loyalty as it died on the road."

"I guess that dog liked you, Mr. Kemp. It must have liked you a lot."

"Of course, I liked the dog, too."

After a long pause, Luke said suddenly. "My father died of a heart attack, Mr. Kemp."

"Is that a fact. I'm sorry, son. I didn't know."

"That's all right, Mr. Kemp. But what you just said about that dog is, well . . . it's an important story," Luke said solemnly.

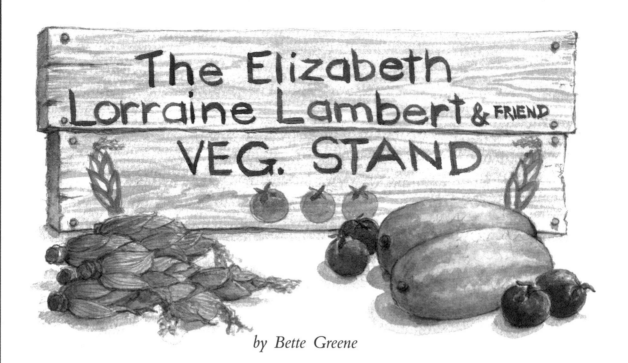

The Elizabeth Lorraine Lambert & FRIEND VEG. STAND

by Bette Greene

Elizabeth Lorraine Lambert wanted to be a veterinarian when she grew up, but her family was poor, and it cost a lot of money to go to college. It didn't take long to think up a way to make some money—but she'd have to grow a lot of vegetables, and she'd need the help of her friend, Philip Hall.

For days and days after the planting I waited for the first green leaves to pop through the earth. First I worried that the seeds weren't going to sprout in such a dry soil. Then we had us some rain and I got to worrying that the moisture was sure to rot the roots. Even Ma noticed my concern, 'cause one day when she was helping me weed, she said that I was fretting more over my garden than Luther does over his "precious pigs."

Still, with all the work I put in, it wasn't until the first seedlings broke earth that I began to believe, really believe, that vegetables were going to grow and that those vegetables were going to make a veget—a veterinarian out of me.

After the seedlings appeared, we got what Pa said was "good growing weather," but that doesn't mean exactly what it sounds like it means. Since farmers are afraid to ever do even the tiniest bit of bragging—thinking that might change their luck for the worse—they say "bad" when what they really mean is "not bad." And when a farmer says "good growing weather," then that's his way of saying it couldn't be more perfect.

Well, the good growing weather brought forth worthy vegetables. Lovely tomatoes, crunchy corn, and watermelon sweeter than a candy bar.

And on the first free day of summer vacation Philip and I built a stand on the gravelly shoulder of the highway by placing some barn boards over a couple of rickety orange crates. When I began to nail on the sign that I had so carefully painted the night before, Philip read out loud: "The Elizabeth Lorraine Lambert & Friend Veg. Stand" in a voice so high that it actually cracked, probably from lack of oxygen. "That's not fair!"

I moved Philip's finger to the word *friend.* "See, I didn't leave you out."

He shook his head. "Not fair!"

"It is *too* fair," I insisted. "Whose idea was it? Who did the planting? The weeding? The picking? You is nothing but a Philip-come-lately."

Philip only gave me a quick look that I couldn't quite read before going on about his business of arranging the tomatoes, watermelons, and corn in the shape of a pyramid on the counter.

"Sure does look nice," I said, hoping that a little appreciation would perk him right up. Philip's face flashed something that could be mistaken for a smile, and just when I was deciding whether or not to count that as progress, a dark blue car came to a stop in front of our stand. Our first customer! Now that was progress, sure enough.

The bald head that poked itself out the car window belonged to the bushy-eyed owner of the Busy Bee Bargain Store.

" 'Lo, Mr. Putterham," I called as he came over to look. "Want to buy some farm-fresh vegetables today?" When he didn't answer, I added, as a sort of extra attraction, " . . . At a bargain?"

Mr. Putterham seemed to take a fancy to one of the ears that was in dead centre of Philip's pyramid. As he gave it a quick yank, it caused the great triangle of corn to level. Philip watched the destruction of his labor with obvious pain, but Mr. Putterham took no more notice of my partner's pain than he did of the great corn levelling. For one thing, he was too busy sniffing the corn, peeling down the shucks, and sniffing some more. Then he looked down at me just as though he had appointed himself the final judge at Judgment Day.

"Thought you said you was selling *fresh* vegetables?"

"An hour ago that corn was still growing on its stalk."

When Mr. Putterham finally drove off, I was one dollar and ninety-five cents richer and a whole lot happier. Philip and I threw our arms around each other, jumped into the air, and made loud and joyful noises.

After the celebrating, I told Philip to mind the store while I made a trip back for more vegetables. Not only had Mr. Putterham bought every last ear of our corn, but he also bought the best two of our three watermelons.

386

At first I got to figuring that he probably bought that second melon to give a friend, but that was before I got to remembering what it is that folks in these parts say about Mr. Cyrus J. Putterham. "Old Putterham is so cheap he wouldn't give nobody nothing, not even a kind word."

I packed the cart, whose long-time missing wheel Luther had replaced as a going-in-business present to me, with a couple dozen ears of corn and two of our biggest melons. But I couldn't get over thinking how peculiar it is that some folks would pay out good money for the same vegetables that they could grow themselves.

As I pulled the rolling produce back along the dusty road, I could see up ahead that a car was parked near our stand. Another customer! I wanted to see him. Wanted to be there when he reached down into his pocket to bring out the money that was going to help pay my way through college.

Running when a person has to play steam engine to a cargo on wheels ain't the easiest thing to do. So while I couldn't exactly run, I did walk just as fast as I could. When I finally reached the highway, the car with a man and woman inside was just driving off.

I gave Philip Hall a congratulating pat on the back. "Reckon you must have sold them a good amount," I said, noticing that the last watermelon was now gone.

He shook his head no.

"What do you mean *no?*"

"What I means to say," said Philip pretending great patience, "is that they didn't buy nothing. And they didn't spend no money. Do you understand now what I mean when I say no?"

"No," I said. " 'Cause I don't see the watermelon. Who bought that?"

His head swirled to look at the place that was now made vacant by the missing melon. "Oh, that one," he said.

"Yep, that one. Who bought it?" I asked just at the moment I caught sight of some watermelon rinds (and only the rinds) lying in the gully. I didn't have to ask another question 'cause now I understood everything. "You good-for-nothing, low-down polecat of a Philip Hall! Those folks stopped to buy a melon, didn't they?"

He looked too surprised to answer so I just went on telling what

I knew to be the truth. "But you didn't have a melon to sell, did you? Cause you already done ate it!"

Philip called me "crazy" and then he stopped talking. And if that wasn't bad enough, the cars too seemed to have stopped stopping. A couple of times, they slowed down and I thought for sure they were going to stop, but they didn't. Don't know why, unless maybe they caught a look at Philip's sourer-than-a-lemon-ball face.

Another thing about this day that wouldn't stop was the sun. One of the real hot ones. I reckon I could've drunk a gallon of ice water. Reckon I could've even drunk a gallon of water without the ice.

Then I heard Philip's voice actually speaking. "We got us another customer. He pointed across the road to a red tow truck with the words WALNUT RIDGE GULF STATION neatly painted on its door.

After the baseball-capped garageman paid me for one melon and a half-dozen ears of corn, I asked him if he knew my grandmother, Miz Regina Mae Forde. "She lives on Route 67 just north of Walnut Ridge."

"No," but he smiled a dimpled smile. "I'm going to be going right past her house to fetch a battery, so I can take you there and back if you've a mind to do some visiting."

I thought about the lemonade that Grandma makes with exactly the right number of sugar granules. I thought about the shade trees that circle her little house. And most of all I thought about Grandma.

I would have gone on thinking, but I was interrupted by my partner's voice. "Let's go, Beth. Please?"

As we walked up Grandma's now grassless path, I got a sudden thought. If she sees me so unexpectedly at her door, she'll right away think I'm bringing bad news. Grandma has been a mite worried about us ever since Calvin Cook Senior was released from jail.

So I stayed hidden in the bushes while friend Philip walked up the front step and knocked hard against the wood door. After a moment's wait he knocked even harder. And when she didn't answer that one, I came out of hiding long enough to ask him to walk around back to see if she wasn't out hanging clothes. Well, he did, but she wasn't.

We sat on a piece of shady grass by the side of the road making bets on who would be coming along first: Grandma or the garageman. Just as I said, "Grandma," as though there wasn't room enough in this world for one speck of doubt, I saw the garageman's arm waving at us through the truck's open window.

About fifteen minutes later, when we came within viewing distance of our stand, I stabbed at the windshield. "What are those damn fool cows doing bunched around our stand?"

"They're our dairy cows," explained Philip as though that was the most natural explanation in the world. "Being brought back from the west pasture for milking."

The garageman hadn't come to a 100 percent complete stop before I was out of that truck flailing my arms as though they had been set into revolving sockets. "Shew! Shew, you dumb cows! Shew! Would you look what you've done to my business!"

All the cows moved leisurely on except one rust-and-white spotted Jersey, who took the only remaining ear of corn into her mouth without even bothering to see what my displeasure was about.

"You're dumb," I yelled at the Jersey. "Dumb, *dumb, dumb!*"

Then just as if to show me how she felt about my name-calling, she backed her perfectly enormous rump into the stand, sending all three melons to the ground. Two of them cracked, but the largest melon miraculously made the fall intact.

"Dumb!" I screamed, and the cow lifted her head as though to demonstrate her complete contempt at my shockingly bad behavior before sending her front foot through the last surviving melon. "Ohhh . . ." I said, feeling violent about the destruction of The Elizabeth Lorraine Lambert & Friend Veg. Stand.

"Her name's Eleanor," said Philip, with what sounded like pride. "She's one cow that always had a mind of her own."

I pointed my finger at him. "You and Eleanor are exactly alike! 'Cause neither of you got the sense God gave you!"

At the supper table I told Pa, Ma, Luther, and Anne about how my vegetable stand was destroyed when Philip Hall made me go with him to Walnut Ridge.

Pa put down his glass of buttermilk. "Show me your scars."

"My what?"

"Your scars," he said again. "'Cause I never knowed nobody who could make my Beth do what she hadn't a mind to do, less'n of course, he beat you with a bull whip." Pa leaned his head back just like he always does when he lets go of a really fat laugh. "So show us your scars." He wasn't laughing alone either. They were all laughing their dang fool heads off. All excepting me.

I jumped up, slapping my hand down upon the oilcloth. "Reckon I should have knowed you folks would rather take sides with Philip Hall than with your own flesh and blood."

Ma gave my hand little taps saying, "Now, now, nobody in this world is taking sides against you."

Tears were coming on, coming on too strong for stopping. I ran into my room to throw myself across my bed. I cried as quietly as I could, wondering why I hadn't seen it before. How they all love Philip Hall better'n me. Well, let them! It don't make me no never mind.

After a while I had to quit crying 'cause it was giving me a headache and I was, truth to tell, plumb tired of lying across the bed. So I tiptoed out the front door so quietly that I didn't have to face a single solitary Lambert.

I passed Pa's garden of the good growing weather, admired the corn stalks which seemed to grow taller and prouder with each sunrise. And on each stalk, ears—lots of corn ripened ears, ready for the picking. Plenty there for a heap of selling. And in the next rows was the tomatoes that should be able to win a blue ribbon at anybody's country fair. But the bluest ribbon should be saved for the watermelon. The reddest, sweetest melons in all of Randolph County.

The sun was lowering, but there was still light enough on the rutty back road that I followed out to the highway. When I reached what remained of The Elizabeth Lorraine Lambert & Friend Veg. Stand, I surveyed the damage. The corn was muddied and bruised; mashed tomatoes littered the gravel shoulder, and the bursted watermelons had become a feast for ants and flies.

The boards and the crates were unbroken although the company sign did suffer from a muddy hoofprint directly across the word *Friend*.

As I replaced the boards across the crates I began thinking about what really happened. I thought about the God-given good growing weather, about Pa's extra planting, about Ma making the time to help me weed my garden. I thought about Luther's repairing the cart, Anne's encouragement, and, God help me, I even thought about Philip Hall who had always been better at talking than at working. And isn't that what I really wanted him for? For company?

Sweet Philip. Did he really force me to go to Walnut Ridge? Although I didn't come close to smiling, I did come closer to understanding what Pa and the rest of the family found funny.

I threw the feast-for-flies melons across the road into the gully and swept away the tomatoes with a willow branch. Then with only one mighty swing with a roadside rock, I nailed the company sign back onto the stand.

As I stepped back to look it all over, I saw only one thing still needed doing. So with my hand I brushed away—carefully brushed away—the mud from the word *Friend*.

The Spaghetti Affair

by Betty Waterton

Quincy Rumpel and her family have just moved to Vancouver and are staying with relatives while Mr. and Mrs. Rumpel look for a new house. Irrepressible Quincy isn't about to admit that her cousin, Gwen, can do anything that she can't do better. . . .

Quincy followed Gwen into the kitchen. "I think I'll make hot cheese biscuits for lunch," said Gwen, putting on an apron, "they're so easy, aren't they?"

"Mmmmm."

"You can make some for supper if you like!"

"Um, no thanks. Actually I like doing more creative things, like spaghetti and stuff." Quincy didn't know what made her say it.

"Gosh! I've never tried anything like that!" said Gwen, mixing up biscuit dough.

"You must be quite a help to your mother," Aunt Ida said to Quincy. She was obviously impressed. Quincy nodded helplessly.

"How would you like to make spaghetti for supper tonight? Uncle George phoned and he needs me over in the shop. There've been a lot of broken umbrellas brought in today because of the wind. It would be a tremendous help if you could!"

"Sure!" answered Quincy, swept along on Aunt Ida's enthusiasm.

After lunch Aunt Ida put out some of the things Quincy would need, including a package of ground meat (frozen) and a big pot.

"You'll need to make quite a lot for eight people. Are you sure you can manage?" she asked.

Now, Quincy said to herself, *tell her NOW that you've never cooked anything more than a fried egg!* But her mouth seemed glued shut, and she just nodded.

"The garlic press is in the drawer, and here's the garlic," went on Aunt Ida. "And if you can't find anything else you need, just ask Gwen. Everybody will be back about five o'clock, I expect. Good luck!" and she dashed out the back door.

"What will *I* do?" asked Morris, after she'd gone.

"You can ride my old bike, if you like," offered Gwen.

"Is it a Moto-Cross?"

"No, it's a girls' three-speed."

"I guess I can stand it," said Morris. "I'll ride in the backyard where no one can see me."

"Do you want some help with the spaghetti?" asked Gwen.

"Um, no thanks," said Quincy, "I can manage."

"Well, in that case I may as well go over to Kim's and do puppets," said Gwen. "See you later!" And she also disappeared out the back door.

"Puppets! I love doing puppets!" exclaimed Quincy as they watched Gwen wheel down the street on her ten-speed.

"She didn't even ask us to go with her!" grumbled Leah. "How come you got mixed up in this spaghetti affair anyways?"

"It's a long story," said Quincy. Suddenly she ran to the mirror in the hall and began taking the elastics off her braids. She combed her hair with her fingers and bunched it up around her face. "How do you think I'd look with short hair?" she asked.

"Pretty good. Better than with braids, anyways."

Quincy stood staring at her reflection and thinking. The more she thought about it, the more she wanted short hair. "I can't stand my hair another minute!" she exclaimed finally, and began hunting for some scissors.

"Shouldn't you ask Mom first? Maybe she'd let you get it cut by a hairdresser."

"I don't want to wait for that—I want to do it now!" Finding a pair of scissors in a kitchen drawer, Quincy pounced on them, exclaiming: "Ha! There you are, my little beauties!" Then she disappeared into the bathroom, locking the door behind her.

"Aw, can't I watch?" moaned Leah.

But Quincy was firm. "You might distract me," she said. Flushed with excitement, she held a strand of hair in one hand, the scissors in the other. She snipped off the first chunk, and as it fell to the floor Quincy got a sudden queer feeling in the pit of her stomach. *Well, I can't stop now,* she said to herself.

Snip, snip, snip! Now one side was shorter than the other! Snip, snip, snip! She kept trying to even it up, but though her hair kept getting shorter and shorter, it was still lopsided.

Quincy kept snipping away—more than she had intended—trying to get it even, and hoping it would curl or something, but it just stuck out in uneven wisps.

She turned on the shower and stuck her head under it hopefully. Her hair didn't frizz.

"Are you finished yet?" asked Leah through the keyhole.

"Almost!" replied Quincy. As her hair dried it stuck out in little sharp points all over her head. There was nothing more she could do.

"You may as well come in," she said, unlocking the door.

"Wow!" gasped Leah, stumbling into the bathroom. "Do you ever look different! Sort of punk rock!"

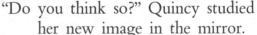

"Do you think so?" Quincy studied her new image in the mirror.

"Mom will have a fit!"

For a moment Quincy's knees felt weak, but quickly putting the thought of her mother out of her head, she began scooping her hair up off the floor and throwing it out the window.

"What are you doing that for?" asked Leah.

"Some bird might want it to put in its nest."

After that she went into the kitchen to think about the spaghetti.

"I'm going to cook the spaghetti first, and get that over with," said Quincy, reading the recipe on the box of pasta. She put some water on to boil.

By three-thirty there was a large pot full of cooked and drained spaghetti. "Don't forget to rinse it in cold water," said Leah, who was perched on a kitchen stool, watching and advising.

"It'll be cool enough by five o'clock without rinsing it now," reasoned Quincy, putting the lid on the pot and setting it on the back of the stove. Then she started on the sauce.

The ground meat was still frozen, so she left it to thaw a little longer. "We'd better double everything," said Quincy, "so we'll be sure to have enough." She got out more onions.

"I wonder what 'sauté' means?" said Leah, reading the recipe. "It says to sauté onion, celery, and garlic in 25 mL of oil."

"I think it means soak," replied Quincy. "But I'm not sure how to measure 25 mL. Aunt Ida hasn't gone metric yet. Oh well, I'll guess . . ." She poured half a bottle of cooking oil into a mixing bowl and added some chopped celery and onions.

"Don't forget the clove of garlic!" said Leah.

Tears streaming down her face from the onions, Quincy said: "I wonder if a clove is the same as a clump?"

Leah didn't have any idea, so Quincy decided to put in the whole clump, just to be sure. She carefully peeled all twenty-three cloves of garlic and mashed them one at a time through the garlic press.

As she was adding them to the oil, Morris came in for his third snack of the afternoon. "Something smells funny in here," he said.

"It's your supper," said Quincy.

"Yuck!" Morris, concerned only with his stomach, hadn't noticed her hair.

It was nearly five o'clock. Quincy put some tomato paste in a pot and heated it up. "Don't you think it looks kind of thick?" asked Leah.

"Maybe." Quincy poured in a few cups of water, then added the frozen hamburger, chipping off the edges that had thawed. "It's supposed to have oregano, but I can't find any," she said.

"When are you going to put in the stuff in the bowl?" wondered Leah.

"I guess it's soaked enough,"
said Quincy, dumping in the celery,
onions, and garlic, and all the oil.
By now it was five o'clock, and everyone
began to arrive home. Gwen was the first. "What
happened to your hair?" she gasped when she saw Quincy.

"Oh," said Quincy, who had almost forgotten about it while in the
throes of making dinner, "I just got tired of it long," and she began to
stir the sauce with great energy.

Suddenly Gwen decided to make cheese biscuits. "We don't need them,
you know," protested Leah, "we've got plenty of spaghetti!"

"I know," replied Gwen, "I smelled it. I still think I'll make hot cheese
biscuits." Grabbing an apron, she got busy.

Then Uncle George came in making jokes about the spaghetti factory,
while Morris ran around holding his nose.

"Never mind them, Quincy!" said Aunt Ida, and began hunting for
the oregano right away. All at once she noticed Quincy's hair. "What
happened to your nice braids?" she asked. "You looked so neat and
wholesome with them!"

Quincy mumbled something like: "They weren't very long ones anyway," but Aunt Ida was busy tasting the sauce, and wasn't listening.

Mr. and Mrs. Rumpel were the last to arrive. "Quincy!" gasped her mother. "What happened to you?" But before Quincy could reply, Aunt Ida said: "This clever girl has just made our supper!"

Mrs. Rumpel's mouth fell open with surprise and she sat down weakly on the nearest chair.

"Quincy made supper!" she told Mr. Rumpel. "Our Quincy!"

"Ah," cried Mr. Rumpel, "that explains the exotic and pungent aromas emanating from the kitchen!" *He's trying to be funny as usual*, thought Quincy. *Oh please, please don't let him say anything about my hair!*

The truth was that Mr. Rumpel had noticed something vaguely different about his daughter, but he couldn't say exactly what it was.

Everybody was hungry, so dinner was dished up promptly. So promptly, in fact, that not all the meat was thawed. The pasta, free at last, plopped out of the pot in a large, solid mass, rather like a soccer ball. It was quite cold. The sauce, however, made up for it. It was runny and very hot.

As Aunt Ida poured it over the spaghetti, Quincy watched anxiously. She thought it looked reasonably presentable, if a little oily. "It's very loose sauce," she explained when the platter was put on the table.

While Uncle George asked the blessing (which the other Rumpels did quite often), Quincy silently added a request of her own: *Please, dear God, let it taste good.*

"It certainly *looks* delicious!" enthused Aunt Ida.

"I think it looks greasy," said Morris, making a face.

"It's certainly er . . . ah, nice and spicy," said Uncle George.

"A Quincy Special!" teased Mr. Rumpel. "Just don't light any matches around here—we all might go up in fumes!"

"I hope you like your spaghetti rare," said Quincy.

"It's very nice, dear," said Mrs. Rumpel bravely. "Maybe somewhat garlicky, but considering it's your first try at cooking . . . not bad."

"First try . . ." Aunt Ida looked shocked, while Gwen nearly dropppped her hot cheese biscuits.

Though there was some spaghetti left over—quite a lot, actually—nobody got sick from eating it.

And that's something at least, thought Quincy gratefully.

BRATS

by X. J. Kennedy

Stealing eggs, Fritz ran afoul
Of an angry great horned owl.
Now she has him—what a catch!—
Seeing if his head will hatch.

Louise, a whiz at curling hair,
Sneaked up on a snoozing bear,
Left its fur all frazzly-frizzly.
My, but its revenge was grisly!

Stephanie, that little stinker,
Skinny-dipped in fabric shrinker.
We will find her yet, we hope,
Once we buy a microscope.

On his motorbike Lars stands
Roaring past us—"Look! no hands!"
Soon with vacant handlebars
Back the bike roars. Look, no Lars!

Hiking in the Rockies, Midge
Meets out on a natural bridge
A long-horned goat. Just one can cross.
Tough luck, Midge: you've lost the toss.

Snickering like crazy, Sue
Brushed a pig with Elmer's Glue
And, to set Aunt Effie squealing,
Stuck it to the kitchen ceiling.
Uncle, gawking, spilled his cup.
"Wow!" he cried. "Has pork gone up!"

Chortling "Ho ho! This'll learn us!"
Gosnold in his grade school's furnace
Hurled a can of kippered herring.
School's been out a whole month, airing.

Ignatz Mott ignored the rule,
"Never stand behind a mule."

In the sky—what can that be?
Haw haw! *Hee-haw!* That is he.

Silver Bullet

by Robert Newton Peck

Janice Riker was the toughest and strongest kid in the whole school. When she knocked Soup and Rob over with her soapbox racer, they vowed they would get even. The trouble was—how? Then Soup got one of his bright ideas, and the Dump was part of his plan.

The Dump was a real neat place to go. It was a clear morning and everything was beautiful, as the sun was shining down on all that wonderful junk.

"Sure is amazing," said Soup.

"What is?"

"Look at all the great stuff people actually throw away. This tire's almost good as new."

"Except for a few holes," I pointed out. "Well, now we're here at the dumping grounds, what are we looking for?"

"Wheels," said Soup.

"Honest?"

"We gotta find four wheels. And I'd say six just might be a bit better."

"Wheels for what?"

"A *tank*," said Soup. "We are declaring war on Janice Riker, and you can't win a war without a tank."

"We can build it ourselves."

"You betcha," said Soup, his voice swollen with confidence. "If old Janice can hammer a soapbox racer together, dumb as she is, you and I could build the Brooklyn Bridge."

"That's in our geography book," I said.

"Right," said Soup, looking at a pile of old coat hangers.

"What kind of a tank will we build?"

"A war tank."

"With guns?"

"Nope," said Soup. "We won't need guns."

"How come?"

"Because we're going to use our tank like a torpedo."

"Like from a submarine."

"You got it. Hey! There's a wheel."

Together we sifted through the mess of discarded materials, and we were rewarded, uncovering an old baby carriage. With three wheels.

"It's missing one, Soup."

"That's okay. We'll find more."

"Wow, look at this." I pointed to an enormous white bathtub. "How about this tub for the body of our tank, Soup? We could ride in it, if the wheels go on."

Soup squinted at the bathtub. I could almost see the blueprints of our war tank spread out in his brain. But then he shook his head.

"Wrong shape."

We saw a stack of old window frames, brass curtain rods, a box of old clothes, a bag of oily rags, a million busted chains, piles and piles of rotten lumber, a pair of red galoshes, an old hat, more tires, a wagon wheel, icebox, ironing board, inner tubes, an old pink sofa with the springs popping out, and lots and lots of spare parts for a car. And an old saddle.

"I wish we could take all this stuff home," I said.

"Wouldn't it be swell," said Soup.

"Can we make a tank?"

"Easy," said Soup. "Curtain rods for axles."

Reaching in his pocket, he produced a roll of black sticky-tape. It was what we always used whenever Soup and I wanted to put something together. Nails and screws were okay, if you have time to hammer. But we were too busy to waste time like that. So we used more than our share of black tape.

"Now," said Soup, "all we gotta find is the *body* of the tank."

"Right," I said.

Sifting through the priceless assembly of discarded chattels, we saw nothing that looked like a suitable chassis. Until we finally turned over an old black hunk of tar paper and *wow!* There it was! All long and shiny, like a great big silver bullet. It must have been two metres long. For a moment or two neither Soup nor I could speak, such was the degree of our enrapt appreciation.

"That's it," said Soup at last.

"A hot water tank."

There wasn't a single farmhouse kitchen in all Vermont that didn't have a big black cookstove. And attached to it, always in the vertical position of a giant silver silo, was a cylindrical tank for hot water.

"Now that," said Soup, "is what I call a tank that looks like a torpedo."

"Just the right shape," I said.

Rapping the old silver tank with a stick, Soup produced the hollow clanks that apparently passed his rigid standards of tank construction.

"Yup," he said, "it's gallonized iron."

"What's gallonized mean?"

"Well," said Soup, "I reckon it means that it holds a lot of gallons."

"Let's get it on wheels."

"Good idea," said Soup, selecting a rod.

We took wheels off a baby carriage, a lawn mower, a bicycle, and a hobbyhorse. Then we removed the circular seat from a piano stool. Nothing seemed to fit until the wire and black tape were added. All told, we had nine wheels on our tank. Some touched the ground and some sort of floated. Our tank resembled a railroad car. It was Soup who added the final touch, throwing the old saddle on the tank as though our vehicle was an iron steed.

"Silver Bullet," said Soup, as his hand reached out to pat our tank softly, as though it was the Lone Ranger's horse.

"Soup?"

"Yeah."

"How'll we steer this old girl?"

"That," said Soup, "might be a minor problem."

We ate our lunch. I don't know how, because we were both so excited. Silver Bullet was some invention, saddle and all. She sure was a beauty, like nothing you'd ever seen before. We just sat on a pile of old clothes as we ate, looking at a tank that was part torpedo, part railroad coach, and part horse, held together with wire and tape.

"Come on," said Soup, gulping down the last of his apple and throwing away the core, "let's attack Janice."

"Never thought the day would come," I said, as we headed toward town, pushing Silver Bullet ahead of us, "I'd ever be looking for Janice Riker."

"Me neither."

There wasn't a kid in town who didn't know where Janice's house was. It was a marked spot. We were up on a hill; behind us, some bushes from where we could look down on the Riker homestead, which was only three houses away from the Baptist Church.

"Hot spit!" said Soup.

Quickly I looked where Soup was pointing. Janice was nowhere in sight, but parked in front of her house was her soapbox racer.

"What'll we do, Soup?"

"Smash it. No sense building a war tank unless you have a good old battle to go along with it."

We stood at the top of Tiller's pasture, looking down a cow path. What a track! All it took was a push here and a tug there to get Silver Bullet pointed down the meadow so that she would hit Janice's car amidships and reduce it to a pile of rubble and poetic justice. Boy, were we clever. I could hardly wait to see Janice Riker's face as Silver Bullet smashed into her soapbox racer. Hers was wood, but *ours* was iron. Gallonized iron!

"Okay," said Soup, "get in the saddle."

"Sure," I said. "You ride behind me."

For a second, for one marrow-chilling moment, I thought Soup was going to suggest that I ride Silver Bullet alone down that hill. But no. He swung his leg up and the two of us occupied the saddle. Slowly at first, we started forward. It seemed sort of high up, but I guess Soup knew what we were doing.

"Don't forget to lean," he said. We hitched our bodies a bit, and Silver Bullet started her descent.

Faster, faster, faster rolled Silver Bullet, exactly as the deadly torpedo it was meant to be, heading straight for Janice's racer. My hands gripped the horn of the saddle, hanging on for dear life, while Soup's arms were around my waist. Silver Bullet gained speed with every split second. I wanted to close my eyes, but I was too scared. We'd got several different sizes of wheels on the darn thing, which made Silver Bullet move less like a torpedo and more like a drunk camel. We weren't on a road. Our trajectory was a cow path down Tiller's pasture that ended up across the road from Janice's house. The ground flew under us.

As I looked down, a wheel came off!

"Lean!" yelled Soup.

We leaned.

But suddenly, so did Silver Bullet. She leaned off to the left so far that she was now way off target. You know, it's a funny thing. But up until now I'd never really pondered much about the fact that Janice Riker

lived next door to Mrs. Stetson. The thought never crossed my mind. But now, as Silver Bullet and Soup and I increased our speed, all I could see ahead of us was Mrs. Stetson's vegetable garden, growing bigger and bigger with every bump. My eyes were watering from the speed.

To tell you the honest truth, had Silver Bullet been actually *shot* from the Lone Ranger's six-shooter, she couldn't have gone any faster. I knew that someday Soup and I would have to die, but I never realized until this very moment, that it would be among Mrs. Stetson's tomato plants. Another wheel came off, and then another. But we were shooting across the road too fast to care.

Janice was yelling.

From the corner of my eye, I saw Janice Riker run toward her car, but we were in no danger of hitting her soapbox racer. All I saw now was flowers, Mrs. Stetson's carefully cultivated marigolds, which we plowed through. Then we mowed down primroses, snapdragons, and day lilies, followed by beds of cosmos and shasta daisies, through a bush of peonies, and into the tomatoes, beans, peas, cabbages, and finally between two rows of tall corn. Falling off, Soup and I skidded to a muddy stop between two hills of potatoes. As I sort of hurt all over from the stun of our sudden stop, I couldn't move much. All I heard was Janice Riker's voice laughing at our crash, but then I heard Mrs. Stetson's voice, and she sure wasn't laughing. Peeking through a potato plant, I saw Mrs. Stetson hit Janice Riker with a broom. Janice was trying to point at us, but as Silver Bullet was totally hidden between the rows of corn, all Mrs. Stetson saw was her torn-up garden and Janice's racer, which was all the evidence she needed.

Being in school with old Janice was sure bad enough, but as far as Mrs. Stetson was concerned, having Janice for a next-door neighbor was no picnic either. The destruction of her garden was the last straw. The straws of Mrs. Stetson's big broom landed on Janice and really gave her a smarting. And then Mrs. Stetson attacked Janice's car, and I heard the wood splinter. As it says in the Bible, it sure was a joyful noise.

I always wondered what Mrs. Stetson said (or thought, or did) when she finally found Silver Bullet, saddle and all, between her rows of corn. Soup and I were not around that long to find out.

Maybe she blamed it on the Lone Ranger.

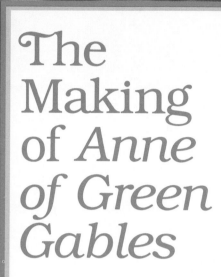

The Making of Anne of Green Gables

by Sheila Dalton

The making of any movie is a challenge, but imagine how hard it would be to turn the story of Anne Shirley, Canada's best-loved fictional heroine, into a TV film. Thousands of people would be waiting to pass judgment, waiting to see if *your* Anne measured up to their idea of her.

Kevin Sullivan, producer and director of CBC Television's *Anne of Green Gables,* and the talented team who worked with him on the film knew just how hard it would be. That only made them more determined to take on the challenge.

Buying the Rights

As producer, Kevin Sullivan's first task was to get permission to turn Lucy Maud Montgomery's novel into a TV movie. Any filmmaker who wants to base a movie on a book must buy rights to use the material from the person or persons who own it. Usually this is the author or the author's family. But in the case of *Anne of Green Gables,* finding the copyright owner became something of a treasure hunt.

Kevin Sullivan soon discovered that L. M. Montgomery had sold the rights to her publisher in 1919. When he enquired further, he was told that two Canadian writers who had written a musical version of the novel in the 1960s now owned the rights. He later found out that because of changes in the law since then all rights belonged once again to Miss Montgomery's family. At last, a year and a half after beginning his search, Sullivan finally succeeded in acquiring TV rights to the book.

Writing the Screenplay

Sullivan's next task was to adapt the novel into a screenplay for television. He remembered loving the book as a child, but when he reread it he encountered problems he hadn't expected. To begin with, the age range for Anne, from eleven to seventeen years of age, was too wide for any actress to handle. His solution was to condense the time span of the story from six years to four years, making Anne thirteen years old at the beginning of the film.

Another problem in writing the screenplay was dealing with the characters' thoughts and feelings. In the novel, L. M. Montgomery simply wrote out what was going on in her characters' heads, but in a film it would seem very odd if the characters spoke their thoughts out loud. Sullivan solved the problem by adding dialogue and whole new scenes. At the beginning of the film he put in scenes to show what life was like for the unhappy young orphan before she came to Green Gables. This allowed the viewers to understand

Anne's feelings when she arrived at Green Gables and to know what the chance of having a real home meant to her.

Choosing the Cast

After the screenplay was completed, casting for the film could begin. As the director, Sullivan had to make the final decision about the actors who would play the characters in his film.

The biggest challenge was choosing the actress who would play Anne. Sullivan auditioned over three thousand girls for the part, and held talent searches in nine cities across Canada, before settling on Canadian actress Megan Follows. Megan was asked to audition because she was a talented actress, and also because she looked the part. She was eager to play Anne and felt that she could play both her chatty side and her more serious side with equal ease. However, Megan had to go through two very demanding auditions before she won the role. In the first audition she was tired and nervous; she had just worked a twelve-hour day on another film and hadn't had enough time to prepare her scenes. The audition didn't go as well as she had hoped. However, a year later, Sullivan still hadn't found the right Anne, and Megan auditioned again. This time she captured Anne's spirit so well that the

director knew the part belonged to her.

For Anne's boyfriend, Gilbert Blythe, the director needed someone who was good-looking, had charisma—and could act. Just when Sullivan had begun to feel discouraged about finding the right person, the casting director saw a talented young actor named Jonathan Crombie in a play at Toronto's Lawrence Park Collegiate. Kevin gave him a screen test, liked what he saw, and offered him the part. Gilbert was Jonathan's first professional role.

The role of Diana Barry, Anne's best friend and "kindred spirit," went to Schuyler Grant, a young actress from the United States who had auditioned to play Anne. In spite of having competed for the same role, she and Megan became good friends during filming, and they often clowned around together between takes.

Casting of the film's main characters was completed when actors Colleen Dewhurst and Richard Farnsworth won the roles of Marilla and Matthew Cuthbert, Anne's adoptive parents. Colleen was particularly thrilled to play Marilla because *Anne* was the very first book her mother read to her when she was a child. Kevin Sullivan believed that Colleen had a great understanding of Marilla's character, and knew exactly where she wanted the role to go. Richard had much less acting experience than Colleen, but he knew a great deal about how movies are made. The director also felt that Richard was the same kind of person as Matthew—sweet, shy, and gentlemanly.

Although some of the cast were seasoned professionals and others, like Jonathan, were beginners, they all got along well together. Megan and Richard, especially, developed a close relationship, and this greatly helped their performances. The deep affection between them on screen is real.

Shooting the Film

Although some of the indoor scenes in *Anne of Green Gables* were shot inside a film studio, most of the movie was done on location—in Ontario! The movie had a small budget, and it would simply have cost too much time and money to move the entire cast and crew to Prince Edward Island for the duration of the filming. So only a few seaside scenes were actually filmed on the Island.

The Green Gables shown in the film is actually two Ontario farmhouses. Both are quaint buildings, their eaves edged with carved wooden gingerbread, their front lawns framed by white picket fences. They look just the way people expect Green Gables to look. A pioneer village near Kitchener, Ontario, and other historical sites around Toronto supplied locations for most of the other outdoor shots.

Anne's period setting and low budget created other problems as well. The story takes place in the 1890s, and it took a lot of special props and artifacts to give the sets the correct period feeling. Finding the right props at the right price was the job of Carol Speir, the art director. It didn't help that one of the props needed was an 1890s train! The props team never did find exactly the right engine, but they did find period cars. They also never found one perfect railway station that looked just right and also had plenty of track to show the train approaching. So train scenes were shot at different stations. The camera crew had to be careful about which angles they shot so that all the different locations would look like the same place!

Scenes were shot according to which location was being used and which characters were appearing in scenes together. This meant that many scenes were not shot in the order in which they would appear in the film, so the actors had to do, and redo, scenes out of sequence. This was particularly complicated for Megan Follows because she sometimes had to make as many as five age changes within the space of a few hours. Megan says that it was hard to be sixteen-year-old Anne in the morning and then go back to being a thirteen-year-old in the afternoon. Nancy Eagles, the film's continuity person, had to keep reminding her how to make the transitions, for example, pitching her voice higher when she played the younger Anne.

Jonathan Crombie had problems of his own because it was his first time in front of a camera. For instance, he was so nervous about his initial scene with Colleen Dewhurst that he says he "went over the first three lines for nine hours." Then when it came time for filming, the director threw out the script and asked him to improvise!

Getting the Right Look

Make-up had to look right for the period and for the characters, and it had to be changed to fit different parts of the story. As Shona Jabour, the make-up artist, says, "Anne's little-girl look had to be done with a very small amount of make-up because she shouldn't really be wearing any at all at that age and in that time period. I concentrated mostly on face shape—shading and highlighting." To mark Anne's transition from gawky girl to assured young woman, Shona phased out her freckles, shaded her nose, and made her skin as smooth and translucent as porcelain.

Marilla's natural outdoorsy look was something Shona hadn't planned on. At the time of filming, Colleen Dewhurst had a fine tan, which she was very proud of. At first Shona intended to conceal the tan with pale make-up, but Colleen suggested that because Marilla was a down-to-earth, hardworking person, she need not look *quite* so pale and delicate as the other female characters in the film. Shona agreed, and made Colleen up to emphasize the healthy, natural look that matched Marilla's personality so well.

Richard Farnsworth's character presented an opposite challenge for Shona. In one scene in the film, he suffers a heart attack. In order to make him look realistic, Shona first studied the appearance of real cardiac patients in hospitals. To create the effect she wanted, she shaded Richard's ear lobes and fingertips blue, and used mellow yellow make-up mixed with gray-green to make him appear drained of color and drawn with pain.

Of course, costumes and hairstyles were also very important in helping create the period "feel" of *Anne*. Most characters wore the same kind of cos-

tumes and hairstyles throughout the film. The appearance of the young characters, though, had to change as they "grew up" on film. As Anne got older, for instance, her clothes became more stylish, her hair changed from red to auburn, and she traded her pigtails for an upswept hairdo.

Wrapping It Up

Filming took most of the summer of 1985. When it was finally over, the cast and crew felt relieved that all the difficulties had been overcome and happy that the filming had gone so well. There was some sadness too. Megan Follows remembers that she felt devastated when it was over. Suddenly, a whole way of life had come to an end. She no longer got up early and rushed to the set, and she was no longer seeing people who had become such a great part of her life.

Once filming was completed, the film editors and sound mixers went to work. The film editors' job was to view all the scenes, which had been shot out of order, and join them into a meaningful sequence. First they noted particular scenes that the director said he wanted in the final film. Then, by running the complete film footage many times and following the script closely, they decided where the scenes should be joined and how long each scene should run.

The last task of all belonged to the sound department. They added the musical score to the other sound tracks so that music, dialogue, and sound effects all flowed smoothly and could be heard without drowning each other out.

At last, *Anne* was complete. *Anne of Green Gables* aired in December of 1985 to the delight of nearly six million viewers. It went on to win twenty-seven international awards, and stole the hearts of audiences all over the world.

Anne of Green Gables *proved to be so popular that Kevin Sullivan decided to put more of Anne's story on film.* Anne of Green Gables—The Sequel *features the same cast as the original film. It was shot during the winter of 1986 and first appeared on Canadian television in December 1987.*

Slake Moves In

by Felice Holman

Nobody cared about Aremis Slake, least of all the "kind of aunt" he boarded with. One day, pursued by a street gang, Slake fled into the subway and hid in a rough alcove he discovered in the tunnel wall. It took him a while to realize that he could make his home there.

In the early hours of the next day it occurred to Slake that he was not being sought by the police, that he was not the main object of a great crime hunt or even part of a general crackdown. The feeling of freedom and release that came to him then was immense. His fast for the last many hours made him dizzy; his cramped position made him unsteady; and both conditions made him weak enough to feel that this revelation had come to him as a vision. A mystical being had entered his cell crying, "Slake, you are free. Arise!" Slake, already arisen, now put his head out of the porthole. Damp but free air came to him in drafts. Dimness and dampness were the primary qualities of this atmosphere of the subway tunnel, but one could also sense other elements. Slake selected something that smelled like gasoline and something that smelled like onions and peanuts. The gasoline didn't interest him, but the peanuts did. Madly.

He put his head out of the porthole and checked the length of the tunnel for oncoming trains. He saw and heard none. Keeping his eye on the great crocodile of the third rail, he eased out of his cave and, holding close to the wall until he was near the mouth of the tunnel, made his way down the track. Then he crossed the track and from below the level of the platform peered up at the dispatcher's office. There was a man in it and Slake was taking no chances. He slid under the overhang of the platform and crept, unseen, down the entire length of the station just under the platform edge. This brought him to the far end of the station. Standing up he could see people waiting for trains down towards the centre stairway, quite a distance from him. He sneaked up the few steps used by track workers and tried to look like someone who had just arrived at the station to catch a train. He was very successful. For one of the few times in his life Slake experienced fleeting confidence. "I'm an actor . . . a great actor." But this was an overstatement and Slake knew it.

Slake now climbed a flight of stairs and near the turnstiles he discovered the aroma that he had thought was gasoline. It wasn't. It was an unbelievably strong disinfectant being used in the men's room, and its intensity singed his nostrils and throat. Slake investigated the facility. The human being who had been selected for this work was just departing, leaving a newly washed floor. His work may have been thankless until then, but Slake was thankful. His experience of school, tenement, and subway lavatories was wide enough to afford him the knowledge that this was a rare moment approaching cleanliness and thus godliness. He took advantage of the situation—lavished water all over his face and arms, drank water from his cupped hands, and used the toilet.

As Slake slapped water about extravagantly, he was aware that this may have been one of the few mornings of his life within memory that he had not been otherwise slapped or shouted into wakefulness, dragged from solitary sleep into the crowded and threatening day. Here he stood, dripping cold water, shivering, but feeling vaguely and oddly unhounded. He ran his wet fingers through his hair, drying them thus, and began to consider his empty stomach. He had no idea what the possibilities might be.

Slake went out into the wide area that served as a concourse for people going in all directions. A mass of passengers coming from the uptown local now surged through and Slake allowed himself to be caught up in the pooled momentum. They seemed to be pushing him into an arcade, but nobody paid the least attention to him.

They don't even notice me, Slake thought. It's like I'm invisible.

But he could see himself reflected in the dirty glass of the still-closed shops and he knew that he was not invisible, though it was a wish he often had. In fact, it surprised him even more to see that, except that he had no jacket, his reflection looked not too different from everyone else's. This reminded him that he was not only hungry, he was quite chilly. Both of these discomforts were familiar to Slake; they were not devastating conditions. They were accepted to a point, like other harassments and discomforts.

And then Slake was passing a glass window behind which some people were standing at a counter or sitting on stools. They seemed to be eating in the quickest way anyone could eat or drink, somewhat the same way Slake ate, standing before the refrigerator most mornings. Slake stopped to watch, pressing his face against the glass so he could see better. Customers tapped impatient coins waiting to be served, and when the coffee came they tossed the liquid down as though there were no need to swallow. Slake watched through the glass as if he were watching a motion picture. One man, leather briefcase between his ankles, waved his hand at the counter girl who moved without nerves to serve the morning brew. Slowly she drew steaming black coffee from the steel urn and set the mug before the man. He threw down a coin and started to sip the coffee. He frowned, and then sipped again. It was too

hot for him. Did he have a more sensitive gullet than the others? He looked at his watch, grabbed his briefcase, and left. Fury was marked in black lines around his eyes and raked upon his forehead. The cup of coffee stood steaming where he had left it. *Slake moved in.*

His heart raced as he put himself in front of the mug. He had never before in his life stood at a counter like this with people dressed for business or whatever. He didn't know what he expected, but it surprised him when it didn't happen. He waited. He reached out and picked up the mug. It was still very hot. Slake noticed people helping themselves to wrapped lumps of sugar from bowls along the counter. He reached out and quickly took a lump. He took another, then watched the cubes absorb the coffee color and essence before they dissolved. Then Slake took a third lump, unwrapped it, and dipped it just a little into the coffee. Then he ate the piece of sugar, which had drawn the hot coffee up into itself. It was delicious. Now he sipped the coffee from the mug and the hot sweet drink warmed Slake in the stomach, throat, neck, and everywhere. His heart stopped racing. When he looked up sideways at the counter girl, she did not seem surprised that he was there.

"She thinks it's my coffee," Slake told himself.

Slake did not hurry. A whole new contingent of coffee drinkers arrived and left while Slake drank his breakfast, dunked six pieces of sugar, and providently slipped two more in his pocket. When Slake left this eatery, he went out into the arcade a warmer boy and a boy less harassed by hunger pains. Indeed, for the moment, Slake felt relatively unharassed by anything at all.

A little farther along, through the turnstiles and up some stairs, Slake found himself in an enormous enclosure—the main concourse of Grand Central Station. The large cold and exposed place made him remember and consider now the need to return to school. As he did, two really terrible feelings swept through him—one down from his throat and the other up from his knees. As the descending and ascending terrible feelings collided in his gut, Slake arrived at a point—not to go back. It wasn't a decision. It was a non-decision, a non-act. Slake simply stopped where he was, and though people pushed past him, surging up from the black gates of the New York Central trains, Slake only swayed or pivoted slightly when jostled. His eyes were fixed at a point, way up on the wall opposite him, where the most enormous screen he had ever seen showed a scene in full color of a magnificent waterfall, the foam and spray so wet and real that Slake felt it would splash down on him.

Slake stood that way a long, long time. But after a while—it may have been the uncomfortable position of his neck—he slowly lowered his head and returned to view the scene around him. The rush hour had passed and he moved without a crowd to guide him, without direction or purpose, and found himself in a bleak waiting room with rows of varnished oak benches, and only an occasional waiting person on each long bench. Slake sat down.

There was a newsstand catering to the needs of travellers—newspapers, magazines, candy bars, chewing gum, cough drops, cigarettes, plastic ducks, automobiles, and airplanes, and countless other merchandise. Slake watched as people bought papers and cigarettes, and then he noticed something. When people rose to leave the benches and resume their journeys, some left their newspapers behind. "Then why did they buy them?" Slake inquired of himself. The answer did not come to him, but when a man, only a short way down the bench from Slake, arose and left his paper, Slake slid down the bench and acquired it. At first he just stared at it, not really reading. Then he folded it, put it under his arm, and started to walk slowly and unobtrusively into the next aisle of seats. There was no paper there, but there was one in the next aisle. The next paper Slake picked up had a lady's glove in it. He held it, looked at it, and then, not knowing what else to do, put it back in the newspaper. In the corner of one bench Slake found a box of cough drops with one cough drop in it. He took that too. He did not know exactly why he was doing this, but Slake had learned early in life that if something is being cast out, acquire it, and determine its use at some other time. With this principle in mind, Slake acquired four copies of *The Daily News* and three copies of *The New York Times* after he had walked past all the benches in the waiting room twice. He also had three buttons, a pencil, and the head of a plastic doll. Slake put the last items in his pocket and then sat down and carefully smoothed and folded the newspapers. When he found the glove again, he put it on his left hand. Then he got up and started walking back through the passage to the subways.

Before he had gone fifteen metres a man, rushing by, grabbed him by the shoulder, stopping him. Slake froze with fear.

"News!" snapped the man. Slake only stared. *"News,* boy!" And without waiting, he grabbed one of Slake's papers, slapped the money into his hand, and hurried on. Slake turned and stared after him. Then he drew in his breath sharply. Though inexperienced, he was not stupid. *Slake knew he was in business.*

Slake now walked with intent towards the part of the subway from which he had earlier emerged. He stood near the turnstiles, keeping a nervous eye on the change-booth attendant. When the man was involved in a transaction, Slake bent down as if to pick something up and slipped under the turnstile. It frightened him to do it. Slake committed crimes no more easily than he performed approved acts of living. He descended the flight of stairs that took him to the uptown platform, and with hesitancy and fear, heart beating in his ears, Slake walked up and down conspicuously. People, leaning against blue pillars, stared straight ahead, or paced impatiently while waiting for their trains.

"They don't see me," Slake told himself, wishing this time to be visible.

And then a man who appeared to be looking at nothing at all finally focussed on Slake.

"Hey, paper?" said Slake, the words pitched at a level and tone that made Slake wonder if they had been heard except in his own head, or even if they had really been uttered.

The man tilted his head. "What's that?" he asked.

"Paper," said Slake, now projecting. And his voice came out so unexpectedly loud that several people turned.

The man said, "No thanks," but another man came across the platform.

"I'll have a *Times,"* he said, and handed Slake the coins. Slake gave him a paper. With the fifteen cents he had just got for the *News,* that made thirty cents and no sweat!

A train came in and the scene changed. The station emptied suddenly like a sink with the plug pulled out. Slake stood quietly, shivering only occasionally as a draft came through the tunnel. Otherwise it was not unduly cold for November. The people travelling the trains did not seem

especially bundled up nor red-faced and teary-eyed as they would become as the winter progressed. It was a gift of mild weather before the icy months.

Now the station started to fill; the blue pillars again supported leaners. A young boy tested his mother's tolerance by seeing how close he could stand to the yellow line at the edge of the station platform. Three working girls laughed wildly about some secret.

Slake cleared his throat and tried his voice again.

"Paper?"

The girls looked at him with absent-minded blinks, and then one said to him, "You better keep an eye out for the transit cops. I never saw anyone peddling papers down here." And then she turned away and picked up her laugh where she'd left it.

"Well, look at that; a paper!" a man said. And he pushed the money into Slake's hand and took a copy of the *News*. Paper was the magic word down here.

When the next local arrived, Slake—dazed with his success and easy fortune—followed the people onto the train. He had no particular aim. Riders who had just boarded the train burrowed out spaces for themselves to sit in, or stood gripping straps that then began to manipulate them like marionettes—lean back, lean forward, lean back. . . . Slake, however, stood close to the doors, and suddenly a man sitting in the end seat signalled him. Slake drew back.

"Paper!" the man said and pushed a quarter into Slake's hand. Slake panicked. Which paper did the man want? He handed the quarter back, shaking his head. He'd have to make change.

"The *Times*," the man said with some impatience.

Slake managed to find a dime in his pocket. That had been an unexpected and exhausting transaction. He got off at Fifty-ninth Street in a hurry.

Weary now from this tense and unusual venture into the world of commerce, Slake wished to go out of business for the time being. He looked at his remaining papers. One was a bit torn, but the others were okay. . . . No, he'd had it, and besides, he had a plan for them. He slipped the remaining papers under his shirt, crossed to the downtown side, and when the train came in, Slake was on it. This time he knew where he was going.

Slake got off at Grand Central. First he went up the stairs and, near the toll booths, he purchased a Nestlé's Crunch for ten cents. Then he went back down the same flight of stairs to the downtown platform. Down the long platform Slake walked until he had reached the end away from the dispatcher's office. Quickly slipping down the stairs, he waited quietly until a train came and went, assuring him that the track would be clear for a few minutes. Then he slid under the edge of the platform and made his way down the track and into the tunnel. He felt around cautiously for the entrance to the room he had occupied the night before. He panicked for just a moment when he could not find it. And then it was there. Through the hole he went. Slake was home.

He got busy immediately, not waiting for his eyes to adjust to the darkness. He took the newspapers from under his shirt and, sheet by sheet, he began to crumple them into soft, loose wads. He put about thirty of these close together in a corner of the room. He laid a couple of the loose pieces of timber around them to keep them from scattering. Then he covered them with three double sheets of newspaper. Slake had a bed.

Now he folded several pieces of the *News* and put them under his shirt again, front and back. He wrapped two other sheets around his arms and tied them with his shoelaces. Then he sat down on his bed and rested from his labors. After a few minutes he reached into his pocket and removed the two lumps of sugar from this morning's coffee, the cough drop, and the candy bar. Slake was hungry but not more so than he had been many times.

It was now that Slake found himself firmly committed to settling on this frontier. It never crossed his mind that life could not be sustained in the subway, but had there been a question, the answer would have been easy for him. Slake knew that life was some persistent weed that grew in gravel, in broken sidewalks, in fetid alleys, and would have no more difficulty doing so here than anywhere he knew.

Liar

by Magda Zalan

There was a girl in our school who wore two long pigtails down to her waist, and strange round spectacles. The other girls all had boyfriends who waited for them after school, but this girl always walked home alone, her hands in her pockets, whistling.

"Girls should not whistle," her classmates told her, with their shiny shoes and their ribbons in their hair.

"And why not?" the girl said and went right on whistling.

"But no!" the other girls exclaimed in unison. "Girls mustn't whistle, it's not ladylike."

"True, they shouldn't, but I have special permission from the Maharaja of Popokatepetl; he gave it to me himself, personally in writing."

"Where is it? Let us see!" they teased, as though they didn't believe her.

"I don't have it with me. I put it in the bank; in a safety deposit box. It's not the sort of thing you carry around with you, like a bus ticket. That's how much you know about the value of a document from the Maharaja of Popokatepetl!"

"I bet you don't even know the Maharaja of Popokatepetl. I bet you've never even *seen* the Maharaja of Popokatepetl," they sneered.

"Of course I know him," the girl told them. "He's a good friend of my father's. Whenever he comes to town, he sleeps on the sofa bed in my father's study."

"A Maharaja on a sofa bed! Imagine it!" laughed the girls. "You're a liar!" And they all ran off together, shouting "Liar! Liar!"

Once the liar was absent from school for several days. When she returned to class, she said that she had been on an expedition to the North Pole, where the ice was hard as rock and bright as a gem. She said that she had spent a whole night digging a hole in the ice to sleep in, and that the blue rays of the polar sunlight came through the walls as if the hole were in the depths of the sea, and when a cloud passed in front of the enormous red globe of the sun, it was as if a ship had passed over the surface of the water, sending its shadow deep into the sea. And mermaids disguised into the shape of wolves sang to the moon as though it pulled their voices from them.

"You're lying!" cried the girls. "You're telling lies!" But they felt a chill down their spines when they thought of the blue and red waters, and the mermaids singing their strange haunting song. And at night, the marvellous polar light lit their boring dreams.

One day one of the girls fell ill. Her classmates went to visit her. The liar went too, though the others did not want her with them. All the other girls bought chocolates, caramels, and flowers for the sick girl. The liar followed along behind them, her empty hands in her pockets, whistling an old sailor's song.

At the bedside of their classmate, the girls lined up to place their gifts on the night table. Last of all, the liar went up to the heap of candy and flowers, piled up one on top of the other, and put down a small gray rock.

"You brought a rock?" said the sick girl with a grimace.

"This isn't a rock," said the liar.

"What is it then?" the girls all asked snidely, in unison.

"Yesterday, early in the morning," the liar began in a soft voice, "I slipped out of the window just before the sun came up and took a walk in the park at the end of our street, where it was still dark amongst the big trees. Suddenly, I saw a tiny beautiful star fall from the sky and land right in front of me, right at my feet. In order to find its way home again, the star had traced a shining streak on the black velvet of the sky. 'Hi,' I called out to it—'How is life up in the heavens?' It told me many interesting things, so in return I told it about our world too. It liked my stories so much that it stayed too long, sitting in the grass, looking about, and forgot to climb back onto its shiny track before the sun rose and erased the dark, and with it the little star's path home.

"I picked it up to throw it back into the clouds, without which I knew it could not survive, but it was already cold and gray in my hand. And so here it is. Maybe it is not dead but only sleeping, and will wake again tonight, when the black velvet of the sky will glitter again with all its playmates, the other stars. I give it to you."

"That's a lie," murmured the sick girl. But she very cautiously picked up the gray rock and let it rest in the palm of her hand. "You're a liar."

The liar shook her head violently. If the sick girl had looked closely she would have seen tears at the corners of her eyes. But she did not look, because she was looking at the rock with a strange smile as if she were happy—very happy.

I was the liar.

Into the Root Cellar

by Janet Lunn

When Rose Larkin's grandmother died, Rose was sent to live with her aunt and uncle and their large noisy family. She didn't like it at all. Right from the start she noticed odd things about the rundown old house the family lived in. She met an old woman named Mrs. Morrissay who spoke to her and then disappeared. Then she saw a girl working in an upstairs room—but the rest of the family said there was no such person. It didn't help much when her cousin Sam said he had seen a strange figure that might be a ghost.

Rose grew more and more uneasy, and at last she decided to ask her grandmother's relatives to find her another home. Just as she finished writing a letter to them she looked up to find old Mrs. Morrissay coming right through her bedroom wall!

"**M**rs. Morrissay!" A shudder like an electric shock ran through Rose. "What are you doing?" she whispered.

Mrs. Morrissay said nothing. She didn't move. She stood half in the twins' room, half in Rose's, a blue and orange kerchief tied around her head, a dust mop in her hand, looking very ill at ease.

Rose was trembling. Her hands were wet with cold sweat and she could hardly focus her eyes. Mrs. Morrissay came the rest of the way through the wall and into the room. She was no longer half-visible. She was solid, three dimensional.

"You're Sam's ghost." Rose heard her own voice, strange and shrill and accusing.

"I ain't no ghost." Mrs. Morrissay was indignant. "I'm just plain myself, minding my own business and it happens."

"Happens?"

"I shift!"

"Shift?"

"Shift. I'm going along minding my own business like I said, hoeing or scrubbing or mopping, and right in the middle I shift. And you needn't be so cross, Rose. You ought to know better. It's not easy for a body to shift. I'm in my kitchen, then quick's a cow's tail after a fly, I'm in yours—or your bedroom." She looked around her. "Oh, Rose, ain't this an awful sight? It was so pretty." She went over to the corner by the window and picked at the layers of wallpaper. "See, this here's the one I put up. It was white with pink roses." Suddenly she smiled at Rose, a warm, embracing smile. Then she looked out the window.

"Ain't it something how them bushes is all grown over. Funny how you can still see where the old garden was."

"Mrs. Morrissay, you have no right to be here!" Rose could barely control her shaking voice. Her sense of how things ought to be had never been so disturbed, not even by her grandmother's death. "You don't belong here, Mrs. Morrissay—" Rose stopped abruptly, her fear, and her shock, subsiding before Mrs. Morrissay's smile. "I suppose it *is* your home?"

"Of course it's my house. I grew up in it. I was married in it. I'm like to die in it and"—Mrs. Morrissay finished with a sigh—"it seems I shift in it."

She reached over and took Rose's hand. Rose snatched it away. "It's all right," said Mrs. Morrissay soothingly. "Rose, I told you, I ain't no ghost. I ain't dead. I'm just shifted, and I don't know how no more than you do. It just happens, like I said. All I know is that if the good Lord sees fit to shift me, I shift. I suppose it's . . . well, I dunno. But I do belong here, and Rose, I want you to make things right in my house for me."

"Mrs. Morrissay, I can't fix your house. It isn't my house and anyway I don't even like this house. I'm not going to stay here. I'm going back to New York."

Rose realized that she was actually talking to the old woman as easily as she had used her name, Mrs. Morrissay. "How do you know so much about me? Who are you?"

But Mrs. Morrissay was staring at Rose in alarm. As if she hadn't heard her question, she said, "Don't talk about going off like that, Rose.

You ain't going to New York, you know you ain't—oh!" Mrs. Morrissay looked at Rose in alarm, opened her mouth to say something, and disappeared, not slowly the way she had come but instantly, like a light being turned off.

Rose started back. Fearfully she put her hand towards the spot where Mrs. Morrissay had been standing. There was no one, nothing. Her mind was in a turmoil. At that moment, through the window, she caught sight of something blue and orange moving across the glade.

"There she is!" Rose spoke aloud in her excitement. "There's her kerchief!"

She flew down the stairs and out of the house. But there was no sign of Mrs. Morrissay in the clearing. Rose slumped down against the little hawthorn tree. "It's true what I wrote Aunt Millicent," she whispered. "They are mad. And now I think I must be mad too."

She sat there, dejectedly scuffing the leaves with her feet, her mind going over and over what had happened. Her toe struck something metal. Surprised, she sat up straight and pushed at it with her foot. It clinked. She went over on her hands and knees to look. She brushed away the leaves and discovered that there were boards underneath with a metal latch of some sort.

"It's a door, a door in the ground, how odd." Excitedly she began to pull at the vines and thick grass that had grown over the boards, and when she had pulled most of them away she saw that, indeed, it was a door, two doors in fact, with rusty hook-and-eye latches that secured them together. With much pulling and wrenching she managed to loosen them and slowly, slowly, with a great deal of straining and heaving she pried them open.

There were steps inside that had been made by cutting away the earth and laying boards across. The boards had all but rotted away but the earth steps were still there. At the bottom, facing her about one metre away, was another door, upright, also fastened with a hook-and-eye latch. The doorway was so low she had to stoop to get through.

Inside she found herself in a kind of closet with shelves along the sides on which stood crockery jars and glass sealers. On the floor stood several barrels with lids on them. The place was cold and damp but it looked to be in use.

I don't understand. If Aunt Nan keeps her pickles and things here, why is it so hard to get into? she thought. She had lifted the lid off one of the crocks and found it full of beets. Another was full of cucumber pickles. She looked up. Someone behind her was blocking the light. Quickly she turned around.

A girl, smaller but probably about the same age as her, stood at the top of the steps with a jar in her hands. It was the girl from the bedroom with the four-poster bed. She wore quite a long dress made of some rough dark brown material, with a white apron over it. On her feet she had awkward-looking ankle-high boots. She had dark brown hair in one long braid down her back, a plain round freckled face, a small nose, a wide mouth—and bright black eyes. They were blinking at Rose in consternation.

"Where'd you come from?" she demanded.

"I . . . I . . . what?"

"You'd best get out of our root cellar." The girl came down the steps. "Missus will be terrible cross." She reached up to the top shelf and brought down one of the crocks. All the while she kept turning around to stare nervously at Rose.

Rose stared back.

"You'd best come along now." The girl frowned. "Honest, Missus don't like having strangers around." She started back up the steps.

"Look"—Rose followed the girl—"look, isn't this—" She'd been going to ask, "Isn't this Aunt Nan's root cellar?" but the words never got spoken. At the top of the steps she found herself standing beside a little garden with rows of young plants set out in it. Behind it the creek bubbled merrily and a neat stone path led from the garden to the kitchen door. Pansies and sweet alyssum bloomed along the walk and there were hollyhocks against the back wall of the house. The bricks looked bright and the trim around the windows and the kitchen door was fresh and white. Chickens and ducks were squawking and flapping to let her know she was intruding and a pair of geese scurried across the grass towards her. Down past the creek a cow and a small flock of sheep were browsing. Beyond, where there should have been a field of crab grass and burdock, was an apple orchard in full bloom.

"This time it's me," whispered Rose. "I've shifted."

Acknowledgments continued from p. 3.

Excerpt from *The Ghost Horse of the Mounties.* Copyright © sean o huigin, 1983. Reprinted by permission of sean o huigin and Black Moss Press.

Excerpt from *The Terrible Churnadryne.* Copyright © 1959 by Eleanor Cameron. Reprinted by permission of Little, Brown and Company in association with the Atlantic Monthly Press.

Excerpt from Chapter Two of *Skateboard Scramble.* Copyright © 1979 Barbara Douglass. Used by permission of The Westminster Press, Philadelphia, PA.

Excerpt from Chapter Ten of *Take a Long Jump.* Copyright © 1971 Marion Renick. Reprinted with the permission of Charles Scribner's Sons, a Division of Macmillan, Inc.

"The Pitcher" by Jeffrey Hovell from *Mysterious Special Sauce—Poems by Canadian Students.* Copyright © The Pandora Charitable Trust of the Canadian Council of Teachers of English. Reprinted by permission of the Canadian Council of Teachers of English.

"The Base Stealer." Copyright © 1960 by Robert Francis. Reprinted from *The Orb Weaver* by permission of Wesleyan University Press.

"My First Home Run" by Margaret Minter. Reprinted with the permission of the author.

Excerpt (pp. 8–15) from *S.O.R. Losers* by Avi. Copyright © 1984 by Avi Wortis. Reprinted with permission of Bradbury Press, an Affiliate of Macmillan, Inc.

Selections "Table Tennis," "Skiing," and "Badminton" from *How Sports Came to Be.* Copyright © 1980 by Don L. Wulffson. Reprinted by permission of Lothrop, Lee & Shepard Books (A Division of William Morrow.)

"The Hockey Sweater" by Roch Carrier from *The Hockey Sweater and Other Stories,* translated by Sheila Fischman (Toronto: House of Anansi Press, 1979). Reprinted by permission of the publisher.

Excerpt from *The Truce of the Games.* Copyright © 1971 Rosemary Sutcliff. Permission to reproduce by the publisher, Hamish Hamilton Ltd., London.

"Arachne" from *The Warrior Goddess Athena.* Copyright © 1972 by Doris Gates. Reprinted by permission of Viking Penguin Inc.

Selections and illustrations (pp. 4–5, 10–19) from *Tales of Pan.* Copyright © 1986 by Mordicai Gerstein. Reprinted by permission of Harper & Row, Publishers, Inc.

Excerpt from *Little Badger and the Fire Spirit* by Maria Campbell. Copyright © 1977 McClelland and Stewart. Used by permission of the Canadian Publishers, McClelland and Stewart, Toronto.

"Savitri and Satyavan" from *Seasons of Splendour.* Copyright © 1985 by Madhur Jaffrey, published in London by Pavilion Books. Reproduced by permission of the publisher.

"Strong Man Who Holds Up the World" from *The Princess and the Sea-Bear and Other Tsimshian Stories* by Joan Skogan. Copyright © Metlakatla Band Council, 1983. Reprinted with the permission of the Metlakatla Band Council.

Excerpt from *Wingman.* Copyright © 1975 by Manus Pinkwater. Reprinted by permission of the author and the author's agents, Writers House Inc., New York.

Chapter Fifteen (pp. 133–145) from *Zeely.* Copyright © 1967 by Virginia Hamilton. Reprinted with permission of Macmillan Publishing Company.

"My Uncle Dan" from *Meet My Folks.* Copyright © 1961, 1973 by Ted Hughes. Reprinted by permission of Faber and Faber Limited, London.

"Michael Built a Bicycle" from *The New Kid on the Block.* Copyright © 1984 by Jack Prelutsky. Reprinted by permission of Greenwillow Books (A Division of William Morrow).

Selections from Chapter Two of *Everything You Want to Know about Inventions: An Amazing Investigation,* copyright © Valerie Wyatt, 1987, an *OWL* Book; and excerpt from *The Wilds of Whip-poor-will Farm,* copyright © Janet Foster, 1982, an *OWL* Book, both reprinted with permission of the publisher, Greey de Pencier Books of Toronto.

Slightly adapted excerpt from "Biruté Galdikas and the Red Apes" in *Wild Animals, Gentle Women.* Copyright © 1978 by Margery Facklam. Reprinted by permission of Harcourt Brace Jovanovich, Inc.

"Blue Lotus Beads" by Jane Adams, copyright © 1985 Potlatch Publications Limited; and "The Painted Caves of Altamira" by Joy Hollamby-Lane, copyright © 1977 Potlatch Publications Limited. Both selections are from *The Canadian Children's Annual* and reprinted with permission of the publisher.

Excerpt from Chapter Four of *The Journey of the Shadow Bairns.* Copyright © 1980 by Margaret Anderson. Reprinted by permission of Alfred A. Knopf., Inc.

Paintings by William Kurelek and captions by Margaret S. Engelhart from *They Sought a New World.* Illustrations copyright © 1985 The Estate of the late William Kurelek, text copyright © 1985 Tundra Books Inc. Reprinted with the permission of the publisher, Tundra Books.

ILLUSTRATIONS AND PHOTOGRAPHS

Paintings used in unit openers:

Charles Pachter *Six Figures in a Landscape* 1978
140 x 215 Private collection

Ken Danby *At the Crease* 1972
71.4 x 101.6 Private collection

Cecil Youngfox *Sunset Dancers* 1984
61 x 76.2 Private collection

Emily M. Carr *Kispiax Village* 1929
92 x 128.9 Art Gallery of Ontario, Toronto

©1986 Ron Bolt

Ron Bolt *Wave Silent* 1986
71.2 x 89 North Editions, Toronto

Courtesy of the Carmen Lamanna Gallery

Paterson Ewen *Northern Lights* 1973
168 x 244.2 Art Gallery of Ontario, Toronto

Jean-Paul Lemieux *The Night Visitor* 1956
80.4 x 110 National Gallery of Canada, Ottawa

Linda Beth Sanderson *And the Spirit Will Guide*
1981 45.7 x 61 Private collection